Workshop on Stylistic Variation 2017

Copenhagen, Denmark
8 September 2017

ISBN: 978-1-5108-4763-7

EMNLP 2017

Workshop on Stylistic Variation

Proceedings of the Workshop

September 8, 2017
Copenhagen, Denmark

Preface

The Workshop on Stylistic Variation (StyVa) at EMNLP 2017 is the first of its kind, offering a new venue for bringing together a large but previously underserved and splintered community within computational linguistics. Our goal in creating this workshop was to attract a variety of perspectives on style from traditional areas within NLP, including authorship attribution, author profiling, genre studies, natural language generation, distributional lexicography, and literary and educational applications; to this end we have defined stylistic variation as broadly as possible, to include any variation in phonological, lexical, syntactic, or discourse realization of particular semantic content, due to differences in extralinguistic variables such as individual speaker, speaker demographics, target audience, genre, etc.

We received 22 submissions, of which we accepted 14 (64%), seven as talks and seven as poster presentations.Though there was indeed a great deal of diversity in the submissions, including at least one submission in several of the major topic areas discussed above, we also noted a clear trend: we received several papers on style-sensitive language generation, particularly using neural network models. This clearly reflects a more general interest in the field, and one we would expect to continue. More generally, we are pleased that this workshop has served as a venue for both traditional and cutting-edge approaches to style.

We'd like to thank the authors for choosing StyVa as a venue for their excellent work, our invited speakers (Ani Nenkova and Walter Daelemans) for their invaluable contribution, and of course the reviews provided by our esteemed Program Committee. We'd also want to thank the ACL workshop organizing committee for giving us this opportunity to bring together the NLP stylistic community.

We look forward to a great workshop in Copenhagen!

Julian Brooke, Moshe Koppel, and Thamar Solorio

Organizers:

Julian Brooke, University of Melbourne
Moshe Koppel, Bar-Ilan University
Thamar Solorio, University of Houston

Program Committee:

Shlomo Argamon, Illinois Institute of Technology
Tim Baldwin, University of Melbourne
Ritwik Banerjee, Stony Brook University
Alberto Barrón-Cedeño, Qatar Computing Research Institute
Yves Bestgen, Université catholique de Louvain
Dasha Bogdanova, Dublin City University
Walter Daelemans, University of Antwerp
Jacob Eisenstein, Georgia Tech
Roger Evans, University of Brighton
Lucie Flekova, Technische Universität Darmstadt
Alexander Gelbukh, Instituto Politécnico Nacional
Rachel Greenstadt, Drexel University
Adam Hammond, San Diego State University
Graeme Hirst, University of Toronto
Dirk Hovy, University of Copenhagen
Eduard Hovy, Carnegie Mellon University
Diana Inkpen, University of Ottawa
Mike Kestemont, University of Antwerp
Ekaterina Kochmar, Cambridge University
Shibamouli Lahiri, University of Michigan
Annie Louis, University of Edinburgh
Suraj Maharjan, University of Houston
Manuel Montes-y-Gomez, Instituto Nacional de Astrofísica, Óptica y Electrónica
Francisco Rangel, Autoritas Consulting, S.A.
Ellie Pavlick, University of Pennsylvania
Barbara Plank, University of Groningen
Martin Potthast, Bauhaus-Universität Weimar
Paolo Rosso, Universitat Politècnica de València
Jan Rybicki, Jagiellonian University
Horacio Saggion, Universitat Pompeu Fabra
Prasha Shrestha, University of Houston
Anders Søgaard, University of Copenhagen
Lucia Specia, University of Sheffield
Efstathios Stamatatos, University of the Aegean
Benno Stein, Bauhaus-Universität Weimar
Joel Tetreault, Grammarly
Oren Tsur, Harvard University
Sandra Uitdenbogerd, RMIT University
Sowmya Vajjala, Iowa State University

Marilyn Walker, UC Santa Cruz
Wei Xu, Ohio State University
Marcos Zampeiri, University of Cologne

Invited Speakers:

Walter Daelemans, University of Antwerp
Ani Nenkova, University of Pennsylvania

Table of Contents

Conference Program

Friday, September 8, 2017

09:00–10:30   Opening Session

09:00–09:10   *Opening remarks*
Julian Brooke, Thamar Solorio, and Moshe Koppel

09:10–10:00   *Invited Talk: Style Analysis for Practical Semantic Interpretation of Text*
Ani Nenkova

10:00–10:30   *From Shakespeare to Twitter: What are Language Styles all about?*
Wei Xu

10:30–11:00   Coffee Break

11:00–12:30   Technical Papers I

11:00–11:30   *Shakespearizing Modern Language Using Copy-Enriched Sequence to Sequence Models*
Harsh Jhamtani, Varun Gangal, Eduard Hovy and Eric Nyberg

11:30–12:00   *Discovering Stylistic Variations in Distributional Vector Space Models via Lexical Paraphrases*
Xing Niu and Marine Carpuat

12:00–12:30   *Harvesting Creative Templates for Generating Stylistically Varied Restaurant Reviews*
Shereen Oraby, Sheideh Homayon and Marilyn Walker

12:30–14:00	**Lunch**
14:00–14:50	*Invited Talk: Problems in Personality Profiling* Walter Daelemans
14:50–15:30	**Poster Session**

Is writing style predictive of scientific fraud?
Chloé Braud and Anders Søgaard

"Deep" Learning : Detecting Metaphoricity in Adjective-Noun Pairs
Yuri Bizzoni, Stergios Chatzikyriakidis and Mehdi Ghanimifard

Authorship Attribution with Convolutional Neural Networks and POS-Eliding
Julian Hitschler, Esther van den Berg and Ines Rehbein

Topic and audience effects on distinctively Scottish vocabulary usage in Twitter data
Philippa Shoemark, James Kirby and Sharon Goldwater

Differences in type-token ratio and part-of-speech frequencies in male and female Russian written texts
Tatiana Litvinova, Pavel Seredin, Olga Litvinova and Olga Zagorovskaya

Modeling Communicative Purpose with Functional Style: Corpus and Features for German Genre and Register Analysis
Thomas Haider and Alexis Palmer

Stylistic Variation in Television Dialogue for Natural Language Generation
Grace Lin and Marilyn Walker

15:30–16:00   **Coffee Break**

16:00–17:30   **Technical Papers II**

16:00–16:30   *Controlling Linguistic Style Aspects in Neural Language Generation*
Jessica Ficler and Yoav Goldberg

16:30–17:00   *Approximating Style by N-gram-based Annotation*
Melanie Andresen and Heike Zinsmeister

17:00–17:30   *Assessing the Stylistic Properties of Neurally Generated Text in Authorship Attribution*
Enrique Manjavacas, Jeroen De Gussem, Walter Daelemans and Mike Kestemont

17:30–17:35   *Closing Remarks*
Julian Brooke, Thamar Solorio, and Moshe Koppel

From Shakespeare to Twitter: What are Language Styles all about?

Wei Xu

Department of Computer Science and Engineering
The Ohio State University
`weixu@cse.ohio-state.edu`

Abstract

As natural language processing research is growing and largely driven by the availability of data, we expanded research from news and small-scale dialog corpora to web and social media. User-generated data and crowdsourcing opened the door for investigating human language of various styles with more statistical power and real-world applications. In this position/survey paper, I will review and discuss seven language styles that I believe to be important and interesting to study: influential work in the past, challenges at the present, and potential impact for the future.

1 Top Three Problems

The top three problems for studying language styles are data, data and data. More specifically, they are data shortage, data fusion, and data annotation problems. The data shortage problem has been improving, which is the main reason that there is surge in the number of research studies on language styles. The data fusion problem is more specific to the area, due to the subtle and often subjective nature of linguistic styles. For instance, while men and women talk in different ways (note this is not the same as talking about different things), they also talk about a lot of things in an indistinguishable way. Moreover, there is also a huge variance from one man to another, one woman to another. The styles are often fused together in the data and not easy to separate out or make black-and-white judgements on. This also leads to challenges in data annotation or data collection, comparing to other NLP tasks (e.g. question answering). Throughout the rest of this paper, we shall see many creative solutions, interesting work, and promising potential.

2 Seven Styles of Language

Disclaimers: (i) We discuss primarily in the context of natural language processing research; (ii) There are certainly more than seven language styles as there are more than seven wonders in the world.

2.1 Simple and Short

Text simplification is one of the earliest topics in computational linguistics that directly deals with language styles, rewriting regular texts into simpler versions for people with limited reading capabilities. The major transition from rule-based to machine learning approach for automatic sentence simplification did not happen until 2010 after Simple English Wikipedia became available. It is worth noting that the Simple Wikipedia data has some issues on the quality and degree of simplicity (Xu et al., 2015b). The shortage of high quality data is becoming gradually alleviated as the Newsela corpus (Xu et al., 2015b) of professionally edited 1000+ articles is released, and as more and more attention and appreciation are given by the research community to data construction (Brunato et al., 2016; Hwang et al., 2015). Multiple studies have shown crowcourcing workers can produce high quality simplifications (Xu et al., 2016; Amancio and Specia, 2014; Pellow and Eskenazi, 2014), though it is costly to scale up. Data will remain a central problem[1] as the data-hungry neural generation models (Nisioi et al., 2017) are a promising direction for future work.

Besides data, another severe problem is evaluation. In fact, one common human evaluation that uses a five point Likert scale on grammaticality, meaning and simplicity should be considered

---

[1] Lexical simplification as a subtask can utilize or bypass the need of parallel data (Glavaš and Štajner, 2015; Paetzold and Specia, 2016; Pavlick and Callison-Burch, 2016).

1

Proceedings of the Workshop on Stylistic Variation, pages 1–9
Copenhagen, Denmark, September 7–11, 2017. ©2017 Association for Computational Linguistics

unacceptable when deletion is involved, as it unfairly biases towards deletions over paraphrasing. There has been some progress on creating automatic evaluation metrics (Xu et al., 2016) and exploring new human evaluation methodologies (Xu et al., 2016; Nisioi et al., 2017; Siddharthan and Mandya, 2014). We are going to need more data, clever ideas and careful evaluation designs.

For the record, everything about sentence simplification is much harder than sentence compression[2] primarily due to the interactions between deletion and paraphrasing. Like simplification, previously, sentence compression also use human evaluation with Likert scale on grammaticality and meaning. However, it is shown to be problematic without controlling for compression ratio (Napoles et al., 2011). Now sentence compression systems are mostly compared at the same compression ratio. It is also worth noting that neural compression is similarly lacking in large-scale parallel data (Toutanova et al., 2016) and currently relies on news headline data which results in headline-like outputs (Filippova et al., 2015; Rush et al., 2015).

2.2 Instructional and Robotic

Despite the fact that instructional language is important in our everyday lives, there have been relatively limited efforts to design automated algorithms that link language to action in real world applications. Largely because of the limited availability of annotated datasets which are much-needed for training and evaluating machine learning models, existing works are primarily on cooking recipes (Tasse and Smith, 2008), airline booking conversations (Zettlemoyer and Collins, 2007), software help documents (Branavan et al., 2009) and robot navigation commands (Chen and Mooney, 2011). In particular, cooking recipe has sprouted a rich line of research as a proxy to robotic instructions (Bollini et al., 2013; Jermsurawong and Habash, 2015; Kiddon et al., 2015). Recent efforts aim to study natural language instructions for biology lab experiments (Kulkarni et al., 2017). Two closely relevant research areas, semantic parsing and dialog, have also both made major advances in recent years to utilize large-scale data via weak supervision (Cai and Yates, 2013; Artzi and Zettlemoyer, 2013) and neural

---

[2]which is closely related to, sometimes used interchangeably with, though different from, abstractive summarization, headline generation, sentence fusion.

network models (Lee et al., 2016; Misra and Artzi, 2016). The 1st Workshop on Language Grounding for Robotics (RoboNLP) will be held at ACL 2017. We shall expect research on instructional language become more and more fruitful in the near future.

2.3 Historical and Evolving

The rise of digital humanities certainly helps to provide more digitized materials for leaning techniques. Historical documents are proven fun (in the other word, hard) to work with. Garrette and Alpert-Abrams (2016) used the following example to present the challenges of having multiple unknown fonts and inking on a single page of a book in the Primeros Libros corpus:

$$a\ a\ a\ a\ a\ a\ a\ a$$

A series of work (Berg-Kirkpatrick et al., 2013; Berg-Kirkpatrick and Klein, 2014; Garrette et al., 2015) have been conducted on this and other corpora to develop historical document optical character recognition (OCR) better handle fonts, offsets, etc, together with language models through unsupervised learning. Unsupervised domain adaptation to historic text was also attempted by Yang and Eisenstein (2015) using feature embedding on the part-of-speech tagging task.

Shakespeare plays in contrast are perfect for investigating a consistent writing style from a single author. Even with a relatively small amount of parallel training data, it is possible to learn paraphrase models which capture stylistic phenomena and can transform the line in the Star Wars *"If you will not be turned, you will be destroyed!"* to Shakespearean style *"If you will not be turn'd, you will be undone!"* (Xu et al., 2012b; Xu, 2014). One can image such stylistic paraphrasing, as it continues to improve, would possibly help preserve privacy and anonymity (Brennan et al., 2012). This is one thing about research on language styles, it often involves a sense of social justice and for social good (e.g. simplification for children, robotics for repetitive wet lab experiments).

Being able to handle evolving language is crucial in natural language processing applications. As the most high-performance systems often utilize fully supervised or weakly supervised learning, the time elapsed from training data to new test data will cause performance deteriorating

(Plank, 2018). The most apparent case is out-of-vocabulary (OOV) words (van der Wees et al., 2015; Seraj et al., 2015), especially new emerging named entities and newly coined words (e.g. *"selfie"*, *"Brexiteers"*). This problem will become more pressing and more feasible to study as more and more time-sensitive online text data is accumulating. Learning up-to-date paraphrases (Lan et al., 2017), vector semantics (Cherry and Guo, 2015) and character-based neural models (Ling et al., 2015; Rei et al., 2016) from online data streams could be plausible solutions that connect unseen data with known expressions.

2.4 Colloquial and Internet

As social media started booming, especially after Twitter released the streaming API for free in 2010 that provides real-time tweets as posted, there is a huge explosion on social media research. Multiple workshops are dedicated to this special type of text including the Workshop on Noisy User-generated Text (WNUT) and Workshop on Making Sense of Microposts (#microposts) that hold annual shared tasks. Before that, most unedited text data (vs. well-edited such as news) is from web forums and blogs, while short message service (SMS) and email data are limited to rather small amounts due to privacy reasons (Baldwin et al., 2013). Interesting research falls into two camps: normalize lexical variants to standard form (Han and Baldwin, 2011; Xu et al., 2013) or develop domain adapted NLP systems (Ritter et al., 2011; Gimpel et al., 2011; Kong et al., 2014; Tabassum et al., 2016). The iconic opinion paper *What to do about bad language on the Internet* by Jacob Eisenstein (2013) highlighted this divide.

There is a third point we have often missed. Besides the noisy hard-to-understand Internet language, many users also use rather standard language on social networks, formal or colloquial. Don't forget that all the traditional news agencies also have Twitter accounts (Hu et al., 2013). Can we make the connections between the formal and colloquial languages as they are heavily mixed on social media? I think the answer is yes, and the twin research topics of paraphrasing and semantic similarity could be part of the solution as many language styles are heavily mixed on social media. For example, in the SemEval shared task PIT-2015 corpus (Xu et al., 2015a), the figurative meaning of the phrase *"on fire"* is captured by the senten-

tial paraphrase of *"Aaaaaaaaand stephen curry is on fire"* and *"What a incredible performance from Stephen Curry"*. Semantic equivalences, as formal as *"fetuses"* and *"fetal tissue"* (Lan et al., 2017) or as informal as *"gets the boot from"* and *"has been sacked by"* (Xu et al., 2014; Xu, 2014), can also be learned automatically from Twitter data. Not to mention that there are also studies that focus on multiword expressions (Schneider and Smith, 2015), idioms (Muzny and Zettlemoyer, 2013), and slang.

2.5 Gendered and Personalized

One unique and exciting opportunity offered by social media data is to learn about the users authoring the texts. Much interesting research on gender difference[3] in language styles appeared in the past few years. Besides gender (Verhoeven et al., 2016; Bamman et al., 2014), other user attributes such as age (Sap et al., 2014), race (Jørgensen et al., 2015) and personality (Schwartz et al., 2013; Ruan et al., 2016; Plank and Hovy, 2015) are also commonly studied for social science and strongly motivated by commercial usages of profiling users and personalized services. Leveraging user demographic factors also shows benefits on improving natural language processing applications such as sentiment analysis (Volkova et al., 2013) and sarcasm detection (Bamman and Smith, 2015).

One particularly interesting challenge is how to handle the situation that stylistic differences (e.g. female users more likely use *"wonderful"* while male users use *"superb"*) are much more subtle than topical preferences (e.g. using word *"husband"* is a strong indicator of female user). Our recent work (Preoţiuc-Pietro et al., 2016) isolated stylistic differences from topic bias by using paraphrase pairs and clusters, and showed their predictive power in user profiling and potential for future work. We also found crowdsourcing workers are surprisingly good at perceiving gender from lexical choices when aggregating their judgments – an infamous phenomenon of so-called *The Wisdom of Crowds* (Surowiecki, 2005). Beyond lexical choice, Johannsen et al. (2015) further showed demographic differences in syntactic variances using multilingual data of online customer reviews and universal dependency parsing.

---

[3]Although unrelated to linguistic styles, the readers may find *He Said, She Said: Gender in the ACL Anthology* (Vogel and Jurafsky, 2012), a paper on gender-based statistics of NLP researchers, interesting.

Another subsequent challenge is how to transfer the subtle style differences into natural language generation and dialog systems. While we were able to transform contemporary texts into Shakespeare style (Xu et al., 2012b), we found gendered language style much harder to impose. It is possibly that because we have not found the right data for evaluation, for instance, it is hard to expect a randomly drawn sentence to be possible to take on a feminine or masculine style. It could also be the case that it is easier for finer-grained language style to show distinctions. One evident example is author recognition based on an individual's frequent word choices (Clark and Hannon, 2007). Another example is persona-based dialog system that not only captures background knowledge of a user (Li et al., 2016) but also speaking style (Mizukami et al., 2015). It is not a coincident that the later work (Mizukami et al., 2015) is on spoken Japanese, which exhibits extensive gender differences as well as honorifics (not as much in written Japanese).

2.6 Pervasive and Framing

The increasing availability of data also make feasible to study the textural characteristics of persuasion, argumentation and framing in realistic (not laboratory) settings and quantitatively. Besides movie quotes, political speeches, and tweets (Guerini et al., 2015), many interesting data are created and discovered, leading to a growing number of studies. Online discussion platforms provide almost ideal real world data with users stating, reasoning and contesting opinions (Somasundaran and Wiebe, 2009), and sometimes even with explicitly marked successful arguments such as ChangeMyView on Reddit. One recent work (Tan et al., 2016) found that in the ChangeMyView data, after controlled for similar arguments, stylistic choices in how the opinion is expressed carry more predictive power on how likely a user to be persuaded than how likely an argument is persuasive. However, predicting pervasiveness turns out to a difficulty task with about 60-65% accuracy using bag-of-words and linguistic features, in constrast of 75-85% accuracy for predicting politeness). Another interesting work (Recasens et al., 2013) utilized Wikipedia edit history to study biased language (e.g. *"stated"* vs. *"claimed"*) as well as framing (e.g. *"pro-life"* vs. *"anti-abortion"*). The recent construction of the Media Frames Corpus (Card et al., 2015)[4] presents another encouraging opportunity to study framing. The legal domain, such as supreme court documents, is another common place for arguments (Sim et al., 2015) and would possibly be used for studying linguistic styles.

2.7 Polite and Abusive

Another angle that has been looked at is the politeness conveyed in language. Unlike many other styles that come in close pairs (e.g. formal vs. informal, feminine vs. masculine), the polite language does not necessarily have an impolite counterpart. In addition, politeness is expressed more through function words. For example, showing gratitude by *"I appreciate that"* or apologizing by *"Sorry to bother you"*. In fact, the phrase *"in fact"* can be negative as *"in fact you did ..."*. Many other cues are identified and annotated (Danescu-Niculescu-Mizil et al., 2013) on the online interchanges of Wikipedia editors and StackExchange QA users, which can train classifier to predict politeness at about 80% accuracy. A recent study (Voigt et al., 2017) also used automatic methods to examine the respectfulness of police officers toward white and black people from transcripts of body-worn camera footage.

In other words, abusive language is closely related to politeness but not the reverse. The targets could vary from one swear word to multi-sentences, such as the mean tweet Barack Obama read on Jimmy Kimmel's show: *"Obama's hair is looking grayer these days. Can't imagine why since he doesn't seem to be one bit worried about all that's going on."* The context-dependent nature makes it challenging to collect data or design experiments. Moreoever, although bullying traces are abundant, it is a tiny fraction out of random samples which is estimated to 0.02∼0.73% of a 95% confidence internal on 2011 TREC Microblog track corpus (Xu et al., 2012a). The compromise is to look at tweets that include keywords *"bully"*, *"bullied"*, *"bullying"* instead, which is inspiring and an important first step, but far from satisfying. Another representative solution is a carefully designed crowdsourcing experiment which reveals patterns of Internet trolling behavior using user comments on CNN.com news website (Cheng et al., 2017). Perhaps, the 1st

---

[4]which is a great example why data resource papers even without learning results should be considered *acceptable* in ACL/EMNLP/NAACL/EACL main conferences.

Workshop on Abusive Language Online (ALW) at ACL 2017 will spark more ideas. I would like to quote an anonymous source who raised a thoughtful question: *"Under what circumstances is language use considered to be an abuse? For example, in many states when a women criticizes her husband in public, this might be considered there as abuse of language or hate speech"*, as a reminder of being aware and mindful of the great social factors and impacts embedded in the research of language styles.

3 Conclusion

At this point of the development, natural language processing research ranges a wide variety of genre, domain, register or type of data. I think the term *style* is an all-in-one umbrella concept to bring researchers and scattered attentions in various NLP subareas to a common place. There are certainly many nuances in language styles besides those mentioned in this paper. For example, connotation (e.g. *"childlike"* vs. *"childish"* vs. *"youthful"*) (Rashkin et al., 2016; Carpuat, 2015) and geographical lexical variations from regional (e.g. *"sode"* vs. *"coke"* vs. *"pop"*) to cross-country (e.g. Austrilian vs. American English) (Eisenstein et al., 2010; Garimella et al., 2016; Han et al., 2016). There are also certainly many other relevant works besides those mentioned in this paper. Last but not least, we would like to point out Dan Jurafsky's recent book *The Language of Food* (2014) and one more paper: *Do Linguistic Style and Readability of Scientific Abstracts Affect their Virality?* (Guerini et al., 2012).

Acknowledgments

I would like to thank three anonymous reviewers for helpful feedback, Julian Brooke, Thamar Solario and Moshe Koppel for organizing the EMNLP 2017 Workshop on Stylistic Variation.

References

Marcelo Amancio and Lucia Specia. 2014. An analysis of crowdsourced text simplifications. In *Proceedings of the 3rd Workshop on Predicting and Improving Text Readability for Target Reader Populations (PITR)*.

Yoav Artzi and Luke Zettlemoyer. 2013. Weakly supervised learning of semantic parsers for mapping instructions to actions. *Transactions of the Association for Computational Linguistics (TACL)* 1:49–62.

Timothy Baldwin, Paul Cook, Marco Lui, Andrew MacKinlay, and Li Wang. 2013. How noisy social media text, how diffrnt social media sources? In *Proceedings of the Sixth International Joint Conference on Natural Language Processing (IJCNLP)*.

David Bamman, Jacob Eisenstein, and Tyler Schnoebelen. 2014. Gender identity and lexical variation in social media. *Journal of Sociolinguistics* 18(2):135–160.

David Bamman and Noah A. Smith. 2015. Contextualized sarcasm detection on Twitter. In *ICWSM*.

Taylor Berg-Kirkpatrick, Greg Durrett, and Dan Klein. 2013. Unsupervised transcription of historical documents. In *Proceedings of the 51st Annual Meeting of the Association for Computational Linguistics (ACL)*.

Taylor Berg-Kirkpatrick and Dan Klein. 2014. Improved typesetting models for historical ocr. In *Proceedings of the 52nd Annual Meeting of the Association for Computational Linguistics (ACL)*.

Mario Bollini, Stefanie Tellex, Tyler Thompson, Nicholas Roy, and Daniela Rus. 2013. Interpreting and executing recipes with a cooking robot. In *Experimental Robotics*. Springer, pages 481–495.

Satchuthananthavale RK Branavan, Harr Chen, Luke S Zettlemoyer, and Regina Barzilay. 2009. Reinforcement learning for mapping instructions to actions. In *Proceedings of the Joint Conference of the 47th Annual Meeting of the ACL and the 4th International Joint Conference on Natural Language Processing (ACL-IJCNLP)*.

Michael Brennan, Sadia Afroz, and Rachel Greenstadt. 2012. Adversarial stylometry: Circumventing authorship recognition to preserve privacy and anonymity. *ACM Transactions on Information and Systems Security* 15(3):12:1–12:22.

Dominique Brunato, Andrea Cimino, Felice Dell'Orletta, and Giulia Venturi. 2016. PaCCSS-IT: A parallel corpus of complex-simple sentences for automatic text simplification. In *Proceedings of the 2016 Conference on Empirical Methods in Natural Language Processing (EMNLP)*.

Qingqing Cai and Alexander Yates. 2013. Large-scale semantic parsing via schema matching and lexicon extension. In *Proceedings of the 51st Annual Meeting of the Association for Computational Linguistics (ACL)*.

Dallas Card, Amber E. Boydstun, Justin H. Gross, Philip Resnik, and Noah A. Smith. 2015. The Media Frames Corpus: Annotations of frames across issues. In *Proceedings of the 53rd Annual Meeting of the Association for Computational Linguistics and the 7th International Joint Conference on Natural Language Processing (ACL-IJCNLP)*.

Marine Carpuat. 2015. Connotation in translation. In *Proceedings of the 6th Workshop on Computational Approaches to Subjectivity, Sentiment and Social Media Analysis*.

David L Chen and Raymond J Mooney. 2011. Learning to interpret natural language navigation instructions from observations. In *Proceedings of the 25th AAAI Conference on Artificial Intelligence (AAAI)*.

Justin Cheng, Michael Bernstein, Cristian Danescu-Niculescu-Mizil, and Jure Leskovec. 2017. Anyone can become a troll: Causes of trolling behavior in online discussions. In *Proceedings of the 2017 ACM Conference on Computer Supported Cooperative Work and Social Computing (CSCW)*.

Colin Cherry and Hongyu Guo. 2015. The unreasonable effectiveness of word representations for Twitter named entity recognition. In *Proceedings of the 2015 Conference of the North American Chapter of the Association for Computational Linguistics: Human Language Technologies (NAACL-HLT)*.

Jonathan Clark and Charles Hannon. 2007. A classifier system for author recognition using synonym-based features. *MICAI 2007: Advances in Artificial Intelligence* pages 839–849.

Cristian Danescu-Niculescu-Mizil, Moritz Sudhof, Dan Jurafsky, Jure Leskovec, and Christopher Potts. 2013. A computational approach to politeness with application to social factors. In *Proceedings of the 51st Annual Meeting of the Association for Computational Linguistics (ACL)*.

Jacob Eisenstein. 2013. What to do about bad language on the Internet. In *Proceedings of the 2013 Conference of the North American Chapter of the Association for Computational Linguistics: Human Language Technologies (NAACL-HLT)*.

Jacob Eisenstein, Brendan O'Connor, Noah A. Smith, and Eric P. Xing. 2010. A latent variable model for geographic lexical variation. In *Proceedings of Empirical Methods for Natural Language Processing (EMNLP)*.

Katja Filippova, Enrique Alfonseca, Carlos A. Colmenares, Lukasz Kaiser, and Oriol Vinyals. 2015. Sentence compression by deletion with LSTMs. In *Proceedings of the 2015 Conference on Empirical Methods in Natural Language Processing (EMNLP)*.

Aparna Garimella, Rada Mihalcea, and James Pennebaker. 2016. Identifying cross-cultural differences in word usage. In *Proceedings of the 26th International Conference on Computational Linguistics (COLING)*.

Dan Garrette and Hannah Alpert-Abrams. 2016. An unsupervised model of orthographic variation for historical document transcription. In *Proceedings of the 2016 Conference of the North American Chapter of the Association for Computational Linguistics: Human Language Technologies (NAACL-HLT)*.

Dan Garrette, Hannah Alpert-Abrams, Taylor Berg-Kirkpatrick, and Dan Klein. 2015. Unsupervised code-switching for multilingual historical document transcription. In *Proceedings of the 2015 Conference of the North American Chapter of the Association for Computational Linguistics: Human Language Technologies (NAACL-HLT)*.

Kevin Gimpel, Nathan Schneider, Brendan O'Connor, Dipanjan Das, Daniel Mills, Jacob Eisenstein, Michael Heilman, Dani Yogatama, Jeffrey Flanigan, and Noah A. Smith. 2011. Part-of-speech tagging for Twitter: Annotation, features, and experiments. In *Proceedings of the 49th Annual Meeting of the Association for Computational Linguistics: Human Language Technologies (ACL-HLT)*.

Goran Glavaš and Sanja Štajner. 2015. Simplifying lexical simplification: Do we need simplified corpora? In *Proceedings of the 53rd Annual Meeting of the Association for Computational Linguistics and the 7th International Joint Conference on Natural Language Processing (ACL-IJCNLP)*.

Marco Guerini, Gözde Özbal, and Carlo Strapparava. 2015. Echoes of persuasion: The effect of euphony in persuasive communication. In *Proceedings of the 2015 Conference of the North American Chapter of the Association for Computational Linguistics: Human Language Technologies (ACL-HLT)*.

Marco Guerini, Alberto Pepe, and Bruno Lepri. 2012. Do linguistic style and readability of scientific abstracts affect their virality? In *Proceedings of the 6th International Conference on Weblogs and Social Media (ICWSM)*.

Bo Han and Timothy Baldwin. 2011. Lexical normalisation of short text messages: Makn sens a #twitter. In *Proceedings of the 49th Annual Meeting of the Association for Computational Linguistics: Human Language Technologies (ACL-HLT)*.

Bo Han, Afshin Rahimi, Leon Derczynski, and Timothy Baldwin. 2016. Twitter geolocation prediction shared task of the 2016 Workshop on Noisy User-generated Text. In *Proceedings of the 2nd Workshop on Noisy User-generated Text (WNUT)*.

Yuheng Hu, Kartik Talamadupula, and Subbarao Kambhampati. 2013. Dude, srsly?: The surprisingly formal nature of Twitter's language. In *Proceedings of the 7th International Conference on Weblogs and Social Media (ICWSM)*.

William Hwang, Hannaneh Hajishirzi, Mari Ostendorf, and Wei Wu. 2015. Aligning sentences from Standard Wikipedia to Simple Wikipedia. In *Proceedings of the 2015 Conference of the North American Chapter of the Association for Computational Linguistics (NAACL)*.

Jermsak Jermsurawong and Nizar Habash. 2015. Predicting the structure of cooking recipes. In *Proceedings of the 2015 Conference on Empirical Methods in Natural Language Processing (EMNLP)*.

Anders Johannsen, Dirk Hovy, and Anders Søgaard. 2015. Cross-lingual syntactic variation over age and gender. In *Proceedings of the Nineteenth Conference on Computational Natural Language Learning (ACL)*.

Anna Jørgensen, Dirk Hovy, and Anders Søgaard. 2015. Challenges of studying and processing dialects in social media. In *Proceedings of the Workshop on Noisy User-generated Text (WNUT)*.

Dan Jurafsky. 2014. *The Language of Food*. W. W. Norton Company, Inc.

Chloé Kiddon, Ganesa Thandavam Ponnuraj, Luke Zettlemoyer, and Yejin Choi. 2015. Mise en Place: Unsupervised interpretation of instructional recipes. In *Proceedings of the 2015 Conference on Empirical Methods in Natural Language Processing (EMNLP)*.

Lingpeng Kong, Nathan Schneider, Swabha Swayamdipta, Archna Bhatia, Chris Dyer, and Noah A. Smith. 2014. A dependency parser for Tweets. In *Proceedings of the 2014 Conference on Empirical Methods in Natural Language Processing (EMNLP)*.

Chaitanya Kulkarni, Wei Xu, Alan Ritter, and Raghu Machiraju. 2017. Taking the first essential steps in automating the wet laboratory: Annotating a corpus of protocols for reproducibility. In *Submission*.

Wuwei Lan, Siyu Qiu, Hua He, and Wei Xu. 2017. A continuously growing dataset of sentential paraphrases from Twitter. In *Proceedings of the 2017 Conference on Empirical Methods in Natural Language Processing (EMNLP)*.

Kenton Lee, Mike Lewis, and Luke Zettlemoyer. 2016. Global neural CCG parsing with optimality guarantees. In *Proceedings of the 2016 Conference on Empirical Methods in Natural Language Processing (EMNLP)*.

Jiwei Li, Michel Galley, Chris Brockett, Georgios Spithourakis, Jianfeng Gao, and Bill Dolan. 2016. A persona-based neural conversation model. In *Proceedings of the 54th Annual Meeting of the Association for Computational Linguistics (ACL)*.

Wang Ling, Chris Dyer, Alan W Black, Isabel Trancoso, Ramon Fermandez, Silvio Amir, Luis Marujo, and Tiago Luis. 2015. Finding function in form: Compositional character models for open vocabulary word representation. In *Proceedings of the 2015 Conference on Empirical Methods in Natural Language Processing (EMNLP)*.

Dipendra Kumar Misra and Yoav Artzi. 2016. Neural shift-reduce CCG semantic parsing. In *Proceedings of the 2016 Conference on Empirical Methods in Natural Language Processing (EMNLP)*.

Masahiro Mizukami, Graham Neubig, Sakriani Sakti, and Tomoki Toda. 2015. Linguistic individuality transformation for spoken language. In *Proceedings of the 6th International Workshop On Spoken Dialogue Systems*.

Grace Muzny and Luke Zettlemoyer. 2013. Automatic idiom identification in Wiktionary. In *Proceedings of the 2013 Conference on Empirical Methods in Natural Language Processing (EMNLP)*.

Courtney Napoles, Benjamin Van Durme, and Chris Callison-Burch. 2011. Evaluating sentence compression: Pitfalls and suggested remedies. In *Proceedings of the Workshop on Monolingual Text-To-Text Generation*.

Sergiu Nisioi, Sanja Štajner, Simone Paolo Ponzetto, and Liviu P. Dinu. 2017. Exploring neural text simplification models. In *Proceedings of the 55th Annual Meeting of the Association for Computational Linguistics (ACL)*.

Gustavo Paetzold and Lucia Specia. 2016. Benchmarking lexical simplification systems. In *Proceedings of the 10th International Conference on Language Resources and Evaluation (LREC)*.

Ellie Pavlick and Chris Callison-Burch. 2016. Simple PPDB: A paraphrase database for simplification. In *Proceedings of the 54th Annual Meeting of the Association for Computational Linguistics (ACL)*.

David Pellow and Maxine Eskenazi. 2014. An open corpus of everyday documents for simplification tasks. In *Proceedings of the 3rd Workshop on Predicting and Improving Text Readability for Target Reader Populations (PITR)*.

Barbara Plank. 2018. What to do about non-standard (or non-canonical) language in nlp. In *Proceedings of the 13th Conference on Natural Language Processing (KONVENS)*.

Barbara Plank and Dirk Hovy. 2015. Personality traits on Twitter -or- how to get 1,500 personality tests in a week. In *Proceedings of the 6th Workshop on Computational Approaches to Subjectivity, Sentiment and Social Media Analysis*.

Daniel Preoţiuc-Pietro, Wei Xu, and Lyle Ungar. 2016. Discovering user attribute stylistic differences via paraphrasing. In *Proceedings of the 30th AAAI Conference on Artificial Intelligence (AAAI)*.

Hannah Rashkin, Sameer Singh, and Yejin Choi. 2016. Connotation frames: A data-driven investigation. In *Proceedings of the 54th Annual Meeting of the Association for Computational Linguistics (ACL)*.

Marta Recasens, Cristian Danescu-Niculescu-Mizil, and Dan Jurafsky. 2013. Linguistic models for analyzing and detecting biased language. In *Proceedings of the 51st Annual Meeting of the Association for Computational Linguistics (ACL)*.

Marek Rei, Gamal Crichton, and Sampo Pyysalo. 2016. Attending to characters in neural sequence labeling models. In *Proceedings of the 26th International Conference on Computational Linguistics (COLING)*.

Alan Ritter, Sam Clark, Mausam, and Oren Etzioni. 2011. Named entity recognition in Tweets: An experimental study. In *Proceedings of the 2011 Conference on Empirical Methods in Natural Language Processing (EMNLP)*.

Xianzhi Ruan, Steven Wilson, and Rada Mihalcea. 2016. Finding optimists and pessimists on Twitter. In *Proceedings of the 54th Annual Meeting of the Association for Computational Linguistics (ACL)*.

Alexander M. Rush, Sumit Chopra, and Jason Weston. 2015. A neural attention model for abstractive sentence summarization. In *Proceedings of the 2015 Conference on Empirical Methods in Natural Language Processing (EMNLP)*.

Maarten Sap, Gregory Park, Johannes Eichstaedt, Margaret Kern, David Stillwell, Michal Kosinski, Lyle Ungar, and Hansen Andrew Schwartz. 2014. Developing age and gender predictive lexica over social media. In *Proceedings of the 2014 Conference on Empirical Methods in Natural Language Processing (EMNLP)*.

Nathan Schneider and Noah A. Smith. 2015. A corpus and model integrating multiword expressions and supersenses. In *Proceedings of the 2015 Conference of the North American Chapter of the Association for Computational Linguistics: Human Language Technologies (NAACL-HLT)*.

H. Andrew Schwartz, Johannes C. Eichstaedt, Margaret L. Kern, Lukasz Dziurzynski, Stephanie M. Ramones, Megha Agrawal, Achal Shah, Michal Kosinski, David Stillwell, Martin E. P. Seligman, and Lyle H. Ungar. 2013. Personality, gender, and age in the language of social media: The open-vocabulary approach. *PLOS One* 8:1–16.

Ramtin Mehdizadeh Seraj, Maryam Siahbani, and Anoop Sarkar. 2015. Improving statistical machine translation with a multilingual paraphrase database. In *Proceedings of the 2015 Conference on Empirical Methods in Natural Language Processing (EMNLP)*.

Advaith Siddharthan and Angrosh Mandya. 2014. Hybrid text simplification using synchronous dependency grammars with hand-written and automatically harvested rules. In *Proceedings of the 14th Conference of the European Chapter of the Association for Computational Linguistics (EACL)*.

Yanchuan Sim, Bryan R. Routledge, and Noah A. Smith. 2015. The utility of text: The case of amicus briefs and the supreme court. In *Proceedings of the 29th AAAI Conference on Artificial Intelligence (AAAI)*.

Swapna Somasundaran and Janyce Wiebe. 2009. Recognizing stances in online debates. In *Proceedings of the Joint Conference of the 47th Annual Meeting of the ACL and the 4th International Joint Conference on Natural Language Processing (ACL-AFNLP)*.

James Surowiecki. 2005. *The Wisdom of Crowds*. Anchor.

Jeniya Tabassum, Alan Ritter, and Wei Xu. 2016. A minimally supervised method for recognizing and normalizing time expressions in Twitter. In *Proceedings of The 2016 Conference on Empirical Methods on Natural Language Processing (EMNLP)*.

Chenhao Tan, Vlad Niculae, Cristian Danescu-Niculescu-Mizil, and Lillian Lee. 2016. Winning arguments: Interaction dynamics and persuasion strategies in good-faith online discussions. In *Proceedings of the 25th International Conference on World Wide Web (WWW)*.

Dan Tasse and Noah A Smith. 2008. SOUR CREAM: Toward semantic processing of recipes. *Carnegie Mellon University, Pittsburgh, Tech. Rep. CMU-LTI-08-005* .

Kristina Toutanova, Chris Brockett, Ke M. Tran, and Saleema Amershi. 2016. A dataset and evaluation metrics for abstractive compression of sentences and short paragraphs. In *Proceedings of the 2016 Conference on Empirical Methods in Natural Language Processing (EMNLP)*.

Marlies van der Wees, Arianna Bisazza, and Christof Monz. 2015. Five shades of noise: Analyzing machine translation errors in user-generated text. In *Proceedings of the Workshop on Noisy User-generated Text (WNUT)*.

Ben Verhoeven, Walter Daelemans, and Barbara Plank. 2016. TwiSty: A multilingual Twitter stylometry corpus for gender and personality profiling. In *Proceedings of the 10th International Conference on Language Resources and Evaluation (LREC)*.

Adam Vogel and Dan Jurafsky. 2012. He said, she said: Gender in the ACL Anthology. In *Proceedings of the ACL 2012 Special Workshop on Rediscovering 50 Years of Discoveries*.

Rob Voigt, Nicholas P. Camp, Vinodkumar Prabhakaran, William L. Hamilton, Rebecca C. Hetey, Camilla M. Griffiths, David Jurgens, Dan Jurafsky, and Jennifer L. Eberhardt. 2017. Language from police body camera footage shows racial disparities in officer respect. *Proceedings of the National Academy of Sciences* 114(25):6521–6526.

Svitlana Volkova, Theresa Wilson, and David Yarowsky. 2013. Exploring demographic language variations to improve multilingual sentiment analysis in social media. In *Proceedings of the 2013 Conference on Empirical Methods in Natural Language Processing (EMNLP)*.

Jun-Ming Xu, Kwang-Sung Jun, Xiaojin Zhu, and Amy Bellmore. 2012a. Learning from bullying traces in social media. In *Proceedings of the 2012 Conference of the North American Chapter of the Association for Computational Linguistics: Human Language Technologies (NAACL-HLT)*.

Wei Xu. 2014. *Data-Drive Approaches for Paraphrasing Across Language Variations*. Ph.D. thesis, Department of Computer Science, New York University.

Wei Xu, Chris Callison-Burch, and William B. Dolan. 2015a. SemEval-2015 Task 1: Paraphrase and semantic similarity in Twitter (PIT). In *Proceedings of the 9th International Workshop on Semantic Evaluation (SemEval)*.

Wei Xu, Chris Callison-Burch, and Courtney Napoles. 2015b. Problems in current text simplification research: New data can help. *Transactions of the Association for Computational Linguistics (TACL)* 3:283–297.

Wei Xu, Courtney Napoles, Ellie Pavlick, Quanze Chen, and Chris Callison-Burch. 2016. Optimizing statistical machine translation for text simplification. *Transactions of the Association for Computational Linguistics (TACL)* 4:401–415.

Wei Xu, Alan Ritter, Chris Callison-Burch, William B Dolan, and Yangfeng Ji. 2014. Extracting lexically divergent paraphrases from Twitter. *Transactions of the Association for Computational Linguistics (TACL)* 2:435–448.

Wei Xu, Alan Ritter, Bill Dolan, Ralph Grishman, and Cherry Colin. 2012b. Paraphrasing for style. In *Proceedings of the 28th International Conference on Computational Linguistics (COLING)*.

Wei Xu, Alan Ritter, and Ralph Grishman. 2013. Gathering and generating paraphrases from Twitter with application to normalization. In *Proceedings of the Sixth Workshop on Building and Using Comparable Corpora (BUCC)*.

Yi Yang and Jacob Eisenstein. 2015. Unsupervised multi-domain adaptation with feature embeddings. In *Proceedings of the 2015 Conference of the North American Chapter of the Association for Computational Linguistics: Human Language Technologies (NAACL-HLT)*.

Luke Zettlemoyer and Michael Collins. 2007. Online learning of relaxed CCG grammars for parsing to logical form. In *Proceedings of the 2007 Joint Conference on Empirical Methods in Natural Language Processing and Computational Natural Language Learning (EMNLP-CoNLL)*.

Shakespearizing Modern Language Using Copy-Enriched Sequence-to-Sequence Models

Harsh Jhamtani [*], **Varun Gangal** [*], **Eduard Hovy, Eric Nyberg**
Language Technologies Institute
Carnegie Mellon University
{jharsh,vgangal,hovy,ehn}@cs.cmu.edu

Abstract

Variations in writing styles are commonly used to adapt the content to a specific context, audience, or purpose. However, applying stylistic variations is still largely a manual process, and there have been little efforts towards automating it. In this paper we explore automated methods to transform text from modern English to Shakespearean English using an end to end trainable neural model with pointers to enable copy action. To tackle limited amount of parallel data, we pre-train embeddings of words by leveraging external dictionaries mapping Shakespearean words to modern English words as well as additional text. Our methods are able to get a BLEU score of 31+, an improvement of $\approx$ 6 points over the strongest baseline. We publicly release our code to foster further research in this area. [1]

1 Introduction

Text is often morphed using a variety of lexical and grammatical transformations, adjusting the degree of formality, usage of catchy phrases, and other such stylistic changes to make it more appealing. Moreover, different text styles appeal to different user segments (Saha Roy et al., 2015) (Kitis, 1997) (Schwartz et al., 2013). Thus there is a need to effectively adapt text to different styles. However, manually transforming text to a desired style can be a tedious process.

There have been increased efforts towards machine assisted text content creation and editing through automated methods for summarization

No	Type	Text
1	MODERN	Oh my, my bones ache so much
	ORIGINAL	Fie, how my bones ache !
	COPY	fie, how my bones ache !
	SIMPLES2S	you'll be, sir, what the bones are tired .
	STAT	Oh my, my bones ache so much .
2	MODERN	I am in a rush .
	ORIGINAL	I stand on sudden haste .
	COPY	i stand on sudden haste .
	SIMPLES2S	i'm stand right here .
	STAT	I am in a Fly
3	MODERN	Give my compliments to your lady
	ORIGINAL	Commend me to thy lady
	COPY	commend me to your lady
	SIMPLES2S	give my regards to your lady
	STAT	give my praises to your lady
4	MODERN	Showing mercy by pardoning killers only causes more murders .
	ORIGINAL	Mercy but murders, pardoning those that kill .
	COPY	mercy but murders, those those who kill us .
	SIMPLES2S	but except the murders to those murders to kill you .
	STAT	of mercy by pardoning killers causes more dire.
5	MODERN	Holy Saint Francis, this is a drastic change !
	ORIGINAL	Holy Saint Francis, what a change is here !
	COPY	holy saint francis, what a change is here !
	SIMPLES2S	it's the holy flute, what's the changed !
	STAT	Holy Saint Francis, this is a drastic change !
6	MODERN	was that my father who left here in such a hurry ?
	ORIGINAL	Was that my father that went hence so fast ?
	COPY	was that my father that went went so fast ?
	SIMPLES2S	was that my father was so that ?
	STAT	was that my father that left here in such a haste ?
7	MODERN	Give me one kiss and I'll go down .
	ORIGINAL	One kiss, and I'll descend .
	COPY	one kiss me, and I'll descend .
	SIMPLES2S	one kiss,and I come down .
	STAT	Give me a kiss, and I'll go down .
8	MODERN	then the window lets day in, and life goes out the window .
	ORIGINAL	Then, window, let day in and life out .
	COPY	then, window out, and day life .
	SIMPLES2S	then she is just a life of life, let me life out of life .
	STAT	then the window will let day in, and life out .

Table 1: Examples from dataset showing modern paraphrases (MODERN) of few sentences from Shakespeare's plays (ORIGINAL). We also show transformation of modern text to Shakespearean text from our models (COPY, SIMPLES2S and STAT).

---

* denotes equal contribution

[1] https://github.com/harsh19/Shakespearizing-Modern-English

Proceedings of the Workshop on Stylistic Variation, pages 10–19
Copenhagen, Denmark, September 7–11, 2017. ©2017 Association for Computational Linguistics

(Rush et al., 2015) , brand naming (Hiranandani et al., 2017), text expansion (Srinivasan et al., 2017), etc. However, there is a dearth of automated solutions for adapting text quickly to different styles. We consider the problem of transforming text written in modern English text to Shakepearean style English. For the sake of brevity and clarity of exposition, we henceforth refer to the *Shakespearean* sentences/side as *Original* and the modern English paraphrases as *Modern*.

Unlike traditional domain or style transfer, our task is made more challenging by the fact that the two styles employ diachronically disparate registers of English - one style uses the contemporary language while the other uses *Early Modern English* [2] from the *Elizabethan Era* (1558-1603). Although *Early Modern English* is not classified as a different language (unlike *Old English* and *Middle English*), it does have novel words (*acknown* and *belike*), novel grammatical constructions (two *second person* forms - *thou* (informal) and *you* (formal) (Brown et al., 1960)), semantically drifted senses (e.g *fetches* is a synonym of *excuses*) and non-standard orthography (Rayson et al., 2007). Additionally, there is a domain difference since the Shakespearean play sentences are from a dramatic screenplay whereas the *parallel* modern English sentences are meant to be simplified explanation for high-school students.

Prior works in this field leverage a language model for the target style, achieving transformation either using phrase tables (Xu et al., 2012), or by inserting relevant adjectives and adverbs (Saha Roy et al., 2015). Such works have limited scope in the type of transformations that can be achieved. Moreover, statistical and rule MT based systems do not provide a direct mechanism to a) share word representation information between source and target sides b) incorporating constraints between words into word representations in end-to-end fashion. Neural sequence-to-sequence models, on the other hand, provide such flexibility.

Our main contributions are as follows:

- We use a sentence level sequence to sequence neural model with a pointer network component to enable direct copying of words from input. We demonstrate that this method performs much better than prior phrase transla-

	Original	Modern
# Word Tokens	217K	200K
# Word Types	12.39K	10.05K
Average Sentence Length	11.81	10.91
Entropy (Type.Dist)	6.15	6.06
∩ Word Types	6.33K	

Table 2: Dataset Statistics

tion based approaches for transforming *Modern* English text to *Shakespearean* English.

- We leverage a dictionary providing mapping between Shakespearean words and modern English words to retrofit pre-trained word embeddings. Incorporating this extra information enables our model to perform well in spite of small size of parallel data.

Rest of the paper is organized as follows. We first provide a brief analysis of our dataset in (§2). We then elaborate on details of our methods in (§3, §4, §5, §6). We then discuss experimental setup and baselines in (§7). Thereafter, we discuss the results and observations in (§8). We conclude with discussions on related work (§9) and future directions (§10).

2 Dataset

Our dataset is a collection of line-by-line modern paraphrases for 16 of Shakespeare's 36 plays (*Antony & Cleopatra, As You Like It, Comedy of Errors, Hamlet, Henry V* etc) from the educational site *Sparknotes*[3]. This dataset was compiled by Xu et al. (2014; 2012) and is freely available on github.[4] 14 plays covering 18,395 sentences form the training data split. We kept 1218 sentences from the play *Twelfth Night* as validation data set. The last play, *Romeo and Juliet*, comprising of 1462 sentences, forms the test set.

2.1 Examples

Table 1 shows some parallel pairs from the test split of our data, along with the corresponding target outputs from some of our models. *Copy* and *SimpleS2S* refer to our best performing attentional S2S models with and without a *Copy* component respectively. *Stat* refers to the best statistical machine translation baseline using off-the-shelf GIZA++ aligner and MOSES. We can see through many of the examples how direct copying from the source side helps the *Copy* generates

[2]https://en.wikipedia.org/wiki/Early_Modern_English

[3]www.sparknotes.com
[4] http://tinyurl.com/ycdd3v6h

better outputs than the *SimpleS2S*. The approaches are described in greater detail in (§3) and (§7).

2.2 Analysis

Table 2 shows some statistics from the training split of the dataset. In general, the *Original* side has longer sentences and a larger vocabulary. The slightly higher entropy of the *Original* side's frequency distribution indicates that the frequencies are more spread out over words. Intuitively, the large number of shared word types indicates that sharing the representation between *Original* and *Modern* sides could provide some benefit.

3 Method Overview

Overall architecture of the system is shown in Figure 1. We use a bidirectional LSTM to encode the input modern English sentence. Our decoder side model is a mixture model of RNN module amd pointer network module. The two individual modules share the attentions weights over encoder states, although it is not necessary to do so. The decoder RNN predicts probability distribution of next word over the vocabulary, while pointer model predicts probability distribution over words in input. The two probabilities undergo a weighted addition, the weights themselves computed based on previous decoder hidden state and the encoder outputs.

Let $\mathbf{x}, \mathbf{y}$ be the some input - output sentence pair in the dataset. Both input $\mathbf{x}$ as well as output $\mathbf{y}$ are sequence of tokens. $\mathbf{x} = \mathbf{x}_1\mathbf{x}_2...\mathbf{x}_{T_{enc}}$, where T_{enc} represents the length of the input sequence $\mathbf{x}$. Similarly, $\mathbf{y} = \mathbf{y}_1\mathbf{y}_2...\mathbf{y}_{T_{dec}}$. Each of $\mathbf{x}_i, \mathbf{y}_j$ is a token from the vocabulary.

4 Token embeddings

Each token in vocabulary is represented by a M dimensional embedding vector. Let vocabulary V be the union of modern English and Shakepearean vocabularies i.e. $V = V_{shakespeare} \cup V_{modern}$. E_{enc} and E_{dec} represent the embedding matrices used by encoder and decoder respectively ($E_{enc}, E_{dec} \in \mathbb{R}^{|V| \times M}$). We consider union of the vocabularies for both input and output embeddings because many of the tokens are common in two vocabularies, and in the best performing setting we share embeddings between encoder and decoder models. Let $E_{enc}(t)$, represent encoder side embeddings of some token t.

For some input sequence $\mathbf{x}$, $E_{enc}(\mathbf{x})$ is given as $(E_{enc}(\mathbf{x}_1), E_{enc}(\mathbf{x}_2), ...)$.

4.1 Pretraining of embeddings

Learning token embeddings from scratch in an end-to-end fashion along with the model greatly increases the number of parameters. To mitigate this, we consider pretraining of the token embeddings. We pretrain our embeddings on all training sentences. We also experiment with adding additional data from PTB (Marcus et al., 1993) for better learning of embeddings. Additionally we leverage a dictionary mapping tokens from Shakespearean English to modern English.

We consider four distinct strategies to train the embeddings. In the cases where we use external text data, we first train the embeddings using both the external data and training data, and then for the same number of iterations on training data alone, to ensure adaptation. Note that we do not directly use off-the-shelf pretrained embeddings such as *Glove* (Pennington et al., 2014) and *Word2Vec* (Mikolov et al., 2013) since we need to learn embeddings for novel word forms (and also different word senses for extant word forms) on the *Original* side.

4.1.1 Plain

This method is the simplest pre-training method. Here, we do not use any additional data, and train word embeddings are trained on the union of *Modern* and *Original* sentences.

4.1.2 PlainExt

In this method, we add all the sentences from the external text source (*PTB*) in addition to sentences in training split of our data.

4.1.3 Retro

We leverage a dictionary L of approximate *Original* $\rightarrow$ *Modern* word pairs (Xu et al., 2012; Xu, 2014), crawled from `shakespeare-words. com`, a source distinct from Sparknotes. We explicitly add the two *2nd persons* and their corresponding forms (thy, thou, thyself etc) which are very frequent but not present in L. The final dictionary we use has 1524 pairs. Faruqui et al (2014) proposed a *retrofitting* method to update a set of word embeddings to incorporate pairwise similarity constraints. Given a set of embeddings $p_i \in P$, a vocabulary V, and a set C of pairwise constraints (i, j) between words, retrofitting tries to learn a

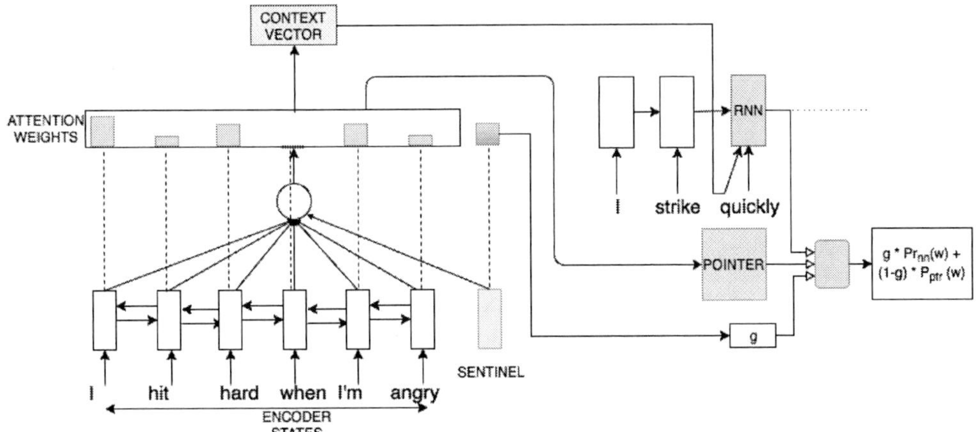

Figure 1: Depiction of our overall architecture (showing decoder step 3). Attention weights are computed using previous decoder hidden state h_2, encoder representations, and sentinel vector. Attention weights are shared by decoder RNN and pointer models. The final probability distribution over vocabulary comes from both the decoder RNN and the pointer network. Similar formulation is used over all decoder steps

new set of embeddings $q_i \in Q$ to minimize the following objective:

$$f(Q) = \delta \sum_{i=1}^{i=|V|} (p_i - q_i)^2 + \omega \sum_{(i,j) \in C} (q_i - q_j)^2 \quad (1)$$

We use their off-the-shelf implementation [5] to encode the dictionary constraints into our pretrained embeddings, setting $C = L$ and using suggested default hyperparameters for δ, ω and number of iterations.

4.1.4 RetroExt

This method is similar to *Retro*, except that we use sentences from the external data (*PTB*) in addition to training sentences.

We use **None** to represent the settings where we do not pretrain the embeddings.

4.2 Fixed embeddings

Fine-tuning pre-trained embeddings for a given task may lead to *overfitting*, especially in scenarios with small amount of supervised data for the task (Madhyastha et al., 2015). This is because embeddings for only a fraction of vocabulary items get updated, leaving the embeddings unchanged for many vocabulary items. To avoid this, we consider fixed embeddings pretrained as per procedures described earlier. While reporting results in Section (§8), we separately report results for fixed

(*FIXED*) and trainable (*VAR*) embeddings, and observe that keeping embeddings fixed leads to better performance.

5 Method Description

In this section we give details of the various modules in the proposed neural model.

5.1 Encoder model

Let $\overrightarrow{LSTM_{enc}}$ and $\overleftarrow{LSTM_{enc}}$ represent the forward and reverse encoder. $\mathbf{h}_t^{\overrightarrow{enc}}$ represent hidden state of encoder model at step t ($\mathbf{h}_t^{\overrightarrow{enc}} \in \mathbb{R}^H$). The following equations describe the model:

$$\mathbf{h}_0^{\overrightarrow{enc}} = \overrightarrow{0}, \mathbf{h}_{|x|}^{\overleftarrow{enc}} = \overrightarrow{0} \quad (2)$$

$$\mathbf{h}_t^{\overrightarrow{enc}} = \overrightarrow{LSTM_{enc}}(\mathbf{h}_{t-1}^{enc}, E_{enc}(\mathbf{x}_t)) \quad (3)$$

$$\mathbf{h}_t^{\overleftarrow{enc}} = \overleftarrow{LSTM_{enc}}(\mathbf{h}_{t+1}^{enc}, E_{enc}(x_t)) \quad (4)$$

$$\mathbf{h}_t^{enc} = \mathbf{h}_t^{\overrightarrow{enc}} + \mathbf{h}_t^{\overleftarrow{enc}} \quad (5)$$

We use addition to combine the forward and backward encoder states, rather than concatenation which is standardly used, since it doesn't add extra parameters, which is important in a low-data scenario such as ours.

5.2 Attention

Let $\mathbf{h}_t^{dec}$ represent the hidden state of the decoder LSTM at step t. Let $E_{dec}(\mathbf{y}_{t-1})$ represent the decoder side embeddings of previous step output. We use special $START$ symbol at $t = 1$.

We first compute a query vector, which is a linear transformation of $\mathbf{h}_{t-1}^{dec}$. A sentinel vector $\mathbf{s} \in \mathbb{R}^{H}$ is concatenated with the encoder states to create $F_{att} \in \mathbb{R}^{(T_{enc}+1) \times H}$, where T_{enc} represents the number of tokens in encoder input sequence $\mathbf{x}$. A normalized attention weight vector α^{norm} is computed. The value g, which corresponds to attention weight over sentinel vector, represents the weight given to the decoder RNN module while computing output probabilties.

$$\mathbf{q} = \mathbf{h}_{t-1}^{dec} W_q \qquad W_q \in \mathbb{R}^{H \times H} \quad (6)$$

$$F_{att} = concat(\mathbf{h}_{1..T_{enc}}^{enc}, \mathbf{s}) \qquad F_{att} \in \mathbb{R}^{(T_{enc}+1) \times H} \quad (7)$$

$$\alpha_i = \sum_{j=1}^{H}(tanh(F_{att}^{(ij)} \mathbf{q}_j)) + \mathbf{b}_i \quad \alpha_i, \mathbf{b}_i \in \mathbb{R} \quad (8)$$

$$\alpha^{norm} = softmax(\alpha) \qquad \alpha^{norm} \in \mathbb{R}^{T_{enc}+1} \quad (9)$$

$$\beta = \alpha_{1,2,\ldots,T_{enc}}^{norm} \qquad \beta \in \mathbb{R}^{T_{enc}} \quad (10)$$

$$g = \alpha_{T_{enc}+1}^{norm} \qquad g \in \mathbb{R} \quad (11)$$

5.3 Pointer model

As pointed out earlier, a pair of corresponding *Original* and *Modern* sentences have significant vocabulary overlap. Moreover, there are lot of proper nouns and rare words which might not be predicted by a sequence to sequence model. To rectify this, pointer networks have been used to enable copying of tokens from input directly (Merity et al., 2016). The pointer module provides location based attention, and output probability distribution due to pointer network module can be expressed as follows:

$$P_t^{PTR}(w) = \sum_{\mathbf{x}_j=w} (\beta_j) \quad (12)$$

5.4 Decoder RNN

Summation of encoder states weighed by corresponding attention weights yields context vector. Output probabilities over vocabulary as per the decoder LSTM module are computed as follows:

$$\mathbf{c}_t = \sum_{i=1}^{T_{enc}} \beta_i \mathbf{h}_i^{enc} \quad (13)$$

$$\mathbf{h}_t^{dec} = LSTM(\mathbf{h}_{t-1}^{dec}, [concat(E_{dec}(\mathbf{y}_{t-1}), \mathbf{c}_t)]) \quad (14)$$

$$P_t^{LSTM} = softmax(W_{out}[concat(\mathbf{h}_t^{dec}, \mathbf{c}_t)] + \mathbf{b}^{out}) \quad (15)$$

During training, we feed the ground truth for $\mathbf{y}_{t-1}$, whereas while making predictions on test data, predicted output from previous step is used instead.

5.5 Output prediction

Output probability of a token w at step t is a weighted sum of probabilities from decoder LSTM model and pointer model given as follows:

$$P_t(w) = g \times P_t^{LSTM}(w) + (1 - g) \times P_t^{PTR}(w) \quad (16)$$

$P_t^{PTR}(w)$ takes a non-zero value only if w occurs in input sequence, otherwise it is 0. Forcing $g = 0$ would correspond to not having a *Copy* component, reducing the model to a plain attentional S2S model, which we refer to as a *SimpleS2S* model.

6 Loss functions

Cross entropy loss is used to train the model. For a data point $(\mathbf{x}, \mathbf{y}) \in \mathcal{D}$ and predicted probability distributions $P_t(w)$ over the different words $w \in \mathbf{V}$ for each time step $t \in \{1, \ldots, T_{dec}\}$, the loss is given by

$$-\sum_{t=1}^{T_{dec}} \log p \left(P_t(\mathbf{y}_t)\right) \quad (17)$$

Sentinel Loss (SL): Following from work by (Merity et al., 2016), we consider additional sentinel loss. This loss function can be considered as a form of *supervised attention*. Sentinel loss is given as follows:

$$-\sum_{t=1}^{T_{dec}} \log(g^{(t)} + \sum_{x_j=y_t} (\beta_j^{(t)})) \quad (18)$$

We report the results demonstrating the impact of including the sentinel loss function (+SL).

7 Experiments

In this section we describe the experimental setup and evaluation criteria used.

7.1 Preprocessing

We lowercase sentences and then use NLTK's PUNKT tokenizer to tokenize all sentences. The *Original* side has certain characters like æwhich are not extant in today's language. We map these characters to the closest equivalent character(s) used today (e.g æ→ ae)

7.2 Baseline Methods

7.2.1 As-it-is

Since both source and target side are English, just replicating the input on the target side is a valid and competitive baseline, with a BLEU of 21+.

7.2.2 Dictionary

Xu et al. (2012) provide a dictionary mapping between large number of Shakespearean and modern English words. We augment this dictionary with pairs corresponding to the 2nd person thou (*thou, thy, thyself*) since these common tokens were not present.

Directly using this dictionary to perform word-by-word replacement is another admittable baseline. As was noted by Xu et al. (2012), this baseline actually performs worse than *As-it-is*. This could be due to its performing aggressive replacement without regard for word context. Moreover, a dictionary cannot easily capture one-to-many mappings as well as long-range dependencies [6].

7.2.3 Off-the-shelf SMT

To train statistical machine translation (*SMT*) baselines, we use publicly available open-source toolkit MOSES (Koehn et al., 2007), along with the GIZA++ word aligner (Och, 2003), as was done in (Xu et al., 2012). For training the target-side LM component, we use the *lmplz* toolkit within MOSES to train a 4-gram LM. We also use *MERT* (Och, 2003), available as part of MOSES, to tune on the validation set.

For fairness of comparison, it is necessary to use the pairwise dictionary and *PTB* while training the SMT models as well - the most obvious way for this is to use the dictionary and *PTB* as additional training data for the alignment component and the target-side LM respectively. We experiment with several SMT models, ablating for the use of both *PTB* and dictionary. In 8, we only report the performance of the best of these approaches.

7.3 Evaluation

Our primary evaluation metric is *BLEU* (Papineni et al., 2002) . We compute *BLEU* using the freely available and very widely used perl script[7] from the MOSES decoder.

We also report *PINC* (Chen and Dolan, 2011), which originates from paraphrase evaluation liter-ature and evaluates how much the target side paraphrases resemble the source side. Given a source sentence s and a target side paraphrase c generated by the system, *PINC(s,c)* is defined as

$$PINC(s,c) = 1 - \frac{1}{N} \sum_{n=1}^{n=N} \frac{|Ngram(c,n) \cap Ngram(s,n)|}{|Ngram(c,n)|}$$

where $Ngram(x,n)$ denotes the set of n-grams of length n in sentence x, and N is the maximum length of ngram considered. We set $N = 4$. Higher the *PINC*, greater the novelty of paraphrases generated by the system. Note, however, that PINC does not measure fluency of generated paraphrases.

7.4 Training and Parameters

We use a minibatch-size of 32 and the *ADAM* optimizer (Kingma and Ba, 2014) with learning rate 0.001, momentum parameters 0.9 and 0.999, and $\epsilon = 10^{-8}$. All our implementations are written in Python using Tensorflow 1.1.0 framework.

For every model, we experimented with two configurations of embedding and LSTM size - S (128-128), ME (192-192) and L (256-256). Across models, we find that the ME configuration performs better in terms of highest validation BLEU. We also find that larger configurations (384-384 & 512-512) fail to converge or perform very poorly [8]. Here, we report results only for the ME configuration for all the models. For all our models, we picked the best saved model over 15 epochs which has the highest validation BLEU.

7.5 Decoding

At test-time we use greedy decoding to find the most likely target sentence[9]. We also experiment with a post-processing strategy which replaces *UNKs* in the target output with the highest aligned (maximum attention) source word. We find that this gives a small jump in *BLEU* of about 0.1-0.2 for all neural models [10]. Our best model, for instance, gets a jump of 0.14 to reach a BLEU of *31.26* from 31.12.

8 Results

The results in Table 3 confirm most of our hypotheses about the right architecture for this task.

---

[6]thou-thyself and you-yourself

[7]http://tinyurl.com/yben45gm

[8]This is expected given the small parallel data

[9]Empirically, we observed that beam search does not give improvements for our task

[10]Since effect is small and uniform, we report BLEU before post-processing in Table 3

- **Copy component**: We can observe from Table 3 that the various *Copy* models each outperform their *SimpleS2S* counterparts by atleast 7-8 BLEU points.

- **Retrofitting dictionary constraints**: The *Retro* configurations generally outperform their corresponding *Plain* configurations. For instance, our best configuration *Copy.Yes.RetroExtFixed* gets a better BLEU than *Copy.Yes.PlainExtFixed* by a margin of atleast 11.

- **Sharing Embeddings**: Sharing source and target side embeddings benefits all the *Retro* configurations, although it slightly deteriorates performance (about 1 BLEU point) for some of the *Plain* configurations.

- **Fixing Embeddings**: *Fixed* configurations always perform better than corresponding *Var* ones (save some exceptions). For instance, *Copy.Yes.RetroExtFixed* get a BLEU of 31.12 compared to 20.95 for *Copy.Yes.RetroExtVar*. Due to fixing embeddings, the former has just half as many parameters as the latter (5.25M vs 9.40M)

- **Effect of External Data**: Pretraining with external data *Ext* works well along with retrofitting *Retro*. For instance, *Copy.Yes.RetroExtFixed* gets a BLEU improvement of 2+ points over *Copy.Yes.RetroFixed*

- **Effect of Pretraining**: For the *SimpleS2S* models, pre-training adversely affects BLEU. However, for the *Copy* models, pre-training leads to improvement in BLEU. The simplest pretrained *Copy* model, *Copy.No.PlainVar* has a BLEU score 1.8 higher than *Copy.No.NoneVar*.

- **PINC scores**: All the neural models have higher PINC scores than the statistical and dictionary approaches, which indicate that the target sentences produced differ more from the source sentences than those produced by these approaches.

- **Sentinel Loss:** Adding the sentinel loss does not have any significant effect, and ends up reducing BLEU by a point or two, as seen with the *Copy+SL* configurations.

8.1 Qualitative Analysis

Figure 2 shows the attention matrices from our best *Copy* model (*Copy.Yes.RetroExtFixed*) and our best *SimpleS2S* model (*SimpleS2S.Yes.Retrofixed*) respectively for the same input test sentence. Without an explicit *Copy* component, the *SimpleS2S* model cannot predict the words *saint* and *francis*, and drifts off after predicting incorrect word *flute*.

Model	Sh	Init	BLEU (PINC)
AS-IT-IS	-	-	21.13 (0.0)
DICTIONARY	-	-	17.00 (26.64)
STAT	-	-	**24.39** (32.30)
SIMPLES2S	×	$NoneVar$	11.66 (85.61)
	×	$PlainVar$	9.27 (86.52)
	×	$PlainExtVar$	8.73 (87.17)
	×	$RetroVar$	10.57 (85.06)
	×	$RetroExtVar$	10.26 (83.83)
	✓	$NoneVar$	11.17 (84.91)
	✓	$PlainVar$	8.78 (85.57)
	✓	$PlainFixed$	8.73 (89.19)
	✓	$PlainExtVar$	8.59 (86.04)
	✓	$PlainExtFixed$	8.59 (89.16)
	✓	$RetroVar$	10.86 (85.58)
	✓	$RetroFixed$	11.36 (85.07)
	✓	$RetroExtVar$	11.25 (83.56)
	✓	$RetroExtFixed$	**10.86** (88.80)
COPY	×	$NoneVar$	18.44 (83.68)
	×	$PlainVar$	20.26 (81.54)
	×	$PlainExtVar$	20.20 (83.38)
	×	$RetroVar$	21.25 (81.18)
	×	$RetroExtVar$	21.57 (82.89)
	✓	$NoneVar$	22.70 (81.51)
	✓	$PlainVar$	19.27 (83.87)
	✓	$PlainFixed$	21.20 (81.61)
	✓	$PlainExtVar$	20.76 (83.17)
	✓	$PlainExtFixed$	19.32 (82.38)
	✓	$RetroVar$	22.71 (81.12)
	✓	$RetroFixed$	**28.86** (80.53)
	✓	$RetroExtVar$	20.95 (81.94)
	✓	$RetroExtFixed$	**31.12** (79.63)
COPY+SL	×	$NoneVar$	17.88 (83.70)
	×	$PlainVar$	20.22 (81.52)
	×	$PlainExtVar$	20.14 (83.46)
	×	$RetroVar$	21.30 (81.22)
	×	$RetroExtVar$	21.52 (82.86)
	✓	$NoneVar$	22.72 (81.41)
	✓	$PlainVar$	21.46 (81.39)
	✓	$PlainFixed$	23.76 (81.68)
	✓	$PlainExtVar$	20.68 (83.18)
	✓	$PlainExtFixed$	22.23 (81.71)
	✓	$RetroVar$	22.62 (81.15)
	✓	$RetroFixed$	27.66 (81.35)
	✓	$RetroExtVar$	24.11 (79.92)
	✓	$RetroExtFixed$	27.81 (84.67)

Table 3: Test BLEU results. *Sh* denotes encoder-decoder embedding sharing (*No*=×,*Yes*=✓) . *Init* denotes the manner of initializing embedding vectors. The -*Fixed* or -*Var* suffix indicates whether embeddings are fixed or trainable. COPY and SIMPLES2S denote presence/absence of *Copy* component. +SL denotes sentinel loss.

Table 1 presents model outputs[11] for some test examples. In general, the *Copy* model outputs re-

---

[11] All neural outputs are lowercase due to our preprocessing. Although this slightly affects BLEU, it helps prevent token occurrences getting split due to capitalization.

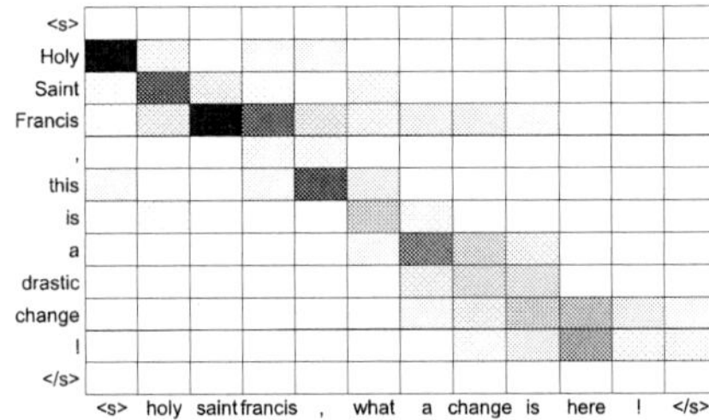

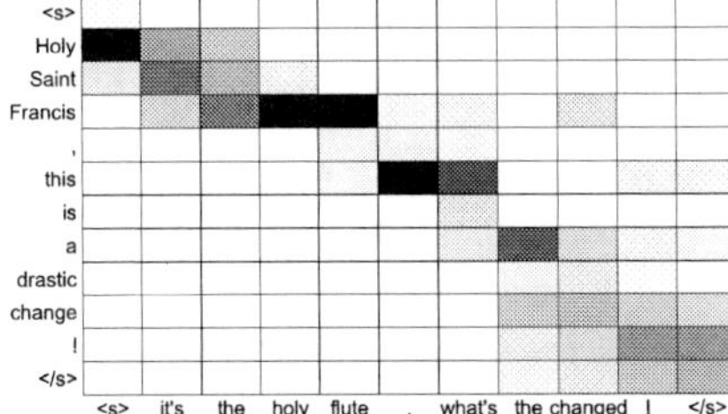

Figure 2: Attention matrices from a *Copy* (top) and a *simple S2S* (bottom) model respectively on the input sentence *"Holy Saint Francis, this is a drastic change!"* . $<s>$ and $</s>$ are start and stop characters. Darker cells are higher-valued.

semble the ground truth more closely compared to *SimpleS2S* and *Stat* . In some cases, it faces issues with repetition (Examples 5 and 7) and fluency (Example 9).

9 Related Work

There have been some prior work on style adaptation. Xu et al. (2012) use phrase table based statistical machine translation to transform text to target style. On the other hand our method is an end-to-end trainable neural network. Saha Roy et al (2015) leverage different language models based on geolocation and occupation to align a text to specific style. However, their work is limited to addition of adjectives and adverbs. Our method can handle more generic transformations including addition and deletion of words.

Pointer networks (Vinyals et al., 2015) allow the use of input-side words directly as output in a neural S2S model, and have been used for tasks like extractive summarization (See et al., 2017) (Zeng et al., 2016) and question answering (Wang and Jiang, 2016). However, pointer networks cannot generate words not present in the input. A mixture model of recurrent neural network and pointer network has been shown to achieve good performance on language modeling task (Merity et al., 2016).

S2S neural models, first proposed by Sutskever et al. (2014), and enhanced with a attention mechanism by Bahdanau et al. (2014), have yielded state-of-the-art results for machine translation (MT), , summarization (Rush et al., 2015), etc. In the context of MT, various settings such as multi-source MT (Zoph and Knight, 2016) and MT with external information (Sennrich et al., 2016) have been explored. Distinct from all of these, our work attempts to solve a Modern English $\rightarrow$ Shakespearean English style transformation task. Although closely related to both paraphrasing and MT, our task has some differentiating characteristics such as considerable source-target overlap in vocabulary and grammar (unlike MT), and different source and target language (unlike paraphrasing). Gangal et al. (2017) have proposed a neural sequence-to-sequence solution for generating a portmanteau given two English root-words. Though their task also involves large overlap in target and input, they do not employ any special copying mechanism. Unlike text simplification and summarization, our task does not involve shortening content length.

10 Conclusion

In this paper we have proposed to use a mixture model of pointer network and LSTM to transform Modern English text to Shakespearean style English. We demonstrate the effectiveness of our proposed approaches over the baselines. Our experiments reveal the utility of incorporating input-copying mechanism, and using dictionary constraints for problems with shared (but non-identical) source-target sides and sparse parallel data.

We have demonstrated the transformation to Shakespearean style English only. Methods have to be explored to achieve other stylistic variations corresponding to formality and politeness of text, usage of fancier words and expressions, etc. We release our code publicly to foster further research on stylistic transformations on text. [12].

---

[12]https://github.com/harsh19/Shakespearizing-Modern-English

Acknowledgements

We thank Taylor Berg-Kirkpatrick and anonymous reviewers for their comments. This research was supported in part by DARPA grant FA8750-12-2-0342 funded under the DEFT program.

References

Dzmitry Bahdanau, Kyunghyun Cho, and Yoshua Bengio. 2014. Neural machine translation by jointly learning to align and translate. *arXiv:1409.0473*.

Roger Brown, Albert Gilman, et al. 1960. The pronouns of power and solidarity. *Article*.

David L Chen and William B Dolan. 2011. Collecting highly parallel data for paraphrase evaluation. In *Proceedings of the 49th Annual Meeting of the Association for Computational Linguistics: Human Language Technologies-Volume 1*, pages 190–200. Association for Computational Linguistics.

Manaal Faruqui, Jesse Dodge, Sujay K Jauhar, Chris Dyer, Eduard Hovy, and Noah A Smith. 2014. Retrofitting word vectors to semantic lexicons. *arXiv preprint arXiv:1411.4166*.

Varun Gangal, Harsh Jhamtani, Graham Neubig, Eduard Hovy, and Eric Nyberg. 2017. Charmanteau: Character embedding models for portmanteau creation. In *Conference on Empirical Methods in Natural Language Processing (EMNLP)*, Copenhagen, Denmark.

Gaurush Hiranandani, Pranav Maneriker, and Harsh Jhamtani. 2017. Generating appealing brand names. *arXiv preprint arXiv:1706.09335*.

Diederik Kingma and Jimmy Ba. 2014. Adam: A method for stochastic optimization. *arXiv preprint arXiv:1412.6980*.

Eliza Kitis. 1997. Adspart of our lives: linguistic awareness of powerful advertising. *Word & Image*, 13(3):304–313.

Philipp Koehn, Hieu Hoang, Alexandra Birch, Chris Callison-Burch, Marcello Federico, Nicola Bertoldi, Brooke Cowan, Wade Shen, Christine Moran, Richard Zens, et al. 2007. Moses: Open source toolkit for statistical machine translation. In *Proceedings of the 45th annual meeting of the ACL on interactive poster and demonstration sessions*, pages 177–180. Association for Computational Linguistics.

Pranava Swaroop Madhyastha, Mohit Bansal, Kevin Gimpel, and Karen Livescu. 2015. Mapping unseen words to task-trained embedding spaces. *arXiv preprint arXiv:1510.02387*.

Mitchell P Marcus, Mary Ann Marcinkiewicz, and Beatrice Santorini. 1993. Building a large annotated corpus of english: The penn treebank. *Computational linguistics*, 19(2):313–330.

Stephen Merity, Caiming Xiong, James Bradbury, and Richard Socher. 2016. Pointer Sentinel Mixture Models. *arXiv preprint arXiv:1609.07843*.

Tomas Mikolov, Kai Chen, Greg Corrado, and Jeffrey Dean. 2013. Efficient estimation of word representations in vector space. *arXiv preprint arXiv:1301.3781*.

Franz Josef Och. 2003. Minimum error rate training in statistical machine translation. In *Proceedings of the 41st Annual Meeting on Association for Computational Linguistics-Volume 1*, pages 160–167. Association for Computational Linguistics.

Kishore Papineni, Salim Roukos, Todd Ward, and Wei-Jing Zhu. 2002. Bleu: a method for automatic evaluation of machine translation. In *Proceedings of the 40th annual meeting on association for computational linguistics*, pages 311–318. Association for Computational Linguistics.

Jeffrey Pennington, Richard Socher, and Christopher D Manning. 2014. Glove: Global Vectors for Word Representation. In *EMNLP*, volume 14, pages 1532–1543.

Paul Rayson, Dawn Archer, Alistair Baron, Jonathan Culpeper, and Nicholas Smith. 2007. Tagging the Bard: Evaluating the accuracy of a modern POS tagger on Early Modern English corpora. *Article*.

Alexander M Rush, Sumit Chopra, and Jason Weston. 2015. A neural attention model for abstractive sentence summarization. *arXiv preprint arXiv:1509.00685*.

Rishiraj Saha Roy, Aishwarya Padmakumar, Guna Prasaad Jeganathan, and Ponnurangam Kumaraguru. 2015. Automated Linguistic Personalization of Targeted Marketing Messages Mining User-Generated Text on Social Media. In *16th International Conference on Intelligent Text Processing and Computational Linguistics 2015 (CICLing '15)*, pages 203–224. Springer International Publishing.

H Andrew Schwartz, Johannes C Eichstaedt, Margaret L Kern, Lukasz Dziurzynski, Stephanie M Ramones, Megha Agrawal, Achal Shah, Michal Kosinski, David Stillwell, Martin EP Seligman, et al. 2013. Personality, gender, and age in the language of social media: The open-vocabulary approach. *PloS one*, 8(9):e73791.

Abigail See, Peter J Liu, and Christopher D Manning. 2017. Get To The Point: Summarization with Pointer-Generator Networks. *arXiv preprint arXiv:1704.04368*.

Rico Sennrich, Barry Haddow, and Alexandra Birch. 2016. Controlling politeness in neural machine translation via side constraints. In *Proceedings of NAACL-HLT*, pages 35–40.

Balaji Vasan Srinivasan, Rishiraj Saha Roy, Harsh Jhamtani, Natwar Modani, and Niyati Chhaya. 2017. Corpus-based automatic text expansion. In *CICLING*.

Ilya Sutskever, Oriol Vinyals, and Quoc V Le. 2014. Sequence to sequence learning with neural networks. In *Neural information processing systems*, pages 3104–3112.

Oriol Vinyals, Meire Fortunato, and Navdeep Jaitly. 2015. Pointer networks. In *Advances in Neural Information Processing Systems*, pages 2692–2700.

Shuohang Wang and Jing Jiang. 2016. Machine comprehension using match-lstm and answer pointer. *arXiv preprint arXiv:1608.07905*.

Wei Xu. 2014. *Data-driven approaches for paraphrasing across language variations*. Ph.D. thesis, New York University.

Wei Xu, Alan Ritter, William B Dolan, Ralph Grishman, and Colin Cherry. 2012. Paraphrasing for style. In *24th International Conference on Computational Linguistics, COLING 2012*.

Wenyuan Zeng, Wenjie Luo, Sanja Fidler, and Raquel Urtasun. 2016. Efficient Summarization with Read-Again and Copy Mechanism. *arXiv preprint arXiv:1611.03382*.

Barret Zoph and Kevin Knight. 2016. Multi-source neural translation. *arXiv preprint arXiv:1601.00710*.

Discovering Stylistic Variations in Distributional Vector Space Models via Lexical Paraphrases

Xing Niu and **Marine Carpuat**
Department of Computer Science
University of Maryland, College Park
`xingniu@cs.umd.edu, marine@cs.umd.edu`

Abstract

Detecting and analyzing stylistic variation in language is relevant to diverse Natural Language Processing applications. In this work, we investigate whether salient dimensions of style variations are embedded in standard distributional vector spaces of word meaning. We hypothesize that distances between embeddings of lexical paraphrases can help isolate style from meaning variations and help identify latent style dimensions. We conduct a qualitative analysis of latent style dimensions, and show the effectiveness of identified style subspaces on a lexical formality prediction task.

1 Introduction

Automatically analyzing and generating natural language requires capturing not only what is said, but also how it is said. Consider the sentences "he shot himself" and "he committed suicide". The first one is less formal than the second one, and carries information beyond its literal meaning, such as the situation in which it might be used. Another example is "stamp show" vs. "philatelic exhibition", English learners with limited vocabulary can use the former term since it is simpler.

As Natural Language Processing systems are deployed in a variety of settings, detecting and analyzing stylistic variations is becoming increasingly important, and is relevant to applications ranging from dialogue systems (Mairesse, 2008) to predicting power differences in social interactions (Danescu-Niculescu-Mizil et al., 2012).

In this work we aim to determine to what extent such stylistic variations are embedded in the topology of distributional vector space models. We focus on dense word embeddings, which provide a compact summary of word usage on the basis of the distributional hypothesis, and have been showed to capture semantic similarity and other lexical semantic relations (Mikolov et al., 2013; Baroni et al., 2014; Levy and Goldberg, 2014).

We hypothesize that differences between embeddings of words that share the same meaning are indicative of style differences. In order to test this hypothesis, we introduce a method based on Principal Component Analysis to identify salient dimensions of variations betwen word embeddings of lexical paraphrases.

Applying our method to word embeddings learned from two large corpora representing distinct genres, we conduct a qualitative analysis of the principal components discovered. It suggests that the principal components indeed discover variations that are relevant to style.

Second, we evaluate the style dimensions more directly, using them to distinguish more formal from less formal words. Formality is considered a key dimension of style variation (Heylighen and Dewaele, 1999), and it encompasses a range of finer-grained dimensions, including politeness, serious-trivial, etc (Irvine, 1979; Brown and Fraser, 1979).

The formality prediction task lets us evaluate empirically the impact of different factors in identifying style-relevant dimensions, including dimensionality of the subspace and the nature of the prediction method. We also conduct an error analysis revealing the limitation of predicting formality based on vector space models.

2 Background

Many studies of style variations have focused on the corpus or sentence level. For instance, multidimensional corpus analysis (Biber, 1995) relies on statistical analysis to identify the salient linguistic

Proceedings of the Workshop on Stylistic Variation, pages 20–27
Copenhagen, Denmark, September 7–11, 2017. ©2017 Association for Computational Linguistics

co-occurrence patterns that underlie register variations. More recently, richer combinations of features have been used to predict style dimensions such as formality: (Pavlick and Tetreault, 2016) provide a thorough study of sentence-level formality and show that classifiers based on features including POS tags and dependency parses can predict formality as defined by the collective intuition of human annotators.

Here, we focus on identifying dimensions of style variations at the lexical level, motivated by the usefulness of word embeddings in many NLP tasks (Mikolov et al., 2013; Baroni et al., 2014), and by recent work that showed that meaningful ultradense subspaces that capture dimensions such as polarity and concreteness can be induced from word embeddings in a supervised fashion (Rothe and Schütze, 2016). Bolukbasi et al. (2016) induced a gender subspace using 10 human-selected gender pairs for reducing stereotypes. In contrast, we aim to discover style relevant dimensions without supervision, using instead lexical paraphrases to discover dimensions of variations that are not explained by semantic differences.

Prior work on evaluation of style factors at the word level has used standard word embeddings as features, and relied on external supervised methods to identify style relevant information in these embeddings. Brooke et al. (2010) proposed to score the formality of a word w by comparing its meaning to that of seed words of known formality using cosine similarity (Turney and Littman, 2003). Other approaches include work by Pavlick and Nenkova (2015) who used a unigram language model to capture the difference between lexical distributions across genres.

Beyond formality, analysis of stylistic variations from the point of view of the lexicon includes predicting term complexity, as annotated by non-native speakers (Paetzold and Specia, 2016). Preotiuc-Pietro et al. (2016) isolated stylistic differences associated with user attributes (gender, age) by using paraphrase pairs and word distributions similar to Pavlick and Nenkova (2015). Xu et al. (2012) used a machine translation model to paraphrasing Shakespeares plays into/from modern English.

3 Approach

Our approach to discovering stylistic variations in vector space models is based on the assumption that these variations cannot be explained by differences in meaning, and they can be captured by salient dimensions of variation in the distributional spaces.

Lexical paraphrases should have the same meaning, and therefore their embeddings should be close to each other. When lexical paraphrases are not in the same location in the vector space, distances between them might be indicative of latent style variations. We discover such latent directions using Principal Component Analysis (PCA).[1]

Concretely, suppose e_i is the word embedding in the vector space for word w_i. Given pairs of word embeddings (e_1, e_2) for lexical paraphrases (w_1, w_2), we subtracted them to get the relative direction $d = e_1 - e_2$.

For a given word pair, the difference vector might capture many things besides style variations. We hypothesize that the regularities among these differences for a large number of examples will reveal stylistic variations. Therefore, we then trained a PCA model on all directional vectors to get principal components (pc_k) capturing latent variations.

4 Qualitative Analysis of Latent Style Dimensions

4.1 Models Settings

The approach outlined above requires two types of inputs: (1) a word embedding space, and (2) a set of lexical paraphrases.

Word Embeddings We used word2vec (Mikolov et al., 2013) to build 300-dimensional vector space models for two corpora representing different genres. As suggested by Brooke et al. (2010), we selected the ICWSM 2009 Spinn3r dataset (English tier-1) as the training corpus (Burton et al., 2009). It consists of about 1.6 billion words in 7.5 million English blogs and is expected to have wide variety of language genres. We also compared it with the pre-trained 300-dimensional model of Google News [2], which represents an even larger training corpus but in a narrower register. By working with two different

---

[1] Other algorithms for dimensionality reduction could also be leveraged to discover latent variations. E.g. multidimensional scaling (MDS) and t-distributed stochastic neighbor embedding (t-SNE).

[2] https://code.google.com/archive/p/word2vec/

k	Representative word pairs
	ICWSM 2009 Spinn3r Blogs
1	annulling • canceling ‖ abolished • canceled ‖ centre • center ‖ emphasise • highlight programme • program ‖ imperatives • essentials ‖ motorway • freeway ‖ labour • labor organised • organize ‖ six-party • six-way ‖ tranquility • serenity ‖ tripartite • three-way
2	spendings • expenditures ‖ summons • subpoenas ‖ anti-malaria • antimalarial doctor • physician ‖ falls • decreases ‖ banned • prohibiting ‖ fallen • decreased
3	decreased • receded ‖ decreased • fallen ‖ decreased • declined ‖ decreased • shrank
4	agreements • understandings ‖ unlimited • unbounded ‖ disruptions • perturbations discriminatory • discriminative ‖ timetable • time-scale ‖ amended • altered ‖ ban • forbidden
5	underscored • underline ‖ eliminated • delete ‖ highlights • underline ‖ widened • expand widened • broaden ‖ emphasises • underline ‖ decreased • reduce ‖ performed • fulfil
6	co-operate • collaborating ‖ interdomain • cross-domain ‖ cooperate • collaborating origin • sourcing ‖ executions • implementations ‖ multifunctional • cross-functional
7	refusing • rebuffs ‖ stopped • halts ‖ stress • underlines ‖ inspected • reviewed withdrawals • withdraws ‖ supervising • oversees ‖ stress • emphasises ‖ refused • rejects
8	restarting • revitalising ‖ co-operation • collaborations ‖ cooperation • collaborations restart • resumes ‖ cleric • clergymen ‖ cooperates • collaborates ‖ expel • expulsions
9	obtain • gain ‖ multi-factor • multifactorial ‖ restricts • hampers ‖ retrieves • recovers obstructs • hampers ‖ revoking • canceling ‖ contravened • breaches ‖ invalidated • canceled
10	delete • eliminate ‖ underline • stresses ‖ underline • emphasises ‖ schema • schemes restarting • revitalising ‖ decreased • reduce ‖ underline • highlight ‖ permissions • permits
	Google News
1	educator • educationist ‖ ousts • deposes ‖ exemptions • derogations ‖ educator • educationalist legal • juridical ‖ truck • lorry ‖ exceptions • derogations ‖ accomplishments • attainments roadway • carriageway ‖ prohibit • proscribe ‖ freeway • motorway ‖ lucrative • remunerative
2	standardize • standardizing ‖ intercept • intercepting ‖ evacuate • evacuating ‖ isolate • isolating
3	destroys • demolishing ‖ solves • resolving ‖ impedes • obstructing ‖ examines • investigating
4	falls • decreases ‖ widens • increases ‖ spends • expenditures ‖ shrinks • decreases
5	infeasible • impracticable ‖ impossible • impracticable ‖ earmarks • allocates unworkable • impracticable ‖ confines • restricts ‖ impractical • impracticable

Table 1: Representative word pairs for top principal components (indexed by k) are listed for both blogs and news corpora. A mixed variation of formality and American-British English (grey-boxed) can be characterized by the first principal component, but the following principal components seem vaguer in terms of interpreting stylistic variations.

corpora, we aim to discover whether they share some common stylistic variations even though they have distinct word distributions.

Lexical Paraphrases PPDB 2.0 (Pavlick et al., 2015) provides automatically extracted lexical paraphrases with entailment annotations. We use the S-size pack and extracted word pairs with `Equivalence` entailment relation, which represent a cleaner subset of the original PPDB. This process yields 9427 paraphrase pairs found in the vocabulary of the blogs embeddings and 6988 pairs found in the vocabulary of the Google news embeddings.

4.2 Analysis

We illustrate the principal components discovered in Table 1. For each of the k-th principal components, we can identify the most representative word pairs for that component by projecting all word pairs on pc_k and ranking pairs based on $d \cdot pc_k$.

The first observation is that the first principal components for both blogs and news corpora capture the pattern of American/British-English variations (grey-boxed in the Table). These might also be related to the formality dimension of style, as British-English can be regarded to be more formal than American-English (Hurtig, 2006). However, not all representative word pairs fall in that category, and the nature of the variation between e.g., "annulling" and "canceling" is harder to characterize.

We can observe clues of stylistic variations in the subsequent (2nd+) principal components, but in general it is difficult to interpret each group. Several word pairs can be seen as illustrating formality variations (e.g., "falls" ↔ "decrease", "delete" ↔ "eliminate"). Many word pairs are literally exchangeable but either one is preferred under certain context, such as "summons" vs. "subpoenas", "decreased" vs. "fallen", etc. Some principal components simply capture groups of words having semantic correlations, such as third PC of blogs and fourth PC of news (all contain "decrease/increase"), due to the biased word distribution of PPDB.

Although blogs and news corpora are expected to have different word distributions, they share the stylistic variation patterns mentioned above. One key difference between the principal components discovered int these two embedding spaces can be found in the second and third principal component of the news corpus, where "base (verb) ↔ present participle" is a dominant pattern, while it cannot be found in the top principal components of the blogs corpus.

Overall, this manual inspection suggests that the principal components do capture information that is relevant to style variations, even if they do not directly align to clear-cut style dimensions. Identifying how many top PCs are style-related (i.e. form a style subspace) is subjective and difficult. Therefore, we now turn to a quantitative evaluation.

5 Extrinsic Evaluation: Lexical Formality Scoring

We evaluate the usefulness of the latent dimensions discovered in Section 4 on a lexical formality prediction task. If the dimensions discovered are relevant to style, they should help predict formality with high accuracy.

5.1 Identifying A Style Subspace

5.1.1 Experimental Setup

Task   Following Brooke et al. (2010), we used a list of 399 synonym pairs from a writing manual – *Choose the Right Word* (CTRW) (Hayakawa, 1994) – to evaluate the formality model. Given a pair of words, such as "hurry" vs. "expedite", the task is to predict which is the more formal of the two.

Ranking method   The predictions were made by linear SVM classifiers (similar to the method proposed by Brooke and Hirst (2014)). They were trained on 105 formal seed words and 138 informal seed words used by Brooke et al. (2010). Each word was represented by a feature vector in word2vec spaces or their subspaces. When ranking two words, we actually compared their distances to the separating hyperplane, i.e. $w \cdot e - \rho$, where w, e and ρ are weight, embedding and bias.

Embedding spaces   We first trained word2vec (W2V) models of blogs corpus with different space sizes (dimensionality=1-10, 15, 20, 25, 30, 35, 40, 45, 50, 100, 150, 200, 250, 300, 350, 400, 450, 500). We then fixed the space size of word2vec models to 300 since it provides large enough original vector space and is a routinely used setting. All subspaces would be extracted from these 300-dimensional original spaces.

Style subspaces   Next, we identified style subspaces (i.e. top PCs) using the PCA method introduced in Section 3. We examined every possible subspace size in the range of $[1, 300]$ and denoted this method as PCA-PPDB.

For comparison, we also trained PCA subspaces using the seed words (PCA-seeds). Since seed words are not paraphrases, the PCA model was simply applied on word vectors. This method is based on the assumption that representative formal/informal words principally vary along the direction of formality.

5.1.2 Results

As illustrated in Figure 1, ✱✱✱ train indicates the training accuracy of SVM classifiers while ✱✱✱ test indicates the CTRW-pairs test accuracy.

The test accuracy of W2V curve has two peaks when dimensionality=10 (accuracy=0.798) and dimensionality=300 (accuracy=0.792). Considering the near-monotonicity of the training accuracy

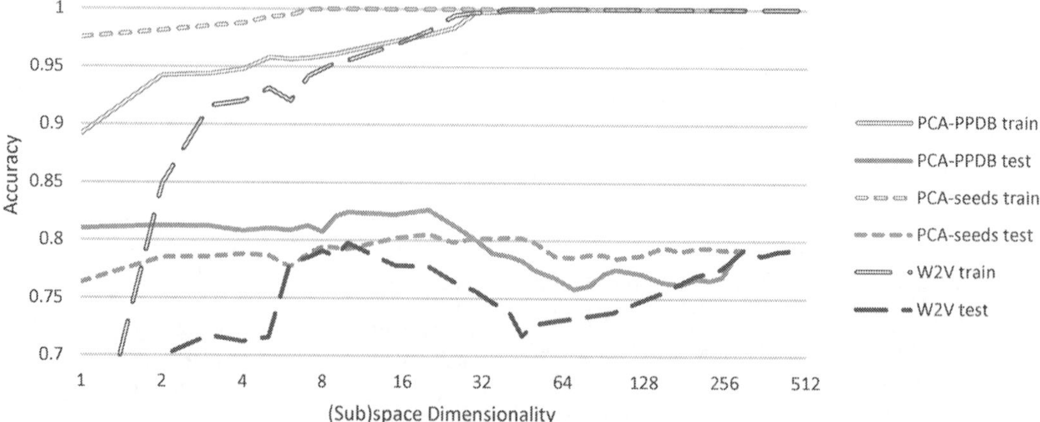

Figure 1: Train accuracy of formal/informal words classification and test accuracy of CTRW word-pair ranking v.s. the (sub)space dimensionality. An SVM-based formality model achieved the best test performance on subspaces identified by PCA on PPDB data.

curve, we attribute the trough around dimensionality=45 to over-fitting (increasing number of features) while attribute the rebound after that to more formality-related dimensions introduced.

Recall that we fixed the original spaces to 300 dimensions. The accuracy curve provides another reason to choose this number: 300-dimensional original spaces can model formality well by itself and the performance converges when dim $\geq$ 300.

Comparing `PCA-PPDB test` and `W2V test`, we can observe clear advantage of using subspaces that capture latent lexical variations. Even a single first principle dimension surpassed original word2vec models of any size, including the full 300-dimensional space which yielded a test accuracy of 0.792. Further improvements were achieved when 9th-21st principle dimensions were introduced (max accuracy=0.826) − back to Table 1, we can notice additional clues of formality variations from 9th PC.

The accuracy curves of `PCA-seeds` indicate that this model can fit the training set better with fewer dimensions than PPDB-based model but does not generalize as well to unseen test data. However, `PCA-seeds` still surpassed original word2vec models of any size.

5.2 SVM-based Ranking vs. Other Formality Models

We have discussed the effectiveness of modeling formality using a subspace of small size (1 for good results and ∼20 for best results). All analy-

ses so far were based on linear SVM, but can other sophisticated methods perform even better on the style-embedded subspaces?

5.2.1 Formality Models

We compare SVM with state-of-the-art lexical formality models based on vector space models, such as `SimDiff` (Brooke et al., 2010) and DENSIFIER (Rothe et al., 2016).

`SimDiff` (Brooke et al., 2010) scores the formality of a word w by comparing its meaning to that of seed words of known formality.[3] Intuitively, w is more likely formal if it is semantically closer to formal seed words than to informal seed words. Formally, given a formal word set S_f and an informal word set S_i, `SimDiff` scores a word w by

$$\text{score}(w) = \frac{1}{|S_f|} \sum_{v \in S_f} e_w \cdot e_v - \frac{1}{|S_i|} \sum_{v \in S_i} e_w \cdot e_v$$

Further manipulations such as score de-biasing and normalization were also introduced in (Brooke et al., 2010), but they would not affect rankings examined by our evaluation.

DENSIFIER (Rothe et al., 2016) is a supervised learning algorithm that transforms word embeddings into pre-defined ultra-dense orthogonal dimensions such as sentiment and concreteness. Under the formality ranking scenario, it optimizes a

---

[3]While Brooke et al. (2010) used cosine to measure the similarity in LSA spaces, we found that dot product yields better results with word2vec embeddings.

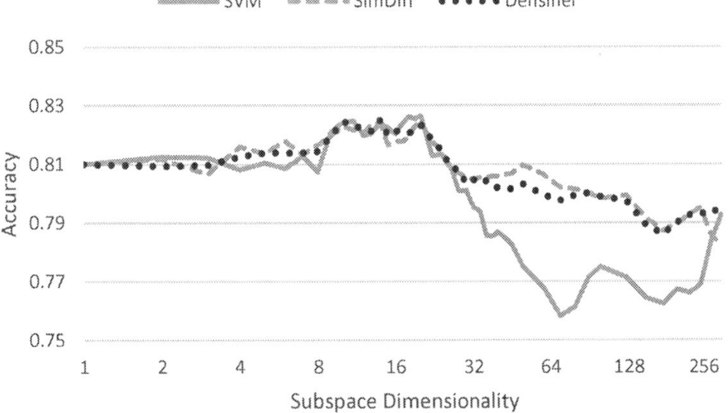

Figure 2: Test accuracy of CTRW word-pair ranking v.s. the subspace dimensionality. All formality models achieved similar performance on subspaces of size 9-21 identified by PCA-PPDB.

Incorrect Examples					Correct Examples				
w_1	w_2	s_1	s_2	$s_2 - s_1$	w_1	w_2	s_1	s_2	$s_2 - s_1$
crony	friend ‡†	0.667	-1.414	-2.081	grill ‡	interrogate	-1.370	1.212	2.581
conceit	vanity ‡	1.107	-0.697	-1.804	excuse ‡	remit	-0.608	2.001	2.609
present †	gift	1.017	-0.732	-1.749	gardening ‡†	tillage	-0.846	1.795	2.641
shiv	knife ‡	0.681	-0.863	-1.543	get ‡†	obtain	-1.435	1.296	2.731
quotation	quote ‡	0.910	-0.594	-1.504	hurry ‡	expedite	-1.632	1.174	2.806
frighten	scare ‡	0.157	-1.244	-1.400	catch ‡†	apprehend	-1.443	1.381	2.824
phony	fake †	0.237	-1.100	-1.337	watch ‡	observe	-1.628	1.264	2.892
parched	dehydrated †	0.173	-1.035	-1.209	loud ‡†	clamorous	-1.304	1.819	3.123
punish ‡	chasen	0.260	-0.697	-0.956	quote ‡‡	adduce	-0.594	2.529	3.123
penetrating ‡	perspicacious	1.527	0.644	-0.883	beach ‡†	littoral	-1.116	2.143	3.259

Table 2: Top (mis-)predicted CTRW word pairs, where s_i is the SVM (formality) score for word w_i. w_2 is supposed to be more formal than w_1. † This word is more frequent than the other in a pair according to the blogs corpus. (‡/ ‡ †/ ‡ ‡ means at least $10/100/1000$ times more.)

formality dimension (transition vector) that aims at separating words in S_f and words in S_i, and grouping words in the same set.

5.2.2 Results

All three formality scoring models (i.e. linear SVM, SimDiff and DENSIFIER) were applied to subspaces extracted from 300-dimensional word2vec spaces using PCA on PPDB data. Figure 2 shows that three models achieves nearly identical accuracy on subspaces with size smaller than 28.[4] Furthermore, we also compared the formality directions discovered by linear SVM (coefficient w) and Densifier (transition vector). For any dimensionality, the cosine similarity between them are larger than 0.8. It is even larger than 0.9

when dim $\geq$ 21. These suggest that the choice of ranking models has marginal impact, therefore identifying the style subspace plays a more critical role in modeling formality.

5.3 Error Analysis

Identified subspaces capture formality decently in terms of ranking lexical formality – as high as 0.826 accuracy in the CTRW dataset (based on the best performing model, i.e. a linear SVM trained on a 20-dimensional subspace identified by PCA-PPDB). The question then arises: what types of errors contribute to the incorrect predictions?

Top (mis-)predicted CTRW word pairs are listed in Table 2, where s_i is the SVM (formality) score for word w_i. w_2 is supposed to be more formal than w_1.

One category of errors roots in the mechanism

---

[4]SVM could also have similar accuracy curve after dimension=28 if an RBF kernel was used.

of vector space models such as word2vec: they are all based on word co-occurrence patterns, which sometimes introduce unwanted biases. For example, "crony" itself is an informal synonym of "friend" in our dataset. However, "crony capitalism" is a tightly glued economy term. For comparison, the formality score of "capitalism" is 0.966, which is very close to 0.667 of "crony".

Ambiguity is another key factor that influences the formality scoring based on vector space models. Arora et al. (2016) pointed out that in the vector space, a word having multiple meanings lies in middle of its senses. Consequently, its formality score is also controlled by all its senses. We can find many ambiguous words in the list of incorrect examples, such as "vanity" (clothing store, singer), "present", "shiv" (Hindu god), "parched" (film), "chasen" (surname, band), etc.

Last but not least, word frequency is a strong signal of predicting formality, but predictions can easily be stereotyped. We used word frequencies in the blogs corpus to rank CTRW word pairs and got an accuracy as high as 0.771 (by arguably treating more frequent as less formal). Projecting to the top (in)correct examples, a † symbol is placed behind the more frequent word in a pair. We can observe that top correctly ranked pairs followed the more-frequent-less-formal rule. However, this rule also biased the prediction to some incorrectly ranked pairs. Frequency information is not designed to be embedded into Word2vec models, but it still can be partially reconstructed (Rothe et al., 2016).

In a nutshell, formality models based on vector space models suffers from the limitation that a word representation is affected by word association, word sense and word frequency.

6 Conclusion

We presented an approach to discovering stylistic variations in distributional vector spaces using lexical paraphrases. Qualitative analysis suggests that the principle components discovered by PCA indeed capture variations related to style. Evaluation on a formality prediction task demonstrates the benefits of the induced subspace to detect style variations. We also compared the impact of different factors in identifying style-relevant dimensions such as the training data for PCA, the dimensionality of subspaces and the nature of prediction methods. Finally, the error analysis indi-

cated some intrinsic limitation of comparing style (formality) based on vector space models.

References

Sanjeev Arora, Yuanzhi Li, Yingyu Liang, Tengyu Ma, and Andrej Risteski. 2016. Linear algebraic structure of word senses, with applications to polysemy. *CoRR*, abs/1601.03764.

Marco Baroni, Georgiana Dinu, and Germán Kruszewski. 2014. Don't count, predict! A systematic comparison of context-counting vs. context-predicting semantic vectors. In *ACL (1)*, pages 238–247. The Association for Computer Linguistics.

Douglas Biber. 1995. *Dimensions of Register Variation: A Cross-Linguistic Comparison*. Cambridge University Press.

Tolga Bolukbasi, Kai-Wei Chang, James Y. Zou, Venkatesh Saligrama, and Adam Tauman Kalai. 2016. Man is to computer programmer as woman is to homemaker? debiasing word embeddings. In *NIPS*, pages 4349–4357.

Julian Brooke and Graeme Hirst. 2014. Supervised ranking of co-occurrence profiles for acquisition of continuous lexical attributes. In *COLING*, pages 2172–2183. ACL.

Julian Brooke, Tong Wang, and Graeme Hirst. 2010. Automatic acquisition of lexical formality. In *COLING (Posters)*, pages 90–98. Chinese Information Processing Society of China.

Penelope Brown and Colin Fraser. 1979. Speech as a marker of situation. In *Social Markers in Speech*, pages 33–62. Cambridge University Press.

Kevin Burton, Akshay Java, and Ian Soboroff. 2009. The ICWSM 2009 Spinn3r dataset. In *Proceedings of the Third Annual Conference on Weblogs and Social Media (ICWSM 2009), San Jose, CA*.

Cristian Danescu-Niculescu-Mizil, Lillian Lee, Bo Pang, and Jon M. Kleinberg. 2012. Echoes of power: language effects and power differences in social interaction. In *WWW*, pages 699–708. ACM.

Samuel Ichiye Hayakawa. 1994. *Choose the right word*. Collins Reference.

Francis Heylighen and Jean-Marc Dewaele. 1999. Formality of language: Definition, measurement and behavioral determinants. *Interner Bericht, Center "Leo Apostel", Vrije Universiteit Brüssel*.

Markus Hurtig. 2006. *Varieties of English in the Swedish classroom*. Karlstad University: Unpublished C-Essay.

Judith T. Irvine. 1979. Formality and informality in communicative events. *American Anthropologist*, 81(4):773–790.

Omer Levy and Yoav Goldberg. 2014. Linguistic regularities in sparse and explicit word representations. In *CoNLL*, pages 171–180. ACL.

François Mairesse. 2008. *Learning to Adapt in Dialogue Systems: Data-Driven Models for Personality Recognition and Generation*. Ph.D. thesis, University of Sheffield, United Kingdom.

Tomas Mikolov, Kai Chen, Greg Corrado, and Jeffrey Dean. 2013. Efficient estimation of word representations in vector space. *CoRR*, abs/1301.3781.

Gustavo Paetzold and Lucia Specia. 2016. Semeval 2016 task 11: Complex word identification. In *SemEval@NAACL-HLT*, pages 560–569. The Association for Computer Linguistics.

Ellie Pavlick and Ani Nenkova. 2015. Inducing lexical style properties for paraphrase and genre differentiation. In *HLT-NAACL*, pages 218–224. The Association for Computational Linguistics.

Ellie Pavlick, Pushpendre Rastogi, Juri Ganitkevitch, Benjamin Van Durme, and Chris Callison-Burch. 2015. PPDB 2.0: Better paraphrase ranking, fine-grained entailment relations, word embeddings, and style classification. In *ACL (2)*, pages 425–430. The Association for Computer Linguistics.

Ellie Pavlick and Joel R. Tetreault. 2016. An empirical analysis of formality in online communication. *TACL*, 4:61–74.

Daniel Preotiuc-Pietro, Wei Xu, and Lyle H. Ungar. 2016. Discovering user attribute stylistic differences via paraphrasing. In *AAAI*, pages 3030–3037. AAAI Press.

Sascha Rothe, Sebastian Ebert, and Hinrich Schütze. 2016. Ultradense word embeddings by orthogonal transformation. In *HLT-NAACL*, pages 767–777. The Association for Computational Linguistics.

Sascha Rothe and Hinrich Schütze. 2016. Word embedding calculus in meaningful ultradense subspaces. In *ACL (2)*. The Association for Computer Linguistics.

Peter D. Turney and Michael L. Littman. 2003. Measuring praise and criticism: Inference of semantic orientation from association. *ACM Trans. Inf. Syst.*, 21(4):315–346.

Wei Xu, Alan Ritter, Bill Dolan, Ralph Grishman, and Colin Cherry. 2012. Paraphrasing for style. In *COLING*, pages 2899–2914. Indian Institute of Technology Bombay.

Harvesting Creative Templates
for Generating Stylistically Varied Restaurant Reviews

Shereen Oraby, Sheideh Homayon, and **Marilyn Walker**

Natural Language and Dialogue Systems Lab
University of California, Santa Cruz
{soraby, shomayon, mawalker}@ucsc.edu

Abstract

Many of the creative and figurative elements that make language exciting are lost in translation in current natural language generation engines. In this paper, we explore a method to harvest templates from positive and negative reviews in the restaurant domain, with the goal of vastly expanding the types of stylistic variation available to the natural language generator. We learn hyperbolic adjective patterns that are representative of the strongly-valenced expressive language commonly used in either positive or negative reviews. We then identify and delexicalize entities, and use heuristics to extract generation templates from review sentences. We evaluate the learned templates against more traditional review templates, using subjective measures of *convincingness*, *interestingness*, and *naturalness*. Our results show that the learned templates score highly on these measures. Finally, we analyze the linguistic categories that characterize the learned positive and negative templates. We plan to use the learned templates to improve the conversational style of dialogue systems in the restaurant domain.

1 Introduction

The restaurant domain has been one of the most common applications for spoken dialogue systems for at least 25 years (Polifroni et al., 1992; Whittaker et al., 2002; Stent et al., 2004; Devillers et al., 2004; Gasic et al., 2008). There has been a tremendous amount of previous work on natural language generation of recommendations and descriptions for restaurants (Howcroft et al., 2013; Wen et al., 2015; Novikova et al., 2016), some of

#	Stars	Review
1	1/5	This place is probably the worst thing that ever happened to the history of the known world. [...] The food, however, I initially would want to call unremarkable but I can't. I can't call it unremarkable because it is so incredibly remarkably terrible. [...]
2	2/5	Can't say anything about the food, as we were never served. We never saw a server, even after sitting at our table for 15 minutes. Unacceptable.
3	3/5	I was back here a couple of days ago with my family. And although I remember The food being a lot better than this time around. I was kind of disappointed. The service was okay since I had no Jose this time. Nothing to mention here just refills chips salsa and beverages when you need and food when it's ready.
4	4/5	I would eat here everyday if I didn't think I'd end up 400 pounds... Minus 1 star because each time I've been here the service has kinda sucked and orders have been messed up. Regardless, their fried chicken on waffles topped with syrup and a slice of Red Velvet cake to top it off......... is sooooooo heavenly.
5	5/5	I only have one warning about this restaurant. The food is so amazing that you cannot eat Mexican food anywhere else. [...] I had chicken and beef enchiladas which had homemade corn tortillas and the most tender meat I had ever tasted. [...] I will be a customer for life here!

Table 1: Restaurant Reviews by Rating from the Yelp Dataset Challenge Corpus

which has even focused on generating stylistically varied restaurant recommendations (Higashinaka et al., 2007b; Mairesse and Walker, 2010; Dethlefs et al., 2014). Given this, it is surprising that previous work has not especially noted that restaurant reviews are a fertile source of creative and figurative language. For example, consider the elaborate descriptions in the restaurant reviews in Table 1[1], e.g. phrases such as *worst thing that*

---

[1]Reviews from the Yelp 2016 dataset challenge:
https://www.yelp.com/dataset_challenge

Proceedings of the Workshop on Stylistic Variation, pages 28–36
Copenhagen, Denmark, September 7–11, 2017. ©2017 Association for Computational Linguistics

ever happened in the history of the known world along with *incredibly remarkably terrible* (Row 1), *eat here everyday if I didn't think I'd end up 400 pounds* and *sooooooo heavenly* (Row 4), and *food so amazing you cannot eat [...] anywhere else* (Row 5). These phrases express extremely valenced reactions to restaurants, their menu items, and related attributes, using figurative language.

The creativity exhibited in these user-generated restaurant reviews can be contrasted with natural language generation (NLG) for the restaurant domain. Methods for NLG typically begin with a structured meaning representation (MR), as shown in Table 2, and map these meaning representations into surface language forms, using a range of different methods, including template-based generation, statistically trained linguistically-informed NLG engines, and neural approaches (Bangalore and Rambow, 2000; Walker and Rambow, 2002). These approaches vary in the degree to which they can generate syntactically and semantically correct utterances, but in most cases the stylistic variation they can generate is extremely limited. Table 2 illustrates sample restaurant domain utterances produced by recent statistical/neural natural language generators (Higashinaka et al., 2007a; Mairesse and Walker, 2007; Wen et al., 2015; Novikova et al., 2016; Dusek and Jurcícek, 2016).

One of the most prominent characteristics of restaurant reviews in the Yelp corpus is the prevalent use of hyperbolic language, such as the phrase *"incredibly remarkably terrible"* in Table 1. Hyperbole is often found in persuasive language, and is classified as a form of figurative language (McCarthy and Carter, 2004; Cano Mora, 2009). Colston and O'Brien describe how an event or situation evokes a scale, and how hyperbole exaggerates a literal situation, introducing a discrepancy between the "truth" and what is said (Colston and Keller, 1998; Colston and O'Brien, 2000). Hyperbole moves the strength of a statement up and down the scale, away from the literal meaning, where the degree of movement reflects the degree of contrast or exaggeration. Depending on what they modify, adverbial intensifiers like *totally, absolutely,* and *incredibly* can shift the strength of the assertion to extreme negative or positive.

Similarly, Kreuz and Roberts (1995) describe a standard frame for hyperbole in English where an adverb modifies an extreme, positive adjective, e.g. *"That was* **absolutely amazing***!"* or *"That*

was **simply the most incredible** *dining experience in my entire life."* Such frames can be seen in the reviews in Table 1, but we also see many other idiomatic hyperbolic expressions such as *out of this world* (Cano Mora, 2009).

Our goal is to develop a natural language generator for the restaurant domain that can harvest and make use of these types of stylistic variations. We explore a data-driven approach to automatically select stylistically varied utterances in the restaurant review domain as candidates for review construction. We empirically learn hyperbolic adjective patterns that are highly correlated with two classes (positive and negative reviews). Using different resources, we also identify and delexicalize *restaurant, cuisine, food, service,* and *staff* entities, and select short, single-entity utterances that are simple to templatize.

Our overall approach is thus similar to Higashinaka et al. (2007a,b), who describe a method for harvesting an NLG dictionary from restaurant reviews, however our focus on learning expressive language, in particular hyperbole as a type of figurative language, is novel. Our framework consists of the following steps:

1. Collect a large number of strongly positive and strongly negative reviews in the restaurant domain;

2. Use a linguistic pattern learner to identify linguistic frames that use hyperbole;

3. Create generation templates from the identified linguistic patterns and infer their contexts of use;

4. Learn to rank the generation templates for convincingness and quality.

We see Steps 1 to 3 as the overgeneration phase, aimed at vastly expanding the types of stylistic variation possible, while Step 4 is the ranking phase, in a classic overgenerate and rank NLG architecture (Langkilde and Knight, 1998; Rambow et al., 2001). We focus in this paper on Steps 1 to 3, expecting to improve these steps before we move on to Step 4.

Thus, in this paper, we conducted an evaluation experiment to compare three different types of NLG templates: pre-defined BASIC templates similar to those used in current NLG engines for the restaurant domain (Walker et al., 2007; Wen et al., 2015), the basic templates stylized with

MR	NLG	System
name[Emilios] foodquality[excellent] location[city centre] cuisine[Italian] decor[decent] service[decent]	*Emilios decor and service are both decent, but its food quality is nothing short of excellent. It serves Italian food and its in the City Centre.*	Seq2Seq NLG (Nayak et al., 2017)
name[The Eagle] eattype[coffee shop] pricerange[moderate] customerrating[3/5] kidsFriendly[yes] near[Burger King]	*The three star coffee shop, The Eagle, gives families a mid-priced dining experience featuring a variety of wines and cheeses. Find The Eagle near Burger King.*	Human annotators (Novikova et al., 2016)
name[X] type[placetoeat] near[Y] food[Continental] food[French]	*X is a restaurant providing french and continental food, near Y.*	Seq2Seq Generation (Dusek and Jurcícek, 2016)
name[Red door cafe] goodformeal[breakfast] area[cathedral hill] kidsallowed[no]	*Red door cafe is a good restaurant for breakfast in the area of cathedral hill and does not allow children .*	LSTM Generation (Wen et al., 2015)
name[Le Marais] cuisine[French] foodquality[good] service[good] decor[decent] price[$44]	*I am sure you would like Le Marais, you know. The atmosphere is acceptable, the servers are nice and it's a fresh, kosher and steak house place. Actually, the food is good, even if its price is 44 dollars.*	PERSONAGE (Mairesse and Walker, 2007)
name[Babbo] foodquality[superb] service[excellent] decor[superb]	*The food is phenomenal and the atmosphere is very unique. Babbo has excellent service. It has the best overall quality among the selected restaurants.*	Unsupervised Method for Lexicon Learning (Higashinaka et al., 2007a)

Table 2: Example Meaning Representations (MR) and Corresponding Natural Language Generation (NLG) Output in the Restaurant Domain

our learned patterns for more HYPERBOLIC templates, and finally a class of CREATIVE templates that incorporate full sentence templates from user reviews. Our expectation was that many of the CREATIVE templates would fail to be appropriate to their contexts, but that our HYPERBOLIC templates would be both appropriate and more interesting and convincing than the BASIC templates. However, our results show that our creative templates are preferred as more convincing, interesting, and natural across the board. We discuss how we can use quantitative metrics associated with the learned templates for future ranking, and analyze characteristic linguistic categories in each class.

2 Data

Our restaurant review data comes from the Yelp dataset challenge, which includes 144K businesses with over 4.1M reviews. We randomly select 10K businesses located in the US that are classified as restaurants, resulting in a set of around 40K reviews. The data consists of around 4K 1 stars, 3.8K 2 stars, 5.6K 3 stars, 11.3K 4 stars, and 15K 5 stars. We divide the reviews by stars, and create three datasets: negative (using all of the 1-2 stars), positive (balancing the number of negative reviews using the 5 stars), and neutral (using all of the 3 stars). Table 3 shows our data distribution.

Split	Stars	Num Reviews
POSITIVE	5	7,853
NEUTRAL	3	5,610
NEGATIVE	1-2	7,853

Table 3: Selected Review Data Distribution

3 Learning Patterns for Hyperbole

Our goal is to learn patterns that are highly associated with the extreme positive and negative reviews, and that exemplify strong, expressive language. To automatically learn such patterns, we use the AutoSlog-TS weakly-supervised extraction pattern learner (Riloff, 1996).

AutoSlog-TS uses a set of syntactic templates

to learn lexically-grounded patterns. AutoSlog does not require fine-grained labels on training data: all it requires is that the training data be divided into two distinct classes. Here, we run two separate AutoSlog experiments, one in which the classes are POSITIVE compared to NEUTRAL, and the other where the NEGATIVE class is compared to NEUTRAL. We hypothesize that in this way, we can surface the most commonly used patterns from each class that are not necessarily sentiment-related.

AutoSlog applies the Sundance shallow parser (Riloff and Phillips, 2004) to each sentence of each review, finds all possible matches for its syntactic templates, and then instantiates the syntactic templates with the words in the sentence to produce a specific lexico-syntactic expression. Most importantly, it uses the labels associated with the data to compute statistics for how frequently each pattern occurs in each class. Thus, for each pattern p, we learn the P(POSITIVE/NEGATIVE$|$ p), the P(NEUTRAL$|$ p), and the pattern's frequency.

Table 4 shows examples of the patterns we learn and sample instantiations, with their respective frequency (F) and probabilities (P). In the pattern template column of Table 4, PassVP refers to passive voice verb phrases (VPs), ActVP refers to active voice VPs, InfVP refers to infinitive VPs, and AuxVP refers to VPs where the main verb is a form of *to be* or *to have*. Subjects (subj), direct objects (dobj), noun phrases (np), and possessives (genitives) can also be extracted by the patterns. Because we are particularly interested in descriptive patterns, we also use ngram pattern templates, `AdjAdj`, `AdvAdj`, `AdvAdvAdj`, as in related work (Oraby et al., 2015, 2016).

Our goal is to find highly reliable patterns without sacrificing linguistic variation. Current statistical methods for training NLG engines typically eliminate linguistic variability by seeking to learn standard, more generic patterns that occur frequently in the data (Liu et al., 2016; Nayak et al., 2017). Since this phase of our work aims to vastly expand the amount of linguistic variation possible, we select instantiations that have a frequency of at least 3, and a probability of at least 0.75 association with the respective class (Oraby et al., 2015, 2016). We hypothesize that patterns that occur at least 3 times should be fairly reliable, and those that have at least a 75% probability of being associated with the positive or negative class should

F	P	Pattern Template	Example Pattern
Positive			
40	1.0	<subj>ActInfVP Dobj	<subj> wait come
19	1.0	ActVP Prep <Np>	tucked in <Np>
54	0.9	AdjAdj	hands down
30	0.9	<subj>ActVP Dobj	<subj> worth wait
20	0.9	NpPrep <Np>	screaming for
10	0.9	<subj> AuxVP Adj	<subj> be scrumptious
416	0.8	AdjNoun	great food
16	0.8	PassVP Prep NP	addicted to
113	0.7	AdvAdj	very fresh
4	0.7	AdjNoun	go-to restaurant
Negative			
17	1.0	<subj> AuxVP Adj	<subj> be impossible
13	1.0	AdjNoun	negative stars
12	1.0	<subj> ActVP Dobj	<subj> got poisoning
23	0.9	AdjNoun	no sense
134	0.8	<subj> AuxVP Adj	<subj> be awful
26	0.8	<subj> AuxVP Adj	<subj> be rubbery
19	0.8	<subj> ActVP	<subj> not waste
107	0.8	AdjNoun	poor service
100	0.8	AdjNoun	no way
201	0.8	<subj> AuxVP Adj	<subj> not be back

Table 4: Examples of Pattern Templates in AutoSlog-TS and Instantiations by Class

be distinctive. Using these filters, we learn 8,320 positive adjective patterns, and 7,839 negative adjective patterns.

We also observe that patterns learned using stricter thresholds (for example, frequency of at least 10 and probability of at least 0.9) also gives us useful patterns, and note that we can use the frequencies and probabilities in our future rank task. For larger coverage, we experiment with our less restrictive thresholds in the current work.

4   Designing Review Templates

To make use of the descriptive adjective patterns we learned, we needed to first identify what entities each of the patterns describes. To do this, we aggregate lexicons for each of five important restaurant entities: *restaurant-type, cuisine, food, service,* and *staff* using Wikipedia[2] and DBpedia[3]. We end up with 14 items for *restaurant-types* (e.g. "cafe"), 45 for *cuisines* (e.g. "Italian"), 4,913 for *foods and ingredients* (e.g. "sushi"), 12 for *staff* (e.g. "waiters"), and 2 for *service* (e.g. "customer service").

4.1   Basic Templates

To construct the most basic set of templates, we use simple relationships between adjectives and the entities they describe to define a set of sentences with entity slots, i.e. *"They had [adj] (entity)."*, *"The (entity) was|is [adj]."*, *"The (entity)*

<hr>

[2] https://www.wikipedia.org/
[3] http://wiki.dbpedia.org/

looked|tasted [adj]." We use basic lists of adjectives commonly found in reviews for these baseline templates. To vary the templates, we alternate between using only simple sentences, and sometimes combine related entities into more complex sentences (e.g. *service* and *staff*, or *restaurant-type* and *cuisine*).

4.2 Hyperbolic Templates

For our hyperbolic templates, we replace the standard adjectives in the basic templates with adjective patterns learned from the restaurant reviews. To select appropriate adjectives patterns for replacement in each basic template, we first delexicalize the sentences that instantiate our learned adjective patterns for each class, and create sets of (entity, adjective pattern) pairs based on the relationship between the adjective and the entity ("is", "was", "tasted", etc.), as above. Using this method, we collect 37 restaurant, 30 cuisine, 247 food, 45 service, and 56 staff patterns for positive and 18 restaurant, 9 cuisine, 221 food, 75 service, and 61 staff patterns for negative. Table 5 shows example patterns in each class for the food and staff entity types.

4.3 Creative Templates

Finally, for our creative templates, we sample from our set of delexicalized sentences for each entity type, as long as they:

- contain a single AutoSlog adjective pattern
- contain a single identifiable entity type
- are between 5-15 words long

We enforce these limitations to gather simple sentences that are short enough to templatize. Thus, we end up with sentence templates for each entity type for both the positive and negative classes, collecting 146 restaurant, 61 cuisine, 743 food, 90 service, and 144 staff patterns for positive and 45 restaurant, 12 cuisine, 480 food, 126 service, and 89 staff patterns for negative. Table 6 shows examples of our templatized sentences for the positive and negative classes, with their AutoSlog-TS adjective patterns between brackets, and capitalized subject extractions when applicable. To construct a full review of a certain polarity, we randomly select a sentence from the sets for each entity type.

We hypothesized that the creative templates would optimize stylistic variation and hence interestingness, but that they would also include cases

Positive	Negative
INSANELY GOOD	ALMOST RAW
SIMPLY PERFECT	VERY FATTY
RIDICULOUSLY GOOD	PREVIOUSLY FROZEN
ALSO INCREDIBLE	COMICALLY BAD
MY FAV	ABSOLUTELY AWFUL
PERFECTLY CRISP	NOT PALATABLE
DEFINITELY UNIQUE	FAIRLY TASTELESS
ALWAYS SO FRESH	PRETTY GENERIC
JUST PHENOMENAL	SO MEDIOCRE
SO DECADENT	SO BLAND
HIGHLY ADDICTIVE	STILL RAW
CONSISTENTLY GREAT	BARELY WARM
WOW AMAZING	PREPACKAGED FROZEN
PERFECT LITTLE	MOST PATHETIC
EXPERTLY PREPARED	SICKLY SWEET
FRESHLY BAKED	LUKE WARM

(a) Sample Learned Adjective Patterns for Foods

Positive	Negative
SUPER HELPFUL	NOT APOLOGETIC
INCREDIBLY FRIENDLY	NOT KNOWLEDGEABLE
SUPER NICE	VERY RUDE
VERY PERSONABLE	TOO BUSY
SO GOOD	FRIENDLY ENOUGH
SO GRACIOUS	JUST HORRIBLE
VERY KNOWLEDGEABLE	NOT ATTENTIVE
SO KIND	VERY PUSH
EXTREMELY PROFESSIONAL	MORE INTERESTED
ALSO FABULOUS	TOO LAZY
EVEN BETTER	EVEN WORSE
STILL AWESOME	EVERY SINGLE
ALWAYS WARM	VERY POOR
ALWAYS ATTENTIVE	SO FEW
ABSOLUTELY BEST	STILL NO
OUR SWEET	VERY UNHAPPY

(b) Sample Learned Adjective Patterns for Staff

Table 5: Sample Learned Adjective Patterns

that would require further refinement, or perhaps elimination by a subsequent ranking phase. Since our focus here is on overgeneration, we include these and evaluate their quality. Table 7 shows examples of each template type we create.

5 Evaluating Template Styles

In order to evaluate our template variations, we choose to focus on three particular criteria: *convincingness, interestingness,* and *naturalness.* We evaluate *convincingness* because creative language such as hyperbole is often used in persuasive language, along with other figurative forms (Kreuz and Roberts, 1995). *Naturalness* is an important concern in generation, so we are also interested in the comparison between the perceived naturalness of each variation style, and we hypothesize that *interestingness* would increase as we used

Entity	Template
Positive	
RESTAURANT	By [FAR MY] favorite <RESTAURANT_ENTITY> I HAVE EVER been to in my life .
CUISINE	Wow what a great [LITTLE <CUISINE_ENTITY>] joint !
FOOD	The <FOOD_ENTITY> is not cheap , but [WELL WORTH] it.
SERVICE	The <SERVICE_ENTITY> is [ALWAYS FRIENDLY] and fast .
STAFF	<STAFF_ENTITY> was [EXTREMELY HELPFUL] and knowledgeable and was on top of everything.
Negative	
RESTAURANT	I was appalled by the experience and will [NOT FREQUENT] this <RESTAURANT_ENTITY> ever again.
CUISINE	[ITS YOUR] typical <CUISINE_ENTITY> buffet , nothing to rave about .
FOOD	<FOOD_ENTITY> smelled [VERY BAD] and tasted worse .
SERVICE	We waited another 5 minutes , [STILL NO] <SERVICE_ENTITY> .
STAFF	I went with 5 friends and our <STAFF_ENTITY> was [REALLY RUDE] .

Table 6: Examples of Learned Creative Sentence Templates by Entity and Polarity

BASIC	The bar is beautiful. They had authentic japanese cuisine. The udon looked excellent. The hosts is dedicated. They had reliable customer service.
HYPERBOLIC	The bar is also very fresh. They had delicious authentic japanese cuisine. The udon looked so delicious. The hosts is also very friendly. They had such amazing customer service.
CREATIVE	This is by far my favorite bar in town. plus there is a great japanese cuisine grocery store that has tons of stuff. The udon is always fresh, delicious and made to order. Hosts was super friendly, looking forward to coming back and trying more items. The customer service is great and the employees are always super nice!

Table 7: Examples of Instantiated Positive Review Variations

more content from organic reviews in our HYPERBOLIC and CREATIVE templates.

To create an evaluation dataset, we instantiate each template type with entities from a hypothetical MR in one of seven popular cuisine types to standardize the content, as illustrated in Table 7. For example, sample slot values could be: {RESTAURANT[BAR], CUISINE[JAPANESE], FOOD[UDON], SERVICE[CUSTOMER SERVICE], STAFF[HOSTS]}.

Our objective is to evaluate whether we can improve upon vanilla-style hand-crafted templates for restaurant reviews by utilizing in hyperbolic and creative elements of organic reviews that we harvest. We set up an annotation experiment on Amazon Mechanical Turk[4], where each Human Intelligence Task (HIT) presents Turkers with a sample of our three review variations, all of the same polarity and instantiated with the same entities. Turkers are asked to judge the reviews based on three criteria: *convincingness* (Do you believe the opinion given?), *interestingness* (Is the review engaging?), and *naturalness* (Is the review coherent?). Turkers are asked to rate each review on a three point scale (*high, medium* and *low*) for each criteria. We release 200 variation triples (100 per polarity class) and ask for five judgements per HIT, tagging a review with a quality if the majority of annotators agree on it (i.e. 3 or more Turkers). Average agreement for individual Turkers with the majority is above 73%.

Figure 1 shows the distribution of *high, medium,* and *low* scores for each of the variation types for each criterion. From the results, we observe that for all criteria, the CREATIVE class has the highest distribution of *high* majority votes. Interestingly, although we hypothesized that the HYPERBOLIC reviews would be better received than the BASIC reviews, we observe that in fact the BASIC reviews receive more *high* votes on *convincingness*. We note that for the future ranking, more context information is necessary when selecting appropriate hyperbolic patterns with which to modify the BASIC reviews. For example, if a learned pattern is OTHER AMAZING, the pattern should only be used when a set of items are being described, and not stand-alone. Similarly, the BASIC reviews are also more *natural* than the HYPERBOLIC ones, although both variation types score very similar percentages for *medium* scores.

For the creative reviews, a crucial next step for ranking is to consider context and develop heuristics for finding the most appropriate entities for lexicalization. For example, for very

---

[4]https://www.mturk.com/

specific creative templates such as: *"I also got one that HAD NOT been separated , so it was [JUST HALF] of a* <FOOD_ENTITY> *.",* or *"The* <FOOD_ENTITY> *were similarly a mix of nearly raw to overly crisp.",* it is necessary to select food items similar to the original instantiations, or to characterize and classify entities based on specific properties.

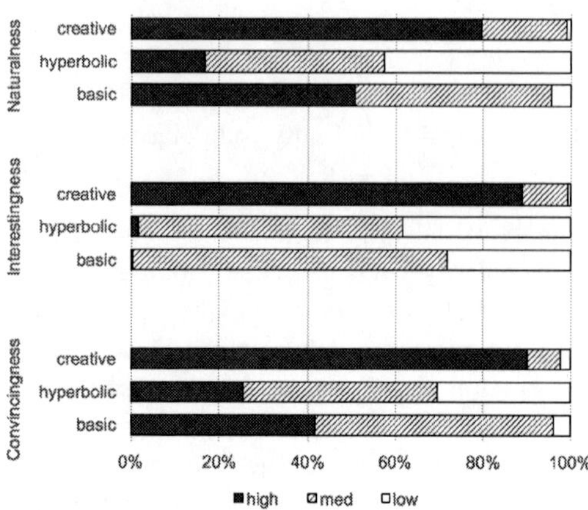

Figure 1: Distribution of Template Variations by Evaluation Criteria

Given the high appeal of the CREATIVE reviews on all counts, we are interested in more closely exploring examples in the data. Table 8 shows two examples of CREATIVE reviews: one that received *high* scores on all criteria, and one that received majority (no creative review received all *lows*). It is clear that the biggest disconnect in the low-scoring *creative* review is the coherence between sentences, which as an important next step to consider as future work given the proof-of-concept presented here. We also note that we can also improve the fully high-scoring review by fixing grammatical errors and applying more informed content selection.

To get a better sense of how grammatically correct the review template variations are, we conduct another evaluation study where we present Turkers with the same set of reviews, and ask them to rate each review based on the content (checking subject-verb agreement, plurality, tense, etc.). Similar to the previous study, we gather 5 judgements for each set of three variations, and aggregate results using majority vote. Average agreement for individual Turkers with the majority in this task is above 80%, higher than the more sub-

ALL HIGH	It is one of my favorite cafe in las vegas. Thank you irma for your amazing mediterranean cuisine cooking! I am always amazed at how fast my falafel arrives. Victor the owner was super nice and cordial our hosts norma was also. Always a great place to go and service is always amazing!
MOSTLY LOW	It's just too bad that the bar itself is not better. Very bad american cuisine.... Guess what came on top of my hotdog? I took my family there for father's day and the hosts was so rude. 555 pm still no customer service.

Table 8: Example of *High* and *Low* Rated Creative Reviews

jective study on convincingness, interestingness, and naturalness.

Figure 2 shows the results of the study. We find that for all three variations, the *med* class receives the majority of the votes, but that the BASIC reviews are the most grammatically correct (since the templates are designed, not harvested). Similarly, the HYPERBOLIC reviews have the largest percentage of *low* scores, since their creation involves modifying templates with learned adjectives. Ranking the best patterns/sentences to use will allow us to improve the grammatical coherence of the templatized utterances for the HYPERBOLIC and CREATIVE classes.

To better understand the linguistic characteristics of the creative reviews by class, we run the Linguistic Inquiry and Word Count (LIWC) tool (Pennebaker et al., 2015) on the full set of 100 POSITIVE and 100 NEGATIVE *creative* reviews. When comparing the linguistic categories for each class, we find that the difference between the POSITIVE and NEGATIVE reviews are significant ($p <$ 0.05, t-test) for many of the categories. Table 9 shows some of the most interesting categories[5].

On average, the POSITIVE templates are char-

---

[5]All of the categories are statistically significant, and are shown in order of most to least significant.

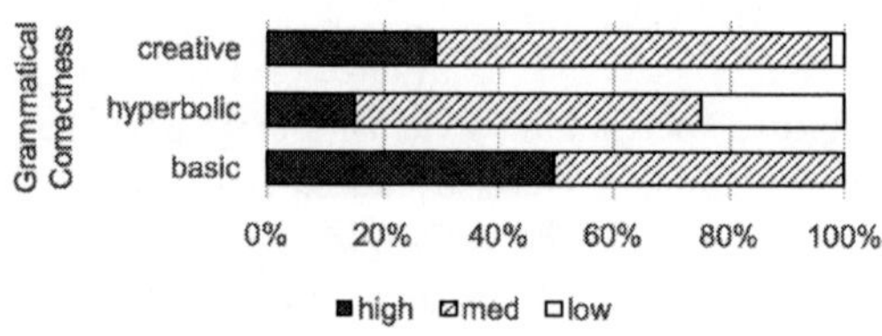

Figure 2: Distribution of Votes on Template Variation Grammar

Positive	Negative
AFFECTIVE PROC.	DIFFERENTIATION
EXCLAMATIONS	RISK
FRIENDS	1st PERSON PLURAL
1st PERSON SINGULAR	ANXIETY
ACHIEVE	ADVERBS
CERTAINTY	ANGER
BIOLOGICAL PROC.	SOCIAL PROC.
INGESTIONS	2nd PERSON
INSIGHT	MOTION
REWARD	COGNITIVE PROC.

Table 9: Statistically Significant LIWC Categories by Polarity

acterized by word classes that exemplify achievement (e.g. *"even better"*, *"champion"*) and certainty (e.g. *"always excellent"*, *"absolutely amazing"*, and *"definitely my go-to place"*). As well as 1st person statements relating to use of the senses (affective processes like *"my favorite place to get rice in Las Vegas!"*, biological processes (*"I just had the most amazingly delicious and freshly prepared couscous!"*), and ingestion (*"good, tasty comfort pizza"*).

The negative contains more oppositional language directed at the second person, often as advice (*"you can get a much better pizza elsewhere at far less cost."*), with categories like differentiation (*"but it's not great"*), and strong emotion indicators like anxiety (*"horrible service, finally just left"*) and anger (*"I was so angry that I contacted the restaurant manager"*).

6   Conclusions

In this paper, we show that we can construct convincing, interesting, and natural restaurant review templates by using a data-driven method to harvest highly descriptive sentences from hyperbolic restaurant reviews. We generate three variations of review templates, ranging from very basic, to hyperbolic, to very creative, and show that the creative ones are more appealing to readers than the others. Future work will focus on ranking the candidate sentence templates we harvest to improve review coherence. As we develop better templates, we will evaluate them against baselines from existing NLG systems to guide our generation of more exciting and expressive stylistically varied reviews.

References

Srinivas Bangalore and Owen Rambow. 2000. Exploiting a probabilistic hierarchical model for generation. In *Proceedings of the 18th conference on Computational linguistics-Volume 1*. Association for Computational Linguistics, pages 42–48.

Laura Cano Mora. 2009. All or nothing: a semantic analysis of hyperbole. *Revista de Lingüística y Lenguas Aplicadas* pages 25–35.

Herbert L. Colston and Shauna B. Keller. 1998. You'll never believe this: Irony and hyperbole in expressing surprise. *Journal of Psycholinguistic Research* 27(4):499–513.

Herbert L. Colston and Jennifer O'Brien. 2000. Contrast and pragmatics in figurative language: Anything understatement can do, irony can do better. *Journal of Pragmatics* 32(11):1557 – 1583.

Nina Dethlefs, Heriberto Cuayáhuitl, Helen F. Hastie, Verena Rieser, and Oliver Lemon. 2014. Cluster-based prediction of user ratings for stylistic surface realisation. In *Proceedings of the 14th Conference of the European Chapter of the Association for Computational Linguistics, EACL 2014, April 26-30, 2014, Gothenburg, Sweden.* pages 702–711.

Laurence Devillers, Hélène Maynard, Sophie Rosset, Patrick Paroubek, Kevin McTait, Djamel Mostefa, Khalid Choukri, Laurent Charnay, Caroline Bousquet, Nadine Vigouroux, Frédéric Béchet, Laurent Romary, Jean-Yves Antoine, Jeanne Villaneau, Myriam Vergnes, and Jérôme Goulian. 2004. The french MEDIA/EVALDA project: the evaluation of the understanding capability of spoken language dialogue systems. In *Proceedings of the Fourth International Conference on Language Resources and Evaluation, LREC 2004, May 26-28, 2004, Lisbon, Portugal.*

Ondrej Dusek and Filip Jurcícek. 2016. Sequence-to-sequence generation for spoken dialogue via deep syntax trees and strings. *CoRR* abs/1606.05491.

Milica Gasic, Simon Keizer, Francois Mairesse, Jost Schatzmann, Blaise Thomson, Kai Yu, and Steve Young. 2008. Training and evaluation of the his pomdp dialogue system in noise. In *Proceedings of the 9th SIGdial Workshop on Discourse and Dialogue*. Association for Computational Linguistics, Association for Computational Linguistics, Columbus, Ohio, page 112–119.

Ryuichiro Higashinaka, Marilyn Walker, and Rashmi Prasad. 2007a. Learning to generate naturalistic utterances using reviews in spoken dialogue systems. *ACM Transactions on Speech and Language Processing (TSLP)* .

Ryuichiro Higashinaka, Marilyn A. Walker, and Rashmi Prasad. 2007b. An unsupervised method for learning generation dictionaries for spoken dialogue systems by mining user reviews. *ACM Transactions on Speech and Language Processing* 4(4).

David Howcroft, Crystal Nakatsu, and Michael White. 2013. Enhancing the expression of contrast in the sparky restaurant corpus. In *Proceedings of the 14th European Workshop on Natural Language Generation*. Association for Computational Linguistics, Sofia, Bulgaria, pages 30–39.

Roger J. Kreuz and Richard M. Roberts. 1995. Two cues for verbal irony: Hyperbole and the ironic tone of voice. *Metaphor and Symbolic Activity* 10(1):21–31.

Irene Langkilde and Kevin Knight. 1998. Generation that exploits corpus-based statistical knowledge. In *Proceedings of the 36th Annual Meeting of the Association for Computational Linguistics and 17th International Conference on Computational Linguistics - Volume 1*. ACL '98, pages 704–710.

Chia-Wei Liu, Ryan Lowe, Iulian Serban, Michael Noseworthy, Laurent Charlin, and Joelle Pineau. 2016. How NOT to evaluate your dialogue system: An empirical study of unsupervised evaluation metrics for dialogue response generation. In *Proceedings of the 2016 Conference on Empirical Methods in Natural Language Processing, EMNLP 2016, Austin, Texas, USA, November 1-4, 2016*. pages 2122–2132.

Francois Mairesse and Marilyn Walker. 2007. Personage: Personality generation for dialogue. In *In Proceedings of the 45th Annual Meeting of the Association for Computational Linguistics (ACL*. pages 496–503.

Francois Mairesse and Marilyn Walker. 2010. Towards personality-based user adaptation: psychologically informed stylistic language generation. *User Modeling and User-Adapted Interaction* pages 1–52.

Michael McCarthy and Ronald Carter. 2004. There's millions of them: hyperbole in everyday conversation. *Journal of Pragmatics* 36(2):149–184.

Neha Nayak, Dilek Hakkani-Tur, Marilyn Walker, and Larry Heck. 2017. To plan or not to plan? discourse planning in slot-value informed sequence to sequence models for language generation. In *Proc. of Interspeech 2017*.

Jekaterina Novikova, Oliver Lemon, and Verena Rieser. 2016. Crowd-sourcing NLG data: Pictures elicit better data. In *INLG 2016 - Proceedings of the Ninth International Natural Language Generation Conference, September 5-8, 2016, Edinburgh, UK*. pages 265–273.

Shereen Oraby, Vrindavan Harrison, Lena Reed, Ernesto Hernandez, Ellen Riloff, and Marilyn A. Walker. 2016. Creating and characterizing a diverse corpus of sarcasm in dialogue. In *Proceedings of the SIGDIAL 2016 Conference, The 17th Annual Meeting of the Special Interest Group on Discourse and Dialogue, 13-15 September 2016, Los Angeles, CA, USA*. pages 31–41.

Shereen Oraby, Lena Reed, Ryan Compton, Ellen Riloff, Marilyn Walker, and Steve Whittaker. 2015. And that's a fact: Distinguishing factual and emotional argumentation in online dialogue. In *Proceedings of the 2nd Workshop on Argumentation Mining at NAACL 2015*. pages 116–126.

James W Pennebaker, Ryan L Boyd, Kayla Jordan, and Kate Blackburn. 2015. The development and psychometric properties of liwc2015. Technical report.

Joseph Polifroni, Lynette Hirschman, Stephanie Seneff, and Victor Zue. 1992. Experiments in evaluating interactive spoken language systems. In *Proceedings of the Workshop on Speech and Natural Language*. Association for Computational Linguistics, Stroudsburg, PA, USA, HLT '91, pages 28–33.

Owen Rambow, Monica Rogati, and Marilyn Walker. 2001. Evaluating a trainable sentence planner for a spoken dialogue travel system. In *Proceedings of the 39th Annual Meeting of the Association for Computational Linguistics (ACL)*.

Ellen Riloff. 1996. Automatically generating extraction patterns from untagged text. In *Proceedings of the Thirteenth National Conference on Artificial Intelligence (AAAI-96)*. pages 1044–1049.

Ellen Riloff and William Phillips. 2004. An introduction to the sundance and autoslog systems. Technical report, Technical Report UUCS-04-015, School of Computing, University of Utah.

Amanda Stent, Rashmi Prasad, and Marilyn Walker. 2004. Trainable sentence planning for complex information presentation in spoken dialogue systems. In *Meeting of the Association for Computational Linguistics*.

Marilyn Walker and Owen Rambow. 2002. Spoken language generation. *Computer Speech & Language* 16(3):273 – 281. Spoken Language Generation.

Marilyn Walker, Amanda Stent, Francois Mairesse, and Rashmi Prasad. 2007. Individual and domain adaptation in sentence planning for dialogue. *Journal of Artificial Intelligence Research (JAIR)* 30:413–456.

Tsung-Hsien Wen, Milica Gasic, Nikola Mrksic, Peihao Su, David Vandyke, and Steve J. Young. 2015. Semantically conditioned lstm-based natural language generation for spoken dialogue systems. *CoRR* abs/1508.01745.

Steve Whittaker, Marilyn Walker, and Johanna Moore. 2002. Fish or fowl: A wizard of oz evaluation of dialogue strategies in the restaurant domain. In *Language Resources and Evaluation Conference*.

Is writing style predictive of scientific fraud?

Chloé Braud and **Anders Søgaard**
CoAStaL DIKU
University of Copenhagen
University Park 5, 2100 Copenhagen
chloe.braud@gmail.com soegaard@di.ku.dk

Abstract

The problem of detecting scientific fraud using machine learning was recently introduced, with initial, positive results from a model taking into account various general indicators. The results seem to suggest that writing style is predictive of scientific fraud. We revisit these initial experiments, and show that the leave-one-out testing procedure they used likely leads to a slight over-estimate of the predictability, but also that simple models can outperform their proposed model by some margin. We go on to explore more abstract linguistic features, such as linguistic complexity and discourse structure, only to obtain negative results. Upon analyzing our models, we do see some interesting patterns, though: Scientific fraud, for examples, contains less comparison, as well as different types of hedging and ways of presenting logical reasoning.

1 Introduction

Cases of scientific misconduct are identified every year. Scientific papers are retracted because of errors, or for suspected fraud, ranging from plagiarism and minor manipulations to faking the data and disguising the results. It has been shown that, however, among the retracted articles indexed in PubMed, only 21.3% are retracted due to error, while 67.4% were removed due to misconduct, among which suspected fraud amounts to 43.4%, the others being due to duplicate publications or plagiarism (Fang et al., 2012).

In a recent paper, Markowitz and Hancock (2015) proposed the first analysis of writing style in fraudulent papers across authors and disciplines. They approached the question of whether these authors have a specific writing style, from a psychological perspective. They found that these papers exhibit a higher rate of jargon, make a higher use of references, and have a lower readability rate, suggesting that the authors try to obfuscate their writing, making them harder to read and analyze. They report classification results using a leave-one-out strategy over the dataset, with a classification accuracy of 57.2%. As suggested in the paper, we propose to improve this performance by evaluating different classification models.

In this paper, we first show that much better results can be obtained using a simple bag-of-words representation and Logistic Regression. Our best model is a syntax-enhanced trigram-model. We also show that the leave-one-out strategy used by the authors leads to an over-estimation of model precision, and we report new results based on a more robust strategy, taking into account the low number of instance available; namely a *nested* cross-validation (Varma and Simon, 2006; Scheffer, 1999). We also considered semantic and discourse features, but we did not observe improvements with such features.

Of course, that a bag-of-words model outperforms a model based on psychologically motivated features, may simply be the result of overfitting. We present an extensive feature analysis to validate our models, as well as to test psychologically motivated hypotheses from the literature.

Contributions (i) We present a simple model with high accuracy, and show that it implicitly captures the previously-proposed psychologically-motivated features. (ii) We show that adding semantics and discourse features does not lead to improvements. (iii) On the other hand, our feature analysis suggests that the models *do* learn to focus on concepts that are intuitively related to scientific

Proceedings of the Workshop on Stylistic Variation, pages 37–42
Copenhagen, Denmark, September 7–11, 2017. ©2017 Association for Computational Linguistics

misconduct, e.g., that scientific fraud contains less comparison.

2   Related work

Markowitz and Hancock (2015) were the first to study writing style in fraudulent papers. They gathered a corpus of 253 articles indexed in PubMed that have been retracted for fraudulent data, as well as 253 unretracted papers (see Section 3). They define five indicators of obfuscation, and show that fraudulent papers tend to demonstrate a higher rate of linguistics obfuscation, corresponding to a lower readability, an higher use of jargon and a higher degree of abstraction. Linked to studies on deception identification, they also report a lower rate of positive emotion terms and a higher rate of causal terms (e.g. "depend", "induce", "manipulated") in fraudulent papers. The readability score was computed using Coh-Metrix (McNamara et al., 2013), while the other scores were based on the Linguistic Inquiry and Word Count (LIWC; (Pennebaker et al., 2007)), a dictionary associating a word to various scores such as abstraction (a word is considered as jargon if it is not found in the dictionary). Finally, they report 57.2% in accuracy using these five indicators as features, a score that we show is probably a little too optimistic, since it is based on a leave-one-out procedure (see Section 5). We extend their work by first showing that a simple unigram model outperforms their model by a large margin, but also by considering more indicators, including discourse and syntax, and by showing, as mentioned, that their scores were probably over-estimated due to their validation strategy.

Our work is also inspired by another related field of research concerned with deception detection. Mihalcea and Strapparava (2009) built three datasets consisting of 100 true and 100 deceptive short statements on three different topics (abortion, death penalty, best friend). Using only unigrams, they report 70.8% accuracy in a 10-fold cross validation. They found that specific word classes, as defined in the LIWC, were predictive of deceptive texts, especially classes indicating detachment from self or related to certainty.

Feng et al. (2012a) investigate syntactic features, using lexicalized and unlexicalized production rules in addition to shallow features (words unigram and bigram, and POS unigram). They experiment on truthful and deceptive reviews from TripAdvisor, either gold (Ott et al., 2011) or retrieved using a fake review detector (Feng et al., 2012b), reviews automatically extracted from Yelp, and the corpus introduced in (Mihalcea and Strapparava, 2009). They report scores between 64.3 and 91.2% accuracy, depending on the dataset. They found that, for all datasets, syntax helps, and that deceptive reviews more frequently use VP, SBAR and WHADVP.

We also consider n-gram features, syntactic features, as well as discourse features. Our task is however a bit different, since authors of fraudulent papers are not directly lying, rather trying to conceal their fraud. Moreover, our documents are longer and are of a different genre, i.e. scientific articles.

3   Data

We use the dataset proposed in (Markowitz and Hancock, 2015) containing 253 publications retracted for data fraud and 253 unretracted publications. These publications were taken from the PubMed archives from 1973 through 2013.

The unretracted papers are extracted by considering one retracted paper and taking a control paper published the same year, in the same journal, and with some common keywords when possible. When no such paper exists (around 19% of the papers), a paper from an adjacent year, or using the same words in the abstract, was selected.

The data used is the pre-processed version presented in (Markowitz and Hancock, 2015): Words were converted from British English to American English forms. Brackets, parentheses, and percent signs were removed. Periods were removed from certains words, such as 'Dr.' or nc.'. The documents only contain the main body text (no section titles, figures, or tables).

4   Methodology

We investigate different types of features, from n-grams to discourse. In large vocabulary feature spaces, we perform feature reduction, to reduce sparsity. We then provide an analysis of the features to identify the most informative indicators.

Word features   We use word n-grams as features, with $n \in \{1, 2, 3\}$. In order to test the hypotheses presented in previous studies, we also use lexicons to extract information about the tokens. We use the General Inquirer (Stone and

Kirsh, 1966) to extract words expressing a *polarity* – the features built represent the polarity between positive, negative, both and neutral –, and words corresponding to a *causal* term. We also use this lexicon to map the words to a more general semantic category (*Inquirer*).

We identify all the personal *pronouns* using manually defined lists. Finally, we also include as features *hedge* and modal words, also using a pre-defined list.[1]

Syntactic features In order to obtain syntactic information, we parse the data using UDPipe[2] (Straka et al., 2016), and a prebuilt model available online for English.[3] We follow (Johannsen et al., 2015) in extracting all subtrees of up to three tokens (*treelets*).

Discourse features Finally, we automatically annotate all the data with discourse connectives and explicit discourse relations using simple models trained on the Penn Discourse Treebank (PDTB) (Prasad et al., 2008), a corpus of news articles from the Wall Street Journal. Discourse coherence is an indicator of the quality of a text (Lin et al., 2011), of its reasoning that could reveal an attempt to deceive. Some specific semantic relations could also be good indicators (e.g. Cause).

We used models to identify the discourse connectives (*Connectives*) and to identify the explicit discourse relation[4] (*Explicit relations*) they trigger, either among the 4 coarse-grained classes (*lvl1*) at the top of the hierarchy of sense or using the 11 more fine-grained relations at the second level (*lvl2*). Our models use Logistic Regression and the connective and the surrounding words and their POS as features (Lin et al., 2009). They are trained on the sections 2-21 of the PDTB. Our results on the section 23 are close to the state-of-the-art (Pitler and Nenkova, 2009; Pitler et al., 2008; Lin et al., 2014): 92.9% in accuracy for identifying the connectives, 95.1% for the level-1 relations, and 86.2% for the level-2 relations.

Feature analysis In addition to presenting accuracies obtained with these feature sets, we

Category	# Orig. feat.	# Selec. feat.
Unigrams	$65,798$	118
2-3-grams	$1,745,188$	154
Polarity	4	–
Causal	68	–
Inquirer	180	–
Pronouns	7	–
Hedges	121	–
Treelets	$50,522$	136
Connectives	70	–
Explicit relations lvl1	4	–
Explicit relations lvl2	10	–

Table 1: Size of the original vocabulary and number of selected features for n-grams and treelets.

also perform a feature analysis. For this purpose we use a combination of correlation coefficients, logistic regression coefficients, and stability selection (Meinshausen and Bühlmann, 2010) – a method that consists in repeatedly fitting the model across different random subsamples, and counting how many times features are selected in ℓ_1-regularized logistic regression models. For stability selection, we use the implementation available in scikit-learn (Pedregosa et al., 2011) with its default parameters, run it on the whole dataset and keep features selected more than 50% of the time.

We indicate the size of the original vocabulary and the number of selected features for each category in Table 1.

5 Classification

Representation We test separately count vectorizations with each set of features – unigrams, 2-3-grams, polarity, causality, Inquirer categories, pronouns (grouping per person, or considering each lemma), treelets, connectives, hedge words, level-1 relations and level-2 relations, and combinations of these features.

Model We use a binary logistic regression classifier, optimizing the norm (ℓ_1 or ℓ_2) and strength ($c \in \{0.001, 0.005, 0.01, 0.1, 0.5, 1, 5, 10, 100\}$ of the regularization term on held-out data.

Validation schemes Markowitz and Hancock (2015) report results with a leave-one-out strategy (LOO). However, LOO often under-estimates the error rate. We compare with a *nested* cross-validation procedure that can provide an almost

---

[1] https://github.com/wooorm/hedges/blob/master/index.json

[2] http://ufal.mff.cuni.cz/udpipe

[3] UD 1.2, https://lindat.mff.cuni.cz/repository/xmlui/handle/11234/1-1659

[4] We ignore the non explicit relations for which the in-domain scores are very low – around 40-57% in accuracy (Rutherford and Xue, 2015; Lin et al., 2014).

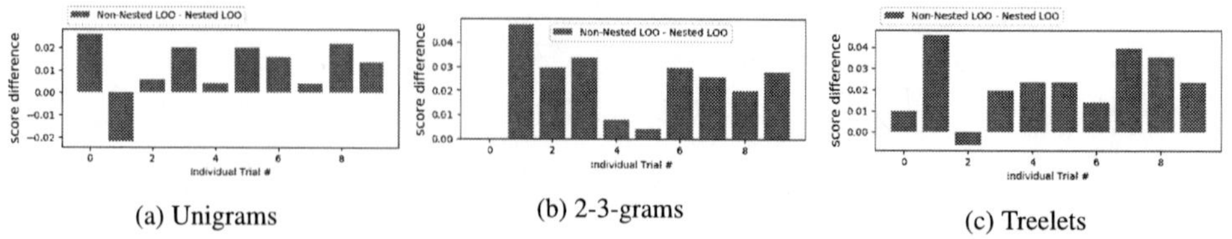

<table>
<tr><td>(a) Unigrams</td><td>(b) 2-3-grams</td><td>(c) Treelets</td></tr>
</table>

Figure 1: Accuracy difference between LOO and Nested LOO for each trial for different features.

System	LOO	N-LOO
(Markowitz and Hancock, 2015)	57.2	-
Unigrams	72.1	71.7
2-3-grams	70.8	69.6
Polarity	50.0	45.3
Causal	59.9	58.4
Inquirer	58.7	54.3
Pronouns	54.5	52.2
Hedges	56.7	54.1
Treelets	72.9	71.7
Connectives	60.1	58.3
Explicit Relations lvl1	54.3	53.2
Explicit Relations lvl2	54.5	54.3
1-2-3-grams+treelets	**76.3**	**76.0**
All	70.3	69.8

Table 2: Results (accuracy, in %).

unbiased estimate of the true error (Varma and Simon, 2006; Scheffer, 1999).

Specifically, we use two cross-validation loops: the inner loop is used for tuning the hyper-parameters, and the outer loop estimates the generalization error. The data are first split into N folds, the fold k ($1 \leq k \leq N$) is the current evaluation set, and the $N - 1$ other folds are used as training data and split into M folds used for model fitting. The best model is then evaluated on fold k. Final scores are averages over the N folds.

For comparison with Markowitz and Hancock (2015), we report performance with LOO and with nested cross-validation using LOO as outer loop, the inner loop being a random 5-fold cross-validation. We repeat each evaluation 10 times, and report a mean over these trials.

Results Our results are summarized in Table 2. Our results are generally higher than the 57.2% reported in (Markowitz and Hancock, 2015), with at best 71.7% with a nested LOO and a single group of features (*unigrams* or *treelets*) and 76.0% when

n-grams and treelets are combined.

Using all the n-grams already leads to a better accuracy score (+1.3%) compared to using only *unigrams* (73.0% in accuracy for *1+2-3-grams* with N-LOO). On the other hand, combining discourse features to the n-grams does not allow improvements over using only the n-grams (72.8% with N-LOO for *1+2-3-grams+Connectives+Explicit Relations lvl1*).

The scores obtained with LOO are over-estimate performance, compared to nested cross-validation, see for example Figure 1: Even if the differences are low, they are consistent across the trials and the feature sets.

6 Feature analysis

We use Pearson's ρ (w. Bonferroni correction) to establish what features are predictive of fraud and non-fraud. We report the values for the features cited in Table 3.

Hedging There is an interesting contrast between adverbial hedges (*conceivably, presumably, surely, effectively*) and verbal hedges (*suggest*) indicative of fraud, and adverbial hedges (*practically, occasionally*) and verbal hedges *assume, speculate*) indicative of non-fraud: It seems adverbs and verbs used in fraud are for interpreting the data on behalf of the reader, whereas the adverbs and verbs indicative of fraud are more observer-aware (e.g., *we speculate*). This suggest that a fraud strategy is to hide observers bias, rather than being explicit about it.

Comparison Both the discourse relation and the Inquirer class for comparison are predictive of non-fraud. Scientific fraud thus seems less likely to compare. On the other hand, neither the causal relations or the presence of causal terms were significantly linked to fraudulent papers.

Therefore vs. since A peculiar, but statistically significant difference between fraud and non-fraud articles, is that fraud articles prefer *therefore* over *since*, and vice versa. We speculate that it may be a fraud strategy to make the reasoning more verbose by separating out premises (because the authors are, consciously or not, afraid the readers will not accept them). This is in slight contrast with or qualifies the main hypothesis in Markowitz and Hancock (2015), that fraudulent writers try to obfuscate their writing.

Other markers of fraud Many technical concepts were highly correlated with fraud, but we suspect these are cases of overfitting. More interestingly, the bigram *described previously* was among the top-5 most highly correlated features, indicating fraud. From our syntactic treelets, proper nouns and interjections were both slightly indicative of fraud ($p < 0.01$).

Other markers of non-fraud From our syntactic treelets, conjunctions of numbers were indicative of non-fraud, suggesting maybe a higher level of technical detail. Non-fraud articles are also more likely to use the pronoun *they*, as compared to *we*, compared to fraud papers.

7 Conclusion

We show that a simple unigram model outperforms previous work on scientific fraud detection. Overall, more high-level linguistic features, beyond syntactic treelets, do not lead to improvements, but we also presented a feature analysis showing, for example, that comparison and explanation (at the semantic and discourse level) are indicators of non-fraud, and that fraudulent writing uses slightly different hedging strategies.

References

Ferric C. Fang, R. Grant Steen, and Arturo Casadevall. 2012. Misconduct accounts for the majority of retracted scientific publications. *Proceedings of the National Academy of Sciences of the United States of America*, 109(42):17028–17033.

Song Feng, Ritwik Banerjee, and Yejin Choi. 2012a. Syntactic stylometry for deception detection. In *Proceedings of the 50th Annual Meeting of the Association for Computational Linguistics: Short Papers-Volume 2*, pages 171–175. Association for Computational Linguistics.

Song Feng, Longfei Xing, Anupam Gogar, and Yejin Choi. 2012b. Distributional footprints of deceptive product reviews. *ICWSM*, 12:98–105.

Hedges		
assume	-0.121	p=0.006
practically	-0.118	p=0.008
occasionally	-0.112	p=0.012
conceivably	0.089	p=0.045
assumed	-0.086	p=0.052
surely	0.077	p=0.083
effectively	0.075	p=0.090
presumably	0.058	p=0.195
Inquirer		
compare	-0.158	p=0.0003
Explicit Relations lvl1		
comparison	-0.096	p=0.031
cause	0.008	p=0.863
Connectives		
since	-0.102	p=0.022
therefore	0.064	p=0.147
2-3-grams		
described previously	0.115	p=0.009
Treelets		
intj	0.126	p=0.004
propn	0.110	p=0.013
Pronouns		
we	0.071	p=0.112
they	-0.059	p=0.182

Table 3: Pearson ρ and original p-value (before Bonferroni correction) for some features.

Anders Trrup Johannsen, Dirk Hovy, and Anders Søgaard. 2015. Cross-lingual syntactic variation over age and gender. In *Proceedings of the Nineteenth Conference on Computational Natural Language Learning*.

Ziheng Lin, Min-Yen Kan, and Hwee Tou Ng. 2009. Recognizing implicit discourse relations in the penn discourse treebank. In *Proceedings of EMNLP*.

Ziheng Lin, Hwee Tou Ng, and Min-Yen Kan. 2011. Automatically evaluating text coherence using discourse relations. In *Proceedings of ACL-HLT*.

Ziheng Lin, Hwee Tou Ng, and Min-Yen Kan. 2014. A pdtb-styled end-to-end discourse parser. *Natural Language Engineering*, 20:151–184.

David M. Markowitz and Jeffrey T. Hancock. 2015. Linguistic Obfuscation in Fraudulent Science. *Journal of Language and Social Psychology*.

DS McNamara, MM Louwerse, Z Cai, and A Graesser. 2013. Coh-metrix version 3.0. *Retrieved [4/1/15] from http://cohmetrix. com.*

Nicolai Meinshausen and Peter Bühlmann. 2010. Stability selection. *Journal of the Royal Statistical Society: Series B (Statistical Methodology)*, 72(4):417–473.

Rada Mihalcea and Carlo Strapparava. 2009. The lie detector: Explorations in the automatic recognition of deceptive language. In *Proceedings of the ACL-IJCNLP 2009 Conference Short Papers*, pages 309–312. Association for Computational Linguistics.

Myle Ott, Yejin Choi, Claire Cardie, and Jeffrey T Hancock. 2011. Finding deceptive opinion spam by any stretch of the imagination. In *Proceedings of ACL HLT*.

F. Pedregosa, G. Varoquaux, A. Gramfort, V. Michel, B. Thirion, O. Grisel, M. Blondel, P. Prettenhofer, R. Weiss, V. Dubourg, J. Vanderplas, A. Passos, D. Cournapeau, M. Brucher, M. Perrot, and E. Duchesnay. 2011. Scikit-learn: Machine learning in Python. *Journal of Machine Learning Research*, 12:2825–2830.

James W Pennebaker, Roger J Booth, and Martha E Francis. 2007. Linguistic inquiry and word count: Liwc. *Austin, TX: Pennebaker Conglomerates.*

Emily Pitler and Ani Nenkova. 2009. Using syntax to disambiguate explicit discourse connectives in text. In *Proceedings of the ACL-IJCNLP*.

Emily Pitler, Mridhula Raghupathy, Hena Mehta, Ani Nenkova, Alan Lee, and Aravind Joshi. 2008. Easily identifiable discourse relations. In *Proceedings of COLING (Posters)*.

Rashmi Prasad, Nikhil Dinesh, Alan Lee, Eleni Miltsakaki, Livio Robaldo, Aravind Joshi, and Bonnie Webber. 2008. The Penn Discourse Treebank 2.0. In *Proceedings of LREC*.

Attapol Rutherford and Nianwen Xue. 2015. Improving the inference of implicit discourse relations via classifying explicit discourse connectives. In *Proceedings of NAACL-HLT*.

Tobias Scheffer. 1999. *Error Estimation and Model Selection*. Ph.D. thesis, Technischen Universitet Berlin, School of Computer Science.

Philip J. Stone and John Kirsh. 1966. *The General Inquirer: A Computer Approach to Content Analysis*. MIT Press.

Milan Straka, Jan Hajič, and Straková. 2016. UDPipe: Trainable Pipeline for Processing CoNLL-U Files Performing Tokenization, Morphological Analysis, POS Tagging and Parsing. In *Proceedings of the Tenth International Conference on Language Resources and Evaluation (LREC'16)*.

Sudhir Varma and Richard Simon. 2006. Bias in error estimation when using cross-validation for model selection. *BMC bioinformatics*.

"Deep" Learning: Detecting Metaphoricity in Adjective-Noun Pairs[*]

Yuri Bizzoni and **Stergios Chatzikyriakidis** and **Mehdi Ghanimifard**

`yuri.bizzoni,stergios.chatzikyriakidis,mehdi.ghanimifard@gu.se`

Abstract

Metaphor is one of the most studied and widespread figures of speech and an essential element of individual style. In this paper we look at metaphor identification in Adjective-Noun pairs. We show that using a single neural network combined with pre-trained vector embeddings can outperform the state of the art in terms of accuracy. In specific, the approach presented in this paper is based on two ideas: a) transfer learning via using pre-trained vectors representing adjective noun pairs, and b) a neural network as a model of composition that predicts a metaphoricity score as output. We present several different architectures for our system and evaluate their performances. Variations on dataset size and on the kinds of embeddings are also investigated. We show considerable improvement over the previous approaches both in terms of accuracy and w.r.t the size of annotated training data.

1 Introduction

The importance of metaphor to characterize both individual and genre-related style has been underlined in several works (Leech and Short, 2007; Simpson, 2004; Goodman, 1975). Studying the kinds of metaphors used in a text can contribute to differentiate between poetic and prosaic style, between different types of fiction, etc. In literary studies, metaphor analysis is often undertaken on a stylistic perspective: "after all, metaphor in literature is a stylistic device and its forms, meanings and use all fall within the remit of stylistics"

(Steen, 2014). Metaphor is thus often taken into consideration qualitative stylistic analyses (Fahnestock, 2009). Nonetheless, it is still very difficult to take metaphors into account in computational stylistics due to the complexity of automatic metaphor identification (Neuman et al., 2013; Klebanov et al., 2015), which is the task of identifying metaphorical usages of text, sentences or subsentential fragments.

This paper's focus of interest is the automatic detection of adjective-noun (AN) pairs like the following:

(1) Clean floor / clean performance

(2) Bright painting / bright idea

(3) Heavy table / heavy feeling

The above examples illustrate that adjectives "normally" used to describe physical characteristics, e.g. a feature that can be perceived through senses like size or weight, are reused to describe more abstract properties. Thus, both a painting and an idea can be bright, both a table and a feeling can be heavy. We will not provide a mean to retrieve AN metaphors in unconstrained texts (e.g. we won't focus on segmentation) but we will study ways to detect metaphoricity in given pairs. Theoretical work on metaphor in the linguistics literature goes back a long way and spans different theoretical paradigms. One of the earliest and most influential works is Conceptual Metaphor Theory (CMT) (Lakoff and Johnson, 2008) (originally published in 1981) and subsequently elaborated in a couple of papers (Lakoff, 1989, 1993). According to CMT, metaphors in natural language can be seen as instances of conceptual metaphors. A conceptual metaphor roughly corresponds to understanding a concept or an idea via association or relation with another idea or concept. Other influential linguistic approaches to metaphor include

[*]This research is funded by the Centre of Linguistic Theory and Studies in Probability at the University of Gothenburg.

43

Proceedings of the Workshop on Stylistic Variation, pages 43–52
Copenhagen, Denmark, September 7–11, 2017. ©2017 Association for Computational Linguistics

pragmatic approaches cast within frameworks like relevance theory (Romero and Soria, 2014; Wilson, 2011), and also approaches where some sort of formal semantics is used (Vogel, 2001). The common denominator in all these approaches is the recognition that there is systematicity in the way metaphorical meanings arise and also that the process of metaphor construction is extremely productive. Thus, given these properties, one would expect metaphors to be quite common in Natural Language (NL). Evidence from corpus linguistics seems to support this claim (Cameron, 2003).

Metaphor detection in statistical NLP has been attempted through several different frames, such as topic modeling (Li and Sporleder, 2010b), semantic similarity graphs (Li and Sporleder, 2010a), distributional clustering (Shutova et al., 2010), vector space based learning (Gutiérrez et al., 2016) and, most of all, feature-based classifiers (Tsvetkov et al., 2014). In the latter case, the challenge consists in selecting the right features to annotate the training data with, and to review their "importance" or weight based on machine learning results.

In this paper we show how using a single-layered neural network combined with pre-trained distributional embeddings can outperform the state of the art in an AN metaphor detection task.

More specifically, this paper's contributions are the following:

- We introduce a system to predict AN metaphoricity and test it on the corpus introduced by (Gutiérrez et al., 2016), showing a significant improvement in accuracy.

- We explore different variations of this model based on ideas found in the literature for composing distributional meaning and we evaluate them under different constraints.

The paper is structured as follows: in Section 2 we present the background on AN metaphor detection and we detail the dataset we use to train our model. In Section 3 we describe our approach, giving a general overview and further describing three alternative architectures on the same model. In Section 4 we present several evaluations of our model. Table 1 and Table 2 synthesize some of our findings. In Section 5 we discuss our findings and possible future applications of the work described in this paper.

2   Background

In the specific task of detecting metaphoricity for AN pairs we find four relevant works that seem to represent the main stages in figurative language detection until now.

The oldest work of the series, (Krishnakumaran and Zhu, 2007), strongly relies on external resources. They adopt a WordNet based approach to recognize Noun-Noun (NN), Noun-Verb (NV) and AN metaphors. Their work is mainly based on qualitative analyses of specific examples and shows that, while they can be useful in such a task, hyponym/hypernym relations are not enough to distinguish metaphors from literal expressions.

More recently, Turney et al. (2011) adopt a two-stage machine learning approach. They first try to learn the words' degree of concreteness and then use this knowledge to detect whether an AN couple is metaphorical or not. They measure their performance on 100 phrases involving 5 adjectives and reach an accuracy of 0.79. It is worth noting that this choice is not random: the authors select the abstract/concrete polarity based on psycholinguistic findings that seem to validate the hypothesis that some kinds of metaphorical expressions are processed as abstract elements.[1]

These results were outperformed by Tsvetkov et al. (2014) through a random forest classifier using DSM vectors, WordNet senses and several accurately selected features, such as abstractness. They also introduce a new set of 200 phrases, on which they declare an F-score of 0.85.

Finally, Gutiérrez et al. (2016) train a distributional model on a corpus of 4.58 billion tokens and test it on an annotated dataset they introduce consisting of 8592 AN phrases. This is the same dataset we are using in this paper and the largest available to date.

They first train distributional vectors for the words in the dataset using positive pointwise mutual information. Then, for each adjective present in the dataset, they divide the literal phrases the adjective occurs in from the metaphorical phrases the same adjective appears in. Then, three different adjective matrices are trained: one to model the adjective's literal sense, one to model its metaphorical sense, and one trained on all the phrases containing this adjective, both literal and metaphorical. They then develop a system to "de-

---

[1]For a more recent study on this issue see (Forgács et al., 2015).

	Accuracy	Feature engineering	Annotated dataset	Embedding
(Turney et al., 2011)	0.79	Yes	100	LSA
(Tsvetkov et al., 2014)	0.85	Yes	200	-
(Gutiérrez et al., 2016)	0.81	No	8592	DSM
Our model	**0.91**	No	8592	Word2Vec

Table 1: The reported accuracy from previous words on AN metaphor detection. The first two studies used different datasets. We are using larger pre-trained vectors than Gutiérrez et al. (2016); at the same time, we don't need a parsed corpus to build our vectors and we don't use adjectival matrices. Given these differences, this comparison should not be considered a "competition".

	Random W	**Trained** W
cat-linear	0.8973	0.9153
cat-relu	0.8763	0.9228
sum-linear	0.8815	0.9068
sum-relu	0.8597	0.9150
mul-linear	0.7858	0.8066
mul-relu	0.7795	0.8186

Table 2: The accuracy results after training the model based on each architecture. In all setups, we trained on 500 samples in 20 epochs. Using a random W is equivalent to preventing our network from learning any form of compositionality (we could consider it as a baseline for models with trained W). As we discuss in the paper, the difference in accuracies with the "baseline" (not training W) shows that training W is helpful.

cide" whether a particular occurrence of an adjective is more likely to relate to the "literal matrix" or the "metaphorical matrix". It is shown that, although such matrices are trained on relatively few examples, they can reach an accuracy of over 0.78.

2.1 Corpus/Experimental Data

The dataset we are using comes from (Gutiérrez et al., 2016). [2] It contains 8592 annotated AN pairs, 3991 being literal and 4601 being metaphorical. The dataset focuses on a set of 23 adjectives that: a) can potentially have both metaphorical and literal meanings, and b) are fairly productive.

The choice of adjectives was based on the test set of (Tsvetkov et al., 2014) and focuses on 23 adjectives.

In details, all adjectives belong to one of the following categories:

1. temperature adjectives (e.g. cold)

2. light adjectives (e.g. bright)

3. texture adjectives (e.g. rough)

4. substance adjectives (e.g. dense)

5. clarity adjectives (e.g. clean)

6. taste adjectives (e.g. bitter)

7. strength adjectives (e.g. strong)

8. depth adjectives (e.g. deep)

The corpus was carefully built in order to avoid non-ambiguous elements: all the AN phrases present in this dataset were extracted from large corpora and all phrases that seemed to require a larger context for their interpretation were filtered out in order to eliminate potentially ambiguous idiomatic expressions such as *bright side*.

In other terms, the corpus was designed to contain elements whose metaphoricity could be deduced by a human annotator without the need of a larger context.

More details about the construction of the dataset and annotation methodology can be found in (Gutiérrez et al., 2016).

3 Describing our approach

3.1 The model framework

Our objective is to build a classifier that disambiguates between metaphoric and literal AN compositions by providing a probability measure between 0 and 1. We based the framework of the model on the following ideas:

1. Transfer learning: we use pre-trained word-vectors to represent AN pairs as input.

2. A neural network as a model of composition for the AN phrase: our model represents

---

[2]The dataset is publicly available here: http://bit.ly/1TQ5czN

phrases with vectors, then based on this representation predicts a metaphoricity score as output. Although we are going to present several variations of this framework, it's important to remember that the basic model is always a standard NN with a single fully connected hidden layer we will call $\mathbf{p}$.

Our approach is thus based on the idea that well-trained distributional vectors contain more valuable information than their reciprocal similarity and, furthermore, that it is possible to treasure such information through machine learning in different tasks. We use 300-dimensional word vectors trained on different corpora (see Evaluation for more details). Our approach can be considered as a way of transferring the learned representation from one task to another. Although it is not possible to point out an explicit mapping between the word-vector learning task (e.g. Word2Vec model) and our metaphoricity task, as it is pointed out by Torrey and Shavlik 2009, we use neural networks which automatically learn how to adapt the feature representations between two tasks (Bengio et al., 2013). In this way we stretch the original embeddings, trained in order to learn lexical similarity, to identify AN metaphors.

Our neural network, being a parameterized function, follows the generalized architecture of word-vector composition similar to (Mitchell and Lapata, 2010):

$$\mathbf{p} = f(\mathbf{u}, \mathbf{v}; \theta) \qquad (4)$$

where $\mathbf{u}$ and $\mathbf{v}$ are two word vector representations to be composed, while $\mathbf{p}$ is the vector representation of their composition with the same dimensions. The function f in our model is parameterized by θ, a list of parameters to be learned as part of our neural network architecture.

Based on the argument by (Mitchell and Lapata, 2010), parameters such as θ are encoded knowledge required by the compositional process. In our case, the gradient based learning in neural networks will find these parameters as an optimization problem where $\mathbf{p}$ is just an intermediate representation in the pipeline of the neural network, which ends with a prediction of a metaphoricity score.

In other words, in order to predict the degree of metaphoricity, we end up learning a specific semantic space for phrase representations $\mathbf{p}$ and a vector $\mathbf{q}$ which actually does not represent a phrase itself, but rather the maximal possible level of metaphoricity given our training set.

The degree of metaphoricity of a phrase can thus be directly computed as cosine similarity between this vector and the phrase vector. However, in the network we used a sigmoid function to produce the measure:

$$\hat{y} = \sigma(\mathbf{p}\cdot\mathbf{q} + b_1) = \frac{1}{1 + e^{-\mathbf{p}\cdot\mathbf{q}+b_1}} \qquad (5)$$

where $\mathbf{q}$ and b_1 are parameters of the final layer and work as metaphoricity indicators, while $\hat{y}$ is the predicted score (*metaphoric* or *literal*) for the composition $\mathbf{p}$. Given a dataset of $D = \{(x_t, y_t)\}_{t\in\{1,...,T\}}$, the composition $\mathbf{p}$ can be formalized as a model for Bernoulli distribution:

$$
\begin{aligned}
y_t &= Pr(x_t \text{ being metaphorical}|D) &\in \{0,1\} \\
\hat{y}_t &= \sigma(\mathbf{p}_t\cdot\mathbf{q} + b_1) \\
&\approx Pr(x_t \text{ being metaphorical}) &\in (0,1)
\end{aligned}
\qquad (6)
$$

where each x_t is an AN pair in the training dataset labeled with a binary value y_t (0 or 1). Given the labels in D, we interpret y_t as a categorical probability score: the probability of a given phrase being metaphorical. Then, for each pair of words in x_t, we use pre-trained word-vector representations such as $\mathbf{u_t}$ and $\mathbf{v_t}$ in the Equation 4 to produce $\mathbf{p}_t$ and, consequently, the score $\hat{y}_t$.

In this formulation, the objective is to minimize the binary cross entropy distance between the estimated $\hat{y}_t$ and the given annotation y_t. Adding $\mathbf{q}$ and b_1 in the list of parameters Θ, we fit all parameters with a small annotated data size T:

$$
\begin{aligned}
\mathbf{x} &= (x_1, ... x_T) \\
\mathbf{y} &= (y_1, ... y_T) \\
\Theta &= (\theta, \mathbf{q}, b_1)
\end{aligned}
\qquad (7)
$$

$$
\mathcal{L}(\Theta; \mathbf{x}, \mathbf{y}) = \begin{aligned}[t] &-\sum_{t=1}^{T}(y_t \log(\hat{y}_t) + \\ &(1 - y_t)\log(1 - \hat{y}_t))\end{aligned} \qquad (8)
$$

where, on each iteration, we update the parameters in Θ using Adam stochastic gradient descent (Kingma and Ba, 2014), with a fixed number of iterations over $\mathbf{x}$ and $\mathbf{y}$ to minimize $\mathcal{L}$.

In this paper, we describe three alternative architectures to implement this framework. All three, with small variations, show a robust ability to generalize on the dataset and perform correct predictions.

3.2 First Architecture

One possible formulation of this frame is similar to additive composition as described in (Mitchell and Lapata, 2010), but instead of performing a scalar modification of each vector, a weight matrix modifies all feature dimensions at once:

$$\mathbf{p} = W_{adj}^T \mathbf{u} + W_{noun}^T \mathbf{v} + b \qquad (9)$$

$$W = \begin{bmatrix} W_{adj} \\ W_{noun} \end{bmatrix} \qquad (10)$$

where the composition function in equation (4) now has $\theta = (W, b)$.

This formulation is very similar to the composition model in (Socher et al., 2011) without the syntactic tree parametrization. As such, instead of the non-linearity function we have linear identity:

$$\mathbf{p} = f_\theta(\mathbf{u}, \mathbf{v}) = W^T \begin{bmatrix} \mathbf{u} \\ \mathbf{v} \end{bmatrix} + b \qquad (11)$$

In practice, this approach represents a simple merging through concatenation: given two words' vectors, we concatenate them before feeding them to a single-layered, fully connected Neural Network.

As a consequence, the network learns a weight matrix that represents linearly the AN combination. To visualize this concept, we could say that, since our pairs always hold the same internal structure (adjective in first position and noun in second position), the first half of the weight matrix is trained on adjectives and the second half of the weight matrix is trained on nouns.

By using 300 dimension pre-trained word vectors, the parameter space for this composition function will be as following: $W \in \mathbb{R}^{300 \times 600}$ and $b \in \mathbb{R}^{300}$.

3.3 Second architecture

The second architecture we describe has the advantage of training a smaller set of parameters with respect to the first. In this model, the weight matrix is shared between the noun and the adjective:

$$\mathbf{p} = f_\theta(\mathbf{u}, \mathbf{v}) = W^T \mathbf{u} + W^T \mathbf{v} + b \qquad (12)$$

Notice that in the case of comparing the vector representations of two different AN phrases, b will be essentially redundant. An advantage of this model is that the learned composition function f can also map all words' vectors, regardless of the part of speech these words belong to, in the new vector space without losing accuracy in the original task. In this new vector space, a simple addition operator composes two vectors:

$$\mathbf{u}' = W^T \mathbf{u} \qquad (13)$$

$$\mathbf{v}' = W^T \mathbf{v} \qquad (14)$$

$$\mathbf{p} = \mathbf{u}' + \mathbf{v}' \qquad (15)$$

Compared to the first architecture, in this architecture we don't assume the need of distinguishing the weight matrix for the adjectives from the weight matrix for the nouns.

It is rather interesting, then, that this architecture doesn't present significant differences in performance with respect to the first one. The number of parameters, however, is smaller: $W \in \mathbb{R}^{300 \times 300}$ and $b \in \mathbb{R}^{300}$.

3.4 Third Architecture

The third architecture, similarly to the second, features a shared composition matrix of weights between the noun and the adjective, but we perform elementwise multiplication between the two vectors:

$$\mathbf{p} = f_\theta(\mathbf{u}, \mathbf{v}) = (\mathbf{u} \times \mathbf{v})W + b \qquad (16)$$

The number of parameters in this case is similar to previous architecture: $W \in \mathbb{R}^{300 \times 300}$ and $b \in \mathbb{R}^{300}$.

3.5 Other Architectures

In all three previous architectures we saw that a weight matrix W can be learned as part of the composing function. Throughout our exploration, we found that W can be a random and a constant uniform matrix (not trained in the network) and still being able to learn $\mathbf{q}$ unless we use a non-linear activation functions over the AN compositions.

$$\mathbf{p} = g(f_\theta(\mathbf{u}, \mathbf{v})) \qquad (17)$$

An intuition is to take W as an identity matrix in Second architecture, the network will take the sum of pre-trained vectors to as features and learn how to predict metaphoricity. A fixed uniform W basically keeps the information in input vectors. For a short overview of all these alternative architectures see Table 2.

4   Evaluation

Our classifier achieved 91.5% accuracy trained on 500 labeled AN-phrases out of 8592 in the corpus and tested on the rest. Training on 8000 and testing on the rest gave us accuracy of 98.5%.[3]

We tested several combinations of the architectures we described in the paper. For each of the three architectures, we also tested the Rectified linear unit (ReLU) as the non-linearity mentioned in Section 3.5. Our test also shows that a random constant matrix W is enough to train the rest of the parameters (reported in Table 2). In general, the best performing combinations involve the use of concatenation (the first architecture), while multiplication led to the lowest results. In any case, all experiments returned accuracies above 75% [4].

To test the robustness of our approach, we have evaluated our model's performance under several constraints:

- Total separation of vocabulary in train and test sets (Table 3) in case of out of vocabulary words.

- Use of different pretrained word embeddings (Figure 3).

- Cross validation (Figure 1).

- Qualitative selection of the training data based on the semantic categories of adjectives (Figure 2).

Finally, we will provide some qualitative insights on how the model works.

Our model is based on the idea of transfer learning: using the learned representation for a new task, in this case the metaphor detection. Our model should generalize very fast with a small set of samples as training data. In order to test this matter, we have to train and test on totally different samples so vocabulary doesn't overlap. The splitting of the 8592 labeled phrases based on vocabulary gives us uneven sizes of training and test phrases[5]. In Table 3 using the pretrained

Word2Vec embeddings trained on Google News (Mikolov et al., 2013) we examined the accuracy, precision and recall of the our trained classifier.

We have used three different word embeddings: Word2Vec embeddings trained on Google News (Mikolov et al., 2013), GloVe embeddings (Pennington et al., 2014) and Levy-Goldberg embeddings (Levy and Goldberg, 2014).

These embeddings are not up-dated during the training process. Thus, the classification task is always performed by learning weights for the preexisting vectors.

The results of our experiment can be seen in Figure 3. All these embeddings have returned similar accuracies both when trained on scarce data (100 phrases) and when trained on half of the dataset (4000 phrases).

Training on 100 phrases indicates the ability of our model to learn from scarce data. One way of checking the consistency of our model under data scarcity is to perform *flipped* cross-validation: this is a cross-validation where, instead of training our model on 90% of the data and testing it on the remaining 10%, we flipped the sizes train it on 10% of the data and test it on the remaining 90%. Results for both classic cross-validation and flipped cross-validation can be seen in Figure 1. Training on 10% of the data proved to consistently achieve accuracies not much lower than 90%. In other terms, a model trained on 90% of the data does not do much better than a model trained on 10%.

Finally, we tried training our model on only one of the semantic categories we introduced at the beginning of the paper and testing it on the rest of the dataset. Results can be seen in Figure 2.

We can wonder "why" our system is working: with respect to more traditional machine learning approaches, there is no direct way to evaluate which features mostly contribute to the success of our system. One way to have an idea of what is happening in the model is to use the "metaphoricity vector" we discussed in Section 3. Such vector represents what is learned by our model and can help making it less opaque for us.

If we compute the cosine similarity between all the nouns in our dataset and this learned vector, we can see that nouns tend to polarize on an abstract/concrete axis: abstract nouns tend to be more similar to the learned vector than concrete nouns.

It is likely that our model is learning nouns'

---

[3]These results are based on the first architecture, the performance of other architectures are not very different in this simple test. The sample code is available on https://guclasp.github.io/anvec-metaphor/

[4]The number of parameters in case of using concatenation (as in first architecture) is 180 601 and other compositions, including addition and multiplication, number of parameters is almost the half: 90 601.

[5]We chose the vocabulary splitting points for every 10% from 10% to 90%, then we applied the splitting separately on nouns and adjective

Test	Train	Accuracy	Precision	Recall
6929	72	0.83	0.89	0.77
5561	299	0.89	0.86	0.93
4406	643	0.91	0.92	0.90
3239	1203	0.90	0.91	0.88
2253	1961	0.91	0.92	0.92
1568	2763	0.89	0.90	0.90
707	4291	0.91	0.94	0.91
313	5494	0.93	0.92	0.95
148	6282	0.93	0.94	0.92

Table 3: This table shows consistent results in accuracy, precision and recall of the classifier trained with different split points of vocabulary instead of phrases. Splitting the vocabulary creates different sizes of training phrases and test phrases.

level of abstractness as a mean to determine phrase metaphoricity. In Table 4 we show the 10 most similar and the 10 least similar nouns obtained with this approach. As can be seen, a concrete-abstract polarity is apparently learned in training.

This factor was amply noted and even used in some feature-based metaphor classifiers, as we discussed in the beginning: the advantage of using continuous semantic spaces probably relies on the possibility of having a more nuanced and complex polarization of nouns along the concrete/abstract axes than using hand-annotated resources.

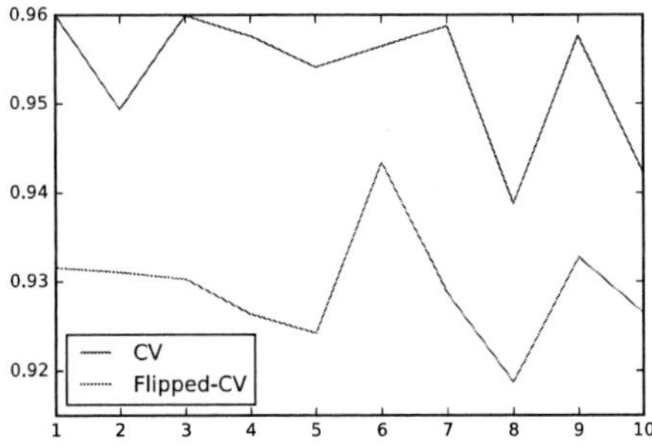

Figure 1: Accuracies for each fold over two complementary approaches: cross-validation (CV) and *flipped* cross-validation ("flipped-CV"). *Flipped* cross-validation takes 90% of our dataset for training. The graph shows that both methods yield good results: in other words training on just 10% of the dataset yields results that are just few points lower than normal cross-validation.

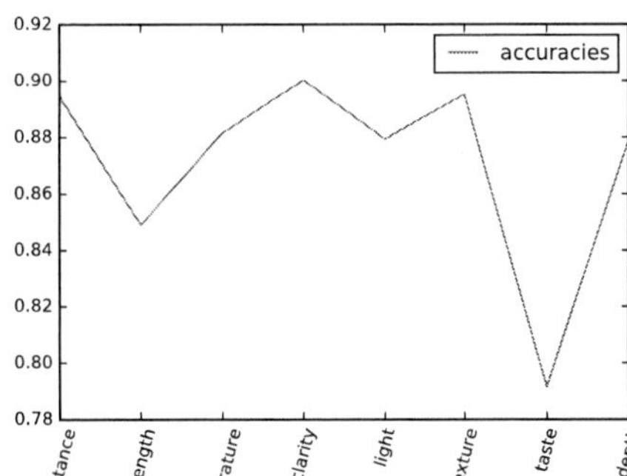

Figure 2: Accuracy training on different categories of adjectives. In this experiment, we train on just one category of the dataset and test on all the others. In general, training on just one category (e.g. *temperature*) and testing on all other categories still yields high accuracy. While the power of generalization of our model is still unclear, we can see that it can detect similar semantic mechanisms even without any vocabulary overlap. The category *taste* is a partial exception: this category seems to be a relative "outlier".

5 Discussion and future work

In this paper we have presented an approach for detecting metaphoricity in AN pairs that outperforms the state of the art without using human annotated data or external resources beyond pretrained word embeddings. We treasured the information captured by Word2Vec vectors through a fully connected neural network able to filter out the "noise" of the original semantic space. We have presented a series of alternative variations of this approach and evaluated its performance under several conditions - different word embeddings, different training data and different training sizes - showing that our model can generalize efficiently and obtain solid results over scarce training data. We think that this is one of the central findings in this paper, since many semantic phenomena similar to metaphor (for example other figures of speech) are under-represented in current NLP resources and their study through supervised classifiers would require systems able to work on small datasets.

The possibility of detecting metaphors and assigning a degree of "metaphoricity" to a snippet of text is essential to automatic stylistic programs designed to go beyond "shallow features" such as sentence length, functional word counting etc.

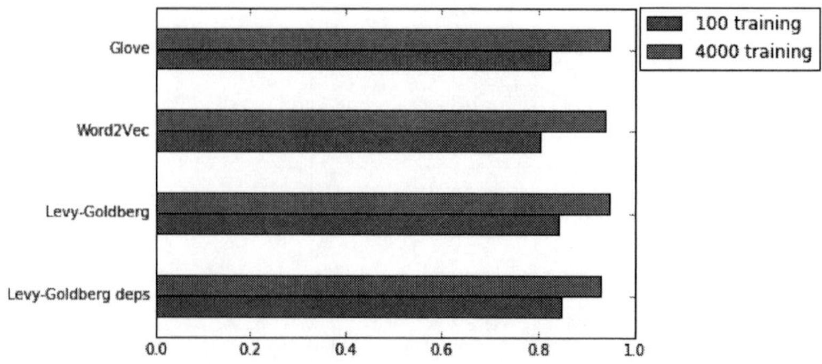

Figure 3: Accuracy on different kinds of embeddings, both training on 100 phrases and 4000 phrases.

Top ten	reluctance, reprisal, resignation, response, rivalry, satisfaction, storytelling, supporter, surveillance, vigilance
Bottom ten	saucepan, flour, skillet, chimney, jar, tub, fuselage, pellet, pouch, cupboard

Table 4: 10 most similar and 10 least similar terms with respect to the "metaphoricity vector", concatenated using an all-zeros vector for the adjective. In practice, this is a way to explore which semantic dimensions are particularly useful to the classifier. A concrete/abstract polarity on the nouns was apparently derived

While such metrics have already allowed powerful studies, the lack of tools to quantify more complex stylistic phenomena is evident (Hughes et al., 2012; Gibbs Jr, 2017). Naturally, this work is intended as a first step: the "metaphoricity" degree our system is learning would mirror the kinds of combination present in this specific dataset, which represents a very specific type of metaphor.

It can be argued that we are not really learning the defining ambiguities of an adjective (e.g. the double meaning of "bright") but that we are probably side-learning nouns' degree of abstraction. This would be in harmony with psycholinguistic findings, since detecting nouns' abstraction seems to be one of the main mechanisms we recur to, when we have to judge the metaphoricity of an expression (Forgács et al., 2015) and is used as a main feature in traditional Machine Learning approaches to this problem. In other terms, our system seems to detect when the same adjective is used with different categories of words (abstract or concrete) and generalize over this distinction; a behavior that might not be too far from the way a human learns to distinguish different senses of a word.

An issue that we would like to further test in the future is metaphoricity detection on different datasets, to explore the ability of generalization of our models. Researching on different datasets could also help us gaining a better insight about the model's learning.

An obvious option is to test verb-adverb pairs (VA, e.g. *think deeply*) using the same approach discussed in this paper. It would then be interesting to see whether having a common training set for both the AN and the VA pairs will allow the model to generalize for both cases or different training on two training sets, one for AN and one for VA, will be needed. Other cases to test include N-N compounds or proposition/sentence level pairs.

Another way such an approach can be extended, is to investigate whether reasoning tasks typically associated with different classes of adjectives can be performed. One task might be to distinguish adjectives that are intersective, subsective or none of the two. In the first case, from $A\,N\,x$ one should infer that x is both an A and an N (something that is a black table is both black and a table), in the second case one should infer that x is N only (for example someone who is a skillful surgeon is only a surgeon but we do not know if s/he is skillful in general), and in the third case neither of the two should be inferred. However, this task is not as simple as giving a training set with instances of AN pairs, to recognize where novel instances of AN pairs belong to. Going beyond logical approaches by having the ability to recognize different uses of an adjective requires a richer notion of context which extends way beyond the AN-pairs.

A further idea we want to pursue in the future is the development of more fine grained datasets, where metaphoricity is not represented as a binary feature but as a gradient property. This means that a classifier should have the ability to predict a degree of metaphoricity and thus allow more fine-grained distinctions to be captured. This is a theoretically interesting side and definitely something that has to be tested since not much literature is available (if at all) on gradient metaphoricity. It seems to us that similar approaches, quantifying a text's metaphoricity and framing it as a supervised learning task, could help having a clear view on the influence of metaphor on style.

References

Yoshua Bengio, Aaron Courville, and Pascal Vincent. 2013. Representation learning: A review and new perspectives. *IEEE transactions on pattern analysis and machine intelligence* 35(8):1798–1828.

Lynne Cameron. 2003. *Metaphor in educational discourse*. A&C Black.

Jeanne Fahnestock. 2009. Quid pro nobis. rhetorical stylistics for argument analysis. *Examining argumentation in context. Fifteen studies on strategic maneuvering* pages 131–152.

Balint Forgács, Megan D. Bardolph, Amsel B.D., DeLong K.A., and M. Kutas. 2015. Metaphors are physical and abstract: Erps to metaphorically modified nouns resemble erps to abstract language. *Front. Hum. Neurosci.* 9(28).

Raymond W Gibbs Jr. 2017. *Metaphor Wars*. Cambridge University Press.

Nelson Goodman. 1975. The status of style. *Critical Inquiry* 1(4):799–811.

E Darío Gutiérrez, Ekaterina Shutova, Tyler Marghetis, and Benjamin K Bergen. 2016. Literal and metaphorical senses in compositional distributional semantic models. In *Proceedings of the 54th Meeting of the Association for Computational Linguistics*. pages 160–170.

James M Hughes, Nicholas J Foti, David C Krakauer, and Daniel N Rockmore. 2012. Quantitative patterns of stylistic influence in the evolution of literature. *Proceedings of the National Academy of Sciences* 109(20):7682–7686.

Diederik Kingma and Jimmy Ba. 2014. Adam: A method for stochastic optimization. *arXiv preprint arXiv:1412.6980* .

Beata Beigman Klebanov, Chee Wee Leong, and Michael Flor. 2015. Supervised word-level metaphor detection: Experiments with concreteness and reweighting of examples. In *Proceedings of the Third Workshop on Metaphor in NLP*. pages 11–20.

Saisuresh Krishnakumaran and Xiaojin Zhu. 2007. Hunting elusive metaphors using lexical resources. In *Proceedings of the Workshop on Computational Approaches to Figurative Language*. Association for Computational Linguistics, Stroudsburg, PA, USA, FigLanguages '07, pages 13–20. http://dl.acm.org/citation.cfm?id=1611528.1611531.

George Lakoff. 1989. Some empirical results about the nature of concepts. *Mind & Language* 4(1-2):103–129.

George Lakoff. 1993. The contemporary theory of metaphor.

George Lakoff and Mark Johnson. 2008. *Metaphors we live by*. University of Chicago press.

Geoffrey N Leech and Mick Short. 2007. *Style in fiction: A linguistic introduction to English fictional prose*. 13. Pearson Education.

Omer Levy and Yoav Goldberg. 2014. Neural word embedding as implicit matrix factorization. In *Advances in neural information processing systems*. pages 2177–2185.

Linlin Li and Caroline Sporleder. 2010a. Linguistic cues for distinguishing literal and non-literal usages. In *Proceedings of the 23rd International Conference on Computational Linguistics: Posters*. Association for Computational Linguistics, pages 683–691.

Linlin Li and Caroline Sporleder. 2010b. Using gaussian mixture models to detect figurative language in context. In *Human Language Technologies: The 2010 Annual Conference of the North American Chapter of the Association for Computational Linguistics*. Association for Computational Linguistics, Stroudsburg, PA, USA, HLT '10, pages 297–300. http://dl.acm.org/citation.cfm?id=1857999.1858038.

Tomas Mikolov, Ilya Sutskever, Kai Chen, Greg S Corrado, and Jeff Dean. 2013. Distributed representations of words and phrases and their compositionality. In *Advances in neural information processing systems*. pages 3111–3119.

Jeff Mitchell and Mirella Lapata. 2010. Composition in distributional models of semantics. *Cognitive science* 34(8):1388–1429.

Yair Neuman, Dan Assaf, Yohai Cohen, Mark Last, Shlomo Argamon, Newton Howard, and Ophir Frieder. 2013. Metaphor identification in large texts corpora. *PloS one* 8(4):e62343.

Jeffrey Pennington, Richard Socher, and Christopher D. Manning. 2014. Glove: Global vectors for word representation. In *Empirical Methods in Natural Language Processing (EMNLP)*. pages 1532–1543. http://www.aclweb.org/anthology/D14-1162.

Esther Romero and Belén Soria. 2014. Relevance theory and metaphor. *Linguagem em (Dis) curso* 14(3):489–509.

Ekaterina Shutova, Lin Sun, and Anna Korhonen. 2010. Metaphor identification using verb and noun clustering. In *Proceedings of the 23rd International Conference on Computational Linguistics*. Association for Computational Linguistics, pages 1002–1010.

Paul Simpson. 2004. *Stylistics: A resource book for students*. Psychology Press.

Richard Socher, Jeffrey Pennington, Eric H Huang, Andrew Y Ng, and Christopher D Manning. 2011. Semi-supervised recursive autoencoders for predicting sentiment distributions. In *Proceedings of the conference on empirical methods in natural language processing*. Association for Computational Linguistics, pages 151–161.

Gerard Steen. 2014. Metaphor and style. *The Cambridge handbook of Stylistics* pages 315–328.

Lisa Torrey and Jude Shavlik. 2009. Transfer learning. *Handbook of Research on Machine Learning Applications and Trends: Algorithms, Methods, and Techniques* 1:242.

Yulia Tsvetkov, Leonid Boytsov, Anatole Gershman, Eric Nyberg, and Chris Dyer. 2014. Metaphor detection with cross-lingual model transfer.

Peter D. Turney, Yair Neuman, Dan Assaf, and Yohai Cohen. 2011. Literal and metaphorical sense identification through concrete and abstract context. In *Proceedings of the Conference on Empirical Methods in Natural Language Processing*. Association for Computational Linguistics, Stroudsburg, PA, USA, EMNLP '11, pages 680–690. http://dl.acm.org/citation.cfm?id=2145432.2145511.

Carl Vogel. 2001. Dynamic semantics for metaphor. *Metaphor and Symbol* 16(1-2):59–74.

Deirdre Wilson. 2011. Parallels and differences in the treatment of metaphor in relevance theory and cognitive linguistics. *Intercultural Pragmatics* 8(2):177–196.

Authorship Attribution with Convolutional Neural Networks and POS-Eliding

Julian Hitschler and **Esther van den Berg** and **Ines Rehbein**
Computational Linguistics
University of Heidelberg
69120 Heidelberg, Germany
{hitschler,vdberg,rehbein}@cl.uni-heidelberg.de

Abstract

We use a convolutional neural network to perform authorship identification on a very homogeneous dataset of scientific publications. In order to investigate the effect of domain biases, we obscure words below a certain frequency threshold, retaining only their POS-tags. This procedure improves test performance due to better generalization on unseen data. Using our method, we are able to predict the authors of scientific publications in the same discipline at levels well above chance.

1 Introduction

Computational authorship identification is a task of great interest for many historical and forensic applications. In order to judge the applicability of current and future authorship identification techniques, they need to have been tested in a variety of realistic settings. As it stands, the accuracy of procedures for automatic authorship attribution varies widely with the setting of the task. Among the variables affecting the accuracy of authorship attribution systems identified by Koppel et al. (2013) are the number of target authors a text is to be attributed to, the presence of an *other*-class in the test set (containing texts not written by any of the authors in the training set), the length of the text segments to be classified, and the amount of training data available.

Another important variable which is frequently unaddressed in the computational authorship attribution literature but which deserves closer attention is the monotonicity or diversity of genres and domains in the data, as well as the domain- and genre-specificity of the writings of individual authors. This work introduces a task setting for authorship attribution that is highly invariant with respect to genre and domain, as well as design ideas for systems adapted to this challenging setting.

We conducted a controlled study on the effects of domain and genre bias on authorship attribution by means of an ablation analysis where words in a text, but not their automatically predicted POS-tag, are obscured at various frequency cutoffs. The aim is the design of a system which can perform authorship attribution of texts which are extremely similar in terms of genre and domain among a large class of target authors, based solely on features extracted from POS-tags and a small core vocabulary. The central research question is how well computational authorship attribution works when based on purely stylometric (as opposed to content) features. In doing so, we shed light on the effect that thematic biases have on results in the area of computational authorship attribution.

2 Related Work

Early work on authorship attribution using statistical methods began as early as the first half of the 20th century (Yule, 1938; Zipf, 1932).[1] Modern authorship attribution was strongly influenced by the work of Mosteller and Wallace (1964) who tried to determine the authors of the Federalist Papers, given a small set of probable candidates. Mosteller and Wallace developed a method based on stylometric features in the texts, such as sentence length, word length, or the distribution of high-frequency function words. For a long time, work on authorship attribution has followed this approach and modeled the task as a closed-set classification problem, assuming that we have access to training data for all the authors in the set.

This setting, however, is highly unrealistic, as has been pointed out by Koppel et al. (2013).

---

[1]For an overview on modern authorship attribution methods, see (Stamatatos, 2009).

Proceedings of the Workshop on Stylistic Variation, pages 53–58
Copenhagen, Denmark, September 7–11, 2017. ©2017 Association for Computational Linguistics

In most realistic scenarios, there will not be a known set of authors to choose from, but an indefinite number of candidates, most of them unknown writers. This means that the closed-set assumption might lead to invalid conclusions, i.e. to consider features as discriminants that are able to model authorship on the closed set, but will not perform well on the large, unseen data that *should be* our test set. In this work, we assume a closed set of authors, however, the set of candidates is large (>800).

Other problems for authorship attribution concern the confusion of author style with genre (Byrnes and Sprang, 2004) and topic (Mikros and Argiri, 2007). The same effects are also relevant for related tasks, e.g. for Native Language Identification (NLI). As shown by Brooke and Hirst (2011), the topic of a document can often bias classification results in an NLI task, even when abstracting away from the context words by using character ngrams. Golcher and Reznicek (2011) reported a similar effect, showing how topic works as a confounding variable when investigating L1 influences in learner language. To assess the real potential of authorship attribution techniques, we need methods that are able to generalize to unseen data, and that are robust against the impact of topic and genre.

Stamatatos (2017) addresses the problem of topic-sensitivity using text distortion. Before extracting token or character ngram features, he masks all tokens that occur below a certain frequency threshold by replacing either the whole token or each character in the token by an asterisk. He tests his approach in an authorship attribution task on texts from different topics and genres (<15 authors), and in an author verification task on data from the PAN 2014 evaluation campaign (Stamatatos et al., 2014). Stamatatos shows that SVMs trained on the features extracted from the distorted texts outperform previous models in a cross-topic scenario. For topic-specific settings, however, where each author is strongly correlated with a specific topic, his approach yields results below the baseline.[2]

So far, only few studies have employed deep neural networks (NN) for authorship attribution. Ge et al. (2016) used a feed-forward NN lan-

guage model to classify short transcripts from 18 coursera lectures that are controlled for topic. Rhodes (2015) trained a convolutional neural network (CNN) on word representations to classify medium-sized texts, and Shrestha et al. (2017) applied a CNN to identify the authors of tweets, based on character ngrams. Bagnall (2015) used a multi-headed recurrent neural network (RNN) language model to estimate character probabilities for each author in the PAN 2015 authorship identification task and outperformed all other models. Their results show the promise of deep NN for improving authorship attribution.

Our approach is similar in spirit to that of Stamatatos (2017). We also obscure words that occur below a certain frequency threshold. In contrast to Stamatatos, however, we use a CNN to classify the texts. We test our approach in a more realistic setting where the author has to be chosen from a much larger set of candidates (>800). To disentangle the influence of topic and genre from author style, we test our method on a highly homogeneous set of scientific articles from the areas of computational linguistics and NLP.

3 Datasets and Tools

In our experiments, we used single-author papers from the ACL Anthology Reference Corpus (Bird et al., 2008). The corpus contains scientific papers published in the proceedings of various conferences and workshops in the areas of computational linguistics and natural language processing. The earliest data is from 1965, the latest data is from 2007. We designated all papers published in the year 2006 as development data and all papers published in 2007 as test data, with the remaining data used for training. New authors without publications before this date were not treated any differently from those which were represented in the training data. We only retained publications from authors with at least two single-author papers, although we do not require both or even one of them to be part of the training data. Our dataset contained 808 distinct authors. We discarded the first 10 lines of each document in order to strip publications of author names, email addresses and workplace information. We also removed any lines containing the author's last name (for example, as part of a self-citation or email ad-

---

[2]The reason for this most probably lies in the closed-class assumption of the setting, and we expect different results for a more realistic test set where the strong correlation between author and topic does not hold.

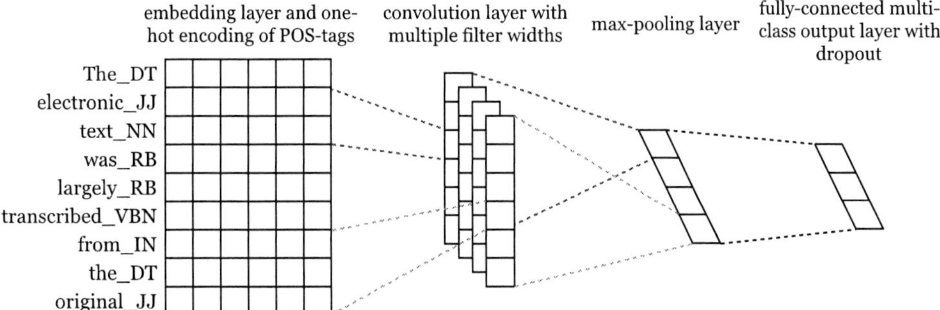

Figure 1: Architecture overview of the convolutional neural network.

dress).[3] We partitioned training, development and test data into segments of 1,500 words each, discarding any segments shorter than 1,500 words at the end of a publication. Authorship prediction is performed on the level of these segments. Table 1 gives an overview of corpus statistics.

	Publications	Segments
Training	1583	5360
Development	210	620
Test	117	323

Table 1: Corpus statistics for the ACL Anthology dataset.

For POS-tagging, we used the Stanford POS-tagger (Toutanova et al., 2003).[4] In addition to POS-tags, we use the pre-trained word embeddings available from Google[5] trained using the skip-gram objective (Mikolov et al., 2013) as input features for our convolutional neural network. Word frequencies were computed on the News Commentary and News Discussions English datasets provided by the WMT15 workshop.[6]

4 Experiments

For authorship prediction, we used a convolutional neural network (CNN) similar to that of Kim (2014). Each sentence is represented as a padded concatenation of word embedding vectors and POS-tag one-hot encodings. The network then applies a single layer of convolving filters with varying window sizes, and a max-over-time pooling layer which retains only the maximum value. The resulting features are passed to a fully-connected softmax layer to obtain a probability distribution over labels. Figure 1 gives an overview of the model architecture.

We used the implementation of Kim (2014),[7] which we modified in a number of ways. We used static channels only and did not modify the pre-trained word embeddings. Our input feature map contained not only the 300-dimensional word embeddings, but also a one-hot representation of POS-tags. We used 100 convolution filters of length 1, 2 and 3 words each and a batch size of 20 sentences. Like that of Kim (2014), our fully connected layer was trained with dropout. The dropout rate was set to 0.5 during training.

The network scans the entire input text of a segment using a sliding-window approach before applying max-pooling over time and making a prediction of authorship based on the prediction of the softmax layer. We tested the following frequency-cutoff settings:

1. Retain only the 1,000 most frequent words in our large, out-of-domain corpus of English, use their word embeddings as input features alongside a one-hot encoding of their POS-tags as predicted by the Stanford POS-tagger. Replace all other words with an unknown token. Generate a separate random embedding for each combination of the unknown token with a particular POS-tag and, in addition, retain the one-hot encoding of the POS-tags of

---

[3]As will become apparent, our procedures of obscuring low-frequency words would eliminate most author names anyway, this step is mainly taken to ensure fair comparison with the full-vocabulary baseline.

[4]Among the available models for English, we chose `english-left3words-distsim.tagger`.

[5]Available for download at `https://code.google.com/archive/p/word2vec/`

[6]Available for download at `http://www.statmt.org/wmt15/translation-task.html`

[7]Available for download at `https://github.com/yoonkim/CNN_sentence`

all unknown tokens.

2-4. Same as (1), but retain the 5,000, 10,000 and 50,000 most frequent words, respectively.

5. Retain all words and use their embeddings as input features, including a 1-hot encoding of their POS-tag. Generate a random word embedding for unknown words, as in Kim (2014).

Training was run for a maximum of 50 epochs. After each epoch, we measured the prediction accuracy on the development data. After training was complete, we tested the model parameters with the best development accuracy on the test data.

In addition to evaluating the authorship predictions of the model, we evaluate rank accuracies as well in order to investigate whether the models are able to reduce the list of possible authors for a segment to a short candidate list which contains the correct author. This can be achieved in a straightforward manner by simply sorting the activations of the softmax layer of the convolutional network for a test segment in order to obtain a ranked candidate list.

Our initial research hypothesis was that (1 - 4) would perform significantly worse than (5), while strongly outperforming a random baseline. This would demonstrate that authorship attribution (in a probabilistic sense) is possible based on stylometric features alone, but not to the same level of accuracy as when content clues are used as well.

5   Results

Table 2 gives an overview of the results for outright prediction of authorship. We find that at a frequency cutoff of 50,000 words, our system outperforms a setting in which the full vocabulary is used, while at lower frequency cutoffs performance is slightly reduced. It should be noted that all of our systems far outperform a random assignment of authors, which would be correct in approximately $\frac{1}{808}$ (0.12%) of cases. Performance in terms of accuracy for our best system is thus two orders of magnitude above random assignment.

Frequency Cutoff	Accuracy on DEV	Accuracy on TEST
$1,000$	11.94%	10.22%
$5,000$	16.61%	10.53%
$10,000$	16.45%	9.29%
$50,000$	15.00%	**13.31%**
None (Full Vocabulary)	15.16%	10.84%

Table 2:   Prediction accuracies for the five frequency cutoffs on development as test data (ACL). The best result is marked in boldface.

Freq. Cutoff	$r = 1$	$r = 5$	$r = 10$	$r = 20$	$r = 50$
$1,000$	10.22%	17.34%	19.50%	26.32%	39.32%
$5,000$	10.53%	20.43%	26.93%	34.37%	46.75%
$10,000$	9.29%	20.12%	26.01%	32.20%	49.23%
$50,000$	**13.31%**	**24.46%**	**30.65%**	**39.32%**	**49.85%**
None	10.84%	19.20%	25.70%	32.82%	44.58%

Table 3:   Rank accuracies for different ranks r on holdout test data (ACL). For example, a result of 24.46% at $r = 5$ means that for 24.46% of segments in the test data, the correct author was among the top-5 predicted authors of the model. Best results are marked in boldface.

For ranked prediction, a similar picture emerges. Table 3 gives an overview of results in this setting. At a frequency cutoff of 50,000 words, our model always outperforms the full-vocabulary baseline and lower frequency cutoffs. However, at higher ranks, there is a tendency for lower frequency cutoffs to outperform the full-vocabulary baseline as well, particularly at a cutoff level of 10,000.

6   Evaluation on Benchmark Dataset

In order to enable meaningful comparison of our models to other work, we additionally tested our approach on a commonly used benchmark dataset. We chose Task I of the PAN 2012 authorship attribution shared task,[8] which involves authorship attribution among a closed class of 14 novelists. The training data was again partitioned into segments of 1,500 words. The training procedure was identical to the one employed on the ACL Anthology dataset. We set aside 200 segments as development data, which left 1,694 segments for training. The test data comprised 14 novel-length texts. Prediction on the test data was performed on segments of a maximum length of 1,500 words, although we allowed for shorter segments at the end

---

[8]`http://pan.webis.de/clef12/pan12-web/author-identification.html`

of texts. For prediction on the text level, we simply aggregated segment-level predictions by majority vote. Results are summarized in table 4. Overall, we observed a similar effect as on the ACL Anthology dataset: The full vocabulary model performed much worse than models with a frequency cutoff. In contrast to the ACL Anthology dataset, the best results were achieved at a frequency cutoff of 1,000.

Frequency Cutoff	Acc. (Segments)	Acc. (Texts)	
1,000	**52.73%**	**78.57%**	11/14
5,000	50.91%	**78.57%**	11/14
10,000	49.90%	71.43%	10/14
50,000	51.82%	**78.57%**	11/14
None (Full Vocabulary)	48.08%	64.29%	9/14

Table 4: Prediction accuracies on PAN 2012, task I on segment and text levels for different frequency cutoffs. Best results are marked in boldface.

7 Discussion and Conclusions

While perhaps initially surprising, the fact that obscuring infrequent words helps system performance can be explained very well by better generalization: The absence of detailed content information may force the system to focus on stylistic features. All of our models achieved performances above 95% on the training data, demonstrating their large modeling capacity and thus their potential for over-fitting. At a frequency cutoff of 50,000 words, performance was improved on the test data, indicating that the model generalized better to unseen data.

In future work, we would like to include an other-class in order to make our setting even more challenging and realistic. We would also like to investigate which, if any, (automatic or manual) obfuscation techniques can be employed by authors to avoid de-anonymization with techniques similar to ours. Furthermore, we would like to investigate the relationship of authorship and native language identification on the ACL Anthology Reference Corpus, as many scientific publications are written by non-native speakers, which can be expected to influence the ease of authorship attribution on datasets of scientific publications.

8 Ethical Considerations

Our work demonstrates that convolutional neural networks have the potential to assign the correct author to very similar documents with some-what remarkable accuracy well above chance. Although the performance of our particular system does not justify a use in legal or forensic settings, as more than 85% of predictions were still incorrect, the public should be made aware that stylistic features, in combination with modern natural language processing methods such as convolutional neural networks have significant potential to de-anonymize text, even when authors write about similar or related topics, and in an ostensibly factual, impersonal register. Since many people value their anonymity as authors, particularly when publishing text online, they should be made aware of the risk that current and future language technology holds for their ability to publish texts anonymously.

For the use of computational authorship attribution as part of historical research, reliable data about the accuracy of such methods is important to good scientific practice. Our work should thus be of interest to historians using such methodologies. In the future, as more powerful techniques are developed, more forensic uses of authorship identification may be justified. Policymakers, legal professionals and the public should have a realistic appraisal of the reliability of authorship identification as a technology in order to make informed judgments about if and when its use could be appropriate. Testing authorship identification technology in difficult, realistic settings such as the one of this work is important to tracking technological progress in this area and giving the public a realistic appraisal of the potential for use and abuse of computational authorship attribution.

References

Douglas Bagnall. 2015. Author Identification using multi-headed Recurrent Neural Networks—Notebook for PAN at CLEF 2015. In Linda Cappellato, Nicola Ferro, Gareth Jones, and Eric San Juan, editors, *CLEF 2015 Evaluation Labs and Workshop – Working Notes Papers, 8-11 September, Toulouse, France*. CEUR-WS.org.

Steven Bird, Robert Dale, Bonnie Dorr, Bryan Gibson, Mark Joseph, Min-Yen Kan, Dongwon Lee, Brett Powley, Dragomir Radev, and Yee Fan Tan. 2008. The ACL Anthology Reference Corpus: A Reference Dataset for Bibliographic Research in Computational Linguistics. In *Proceedings of the Sixth International Conference on Language Resources and Evaluation (LREC-08)*. Marrakech, Morocco.

Julian Brooke and Graeme Hirst. 2011. Native Language Detection with Cheap Learner Corpora. In

Conference of Learner Corpus Research. Louvain-la-Neuve, Belgium, LCR2011.

Heidi Byrnes and Katherine A. Sprang. 2004. Fostering advanced L2 literacy; A genre-based, cognitive approach. In Heidi Byrnes and Hiram H. Maxim, editors, *Advanced foreign language learning: A challenge to college programs*, Boston: Heinle Thomson, pages 47–85.

Zhenhao Ge, Yufang Sun, and Mark J. T. Smith. 2016. Authorship Attribution Using a Neural Network Language Model. *CoRR* abs/1602.05292. http://arxiv.org/abs/1602.05292.

Felix Golcher and Marc Reznicek. 2011. Stylometry and the Interplay of Topic and L1 in the Different Annotation Layers in the Falko Corpus. In *Quantitative Investigations in Theoretical Linguistics*. Berlin, Germany, QITL 4.

Yoon Kim. 2014. Convolutional Neural Networks for Sentence Classification. In *Proceedings of the 2014 Conference on Empirical Methods in Natural Language Processing (EMNLP)*. Association for Computational Linguistics, Doha, Qatar, pages 1746–1751.

M. Koppel, J. Schler, and S. Argamon. 2013. Authorship Attribution: Whats Easy and Whats Hard? *Journal of Law and Policy* 21(2):317 – 332.

Tomas Mikolov, Ilya Sutskever, Kai Chen, Greg S Corrado, and Jeff Dean. 2013. Distributed Representations of Words and Phrases and their Compositionality. In C. J. C. Burges, L. Bottou, M. Welling, Z. Ghahramani, and K. Q. Weinberger, editors, *Advances in Neural Information Processing Systems 26*, Curran Associates, Inc., pages 3111–3119.

George K. Mikros and Eleni K. Argiri. 2007. Investigating Topic Influence in Authorship Attribution. In Benno Stein, Moshe Koppel, and Efstathios Stamatatos, editors, *SIGIR 07 Workshop Workshop on Plagiarism Analysis, Authorship Identification, and Near-Duplicate Detection*. PAN 2007.

Frederick Mosteller and David L. Wallace. 1964. Inference and Disputed Authorship: The Federalist. *Journal of the American Statistical Association* 58(302):275–309.

Dylan Rhodes. 2015. Author Attribution with CNNs. Technical report. http://cs224d.stanford.edu/reports/RhodesDylan.pdf.

Prasha Shrestha, Sebastian Sierra, Fabio A. Gonzalez, Manuel Montes y Gmez, and Thamar Solorio. 2017. Convolutional Neural Networks for Authorship Attribution of Short Texts. In *Proceedings of the EACL*. EACL, Valencia, Spain. https://www.aclweb.org/anthology/E/E17/E17-2106.pdf.

Efstathios Stamatatos. 2009. A Survey of Modern Authorship Attribution Methods. *Journal of the American Society for Information Science and Technology* 60(3):538–556. https://doi.org/10.1002/asi.v60:3.

Efstathios Stamatatos. 2017. Authorship Attribution Using Text Distortion. In *Proceedings of the 15th Conference of the European Chapter of the Association for the Computational Linguistics*. Valencia, Spain, EACL 2017.

Efstathios Stamatatos, Walter Daelemans, Ben Verhoeven, Martin Potthast, Benno Stein, Patrick Juola, Miguel A. Sanchez-Perez, and Alberto Barrón-Cedeño. 2014. Overview of the Author Identification Task at PAN 2014. In Linda Cappellato, Nicola Ferro, Martin Halvey, and Wessel Kraaij, editors, *CLEF 2014 Evaluation Labs and Workshop – Working Notes Papers, 15-18 September, Sheffield, UK*.

Kristina Toutanova, Dan Klein, Christopher Manning, and Yoram Singer. 2003. Feature-Rich Part-of-Speech Tagging with a Cyclic Dependency Network. In *Proceedings of the Conference of the North American Chapter of the Association for Computational Linguistics: Human Language Technologies (NAACL HLT)*. Edmonton, Alberta, Canada.

G. Udny Yule. 1938. On Sentence-Length as a Statistical Characteristic of Style in Prose: With Application to Two Cases of Disputed Authorship. *Biometrika* 30:363–390.

George K. Zipf. 1932. *Selective Studies and the Principle of Relative Frequency in Language*. Harvard University Press.

Topic and audience effects on distinctively Scottish vocabulary usage in Twitter data

Philippa Shoemark[*]
p.j.shoemark@ed.ac.uk

James Kirby[†]
j.kirby@ed.ac.uk

Sharon Goldwater[*]
sgwater@inf.ed.ac.uk

[*]School of Informatics
University of Edinburgh

[†]Dept. of Linguistics and English Language
University of Edinburgh

Abstract

Sociolinguistic research suggests that speakers modulate their language style in response to their audience. Similar effects have recently been claimed to occur in the informal written context of Twitter, with users choosing less region-specific and non-standard vocabulary when addressing larger audiences. However, these studies have not carefully controlled for the possible confound of topic: that is, tweets addressed to a broad audience might also tend towards topics that engender a more formal style. In addition, it is not clear to what extent previous results generalize to different samples of users. Using mixed-effects models, we show that audience and topic have independent effects on the rate of distinctively Scottish usage in two demographically distinct Twitter user samples. However, not all effects are consistent between the two groups,underscoring the importance of replicating studies on distinct user samples before drawing strong conclusions from social media data.

1 Introduction

Linguistic variation in social media is a growing research area, with interest stemming both from the engineering goal of developing tools that work well across different styles and dialects (Hovy, 2015; Stoop and van den Bosch, 2014; Vyas et al., 2014; Huang and Yates, 2014), and from the social science goal of studying user behaviour (Bamman et al., 2014; Eisenstein, 2015; Huang et al., 2016; Nguyen et al., 2015). However, this type of research is often complicated by the messy nature of social media data, which can make it hard to control for different explanatory factors and to know whether results obtained on a particular user sample generalize to another sample.

For example, previous studies have suggested that Twitter users modulate their use of regional and non-standard language depending on the expected size of the audience (operationalized as whether a Tweet contains hashtags, @-mentions, or neither) (Pavalanathan and Eisenstein, 2015a; Shoemark et al., 2017). However, these studies did not sufficiently control for possible effects of topic, which may be confounded with audience size: e.g., users may use more hashtags when discussing political events than when discussing daily routines. These studies also did not look at the degree to which their results generalize across different populations of users.

In this work we study two largely disjoint groups of (mainly) Scottish Twitter users: one group sent tweets geotagged within Scotland, while the other used hashtags related to the 2014 Scottish independence referendum. We use mixed-effects models to tease apart the effects of audience and topic on their choice of Scottish-specific terms. We find that in both user groups, topic and audience have independent effects on the rate of Scottish usage, providing stronger evidence than in previous work that users are indeed sensitive to their audience.

Nevertheless, our study does not confirm all aspects of previous work. When comparing our two user groups, the effect of topic is qualitatively similar: tweets about lifestyle or politics have lower rates of Scottish usage than "chitchat" tweets. However, the effects of audience differ between the two groups. For the geotagged users, rates of Scottish usage follow the pattern predicted by previous research: lowest among tweets with the largest expected audience, and rising as the expected audience size shrinks. In contrast, the independence referendum group showed a less consistent and less pronounced pattern which does not align cleanly

Proceedings of the Workshop on Stylistic Variation, pages 59–68
Copenhagen, Denmark, September 7–11, 2017. ©2017 Association for Computational Linguistics

with audience size. We were unable to find a clear explanation of this difference. Nevertheless, it highlights the difficulty of sampling representative groups from social media data and the need to interpret results with caution until they are shown to generalize across several different populations.

2 Background

Bell's (1984) Audience Design theory posits that intra-speaker stylistic variation is primarily conditioned by the audience of the interaction. Bell argues that stylistic variation across topics derives from so-called 'reference groups' whom the speaker associates with the topics in question, and predicts that effects of topic on style variation will be weaker than direct effects of audience. However, later studies of spoken conversation (e.g. Rickford and McNair-Knox, 1994) have suggested that both topic and audience affect a speaker's style, and that topic may even have a greater effect. Topic also appears to influence stylistic variation in computer-mediated communication—for example, statistical associations between lexical features and author attributes such as gender are often mediated by the topic of discourse (Herring and Paolillo, 2006; Bamman et al., 2014).

Our work is primarily inspired by two previous studies of Twitter users and how their use of regional lexical variants is influenced by either audience (Pavalanathan and Eisenstein, 2015a) or topic (Shoemark et al., 2017). In the first of these, Pavalanathan and Eisenstein (2015a) studied lexical items that were strongly associated with tweets from specific regions of the US, as determined by a data-driven approach (Eisenstein et al., 2011). They found that users were less likely to use these regional terms, as well as other nonstandard terms, in tweets containing hashtags, and more likely to do so in tweets containing @-mentions (i.e., other users' IDs). They attributed these findings to style-shifting in relation to audience size, since tweets with hashtags are more likely to be viewed by users outside of the author's follower group, while by default tweets which begin with a mention are shown only to the author, the mentioned user, and their mutual followers.

While suggestive, there are alternative explanations for this finding. For example, in their study of Scottish tweets, Shoemark et al. (2017) pointed out that if users use the word 'masel' (a Scottish variant of standard English 'myself') less frequently in tweets with hashtags, it could be simply because people talk about themselves less in tweets with hashtags, not because they are modulating the use of a regionally specific variant.

Shoemark et al. (2017) focused mainly on effects of topic rather than audience, but to avoid similar confounds, they measured the frequencies of regional variants of lexical variables[1] *relative* to their standard variants. They found that, amongst users who tweeted about the Scottish independence referendum, both pro- and anti-independence users decreased their use of Scottish-specific terms in tweets containing referendum-related hashtags, compared to other tweets. A follow-up analysis suggested that this effect might be due to the larger audience obtained by using referendum-related hashtags, but the evidence was indirect as the original study was not designed to test that hypothesis.

Our work extends these two previous studies by building models that include factors for both topic and audience. We follow Shoemark et al. (2017) in focusing on variables that alternate between Scottish English and Standard English variants, but use a wider range of topics identified with a topic model rather than just hashtags. We use mixed-effects logistic regression in order to establish whether there are independent effects of audience and topic, whilst controlling for variation in the base rate of Scottish-variant usage across different users and variables. In addition, we explicitly examine how different methods of sampling users might affect results, by performing the same study on two user groups gathered in different ways.

3 Data

3.1 Lexical variables

We use 50 of the 51 lexical variables identified by Shoemark et al. (2017). Each variable consists of one or more distinctively Scottish variants and one or more Standard English variants, all of which are referentially and syntactically equivalent; examples are shown in Table 1. From the original 51 variables, we discard **SHIT**, since the variant identified as Scottish-specifc, SHITE, is used at a higher rate than the Scottish-specific forms of the other variables (e.g. 27% of **SHIT** occurences in Shoemark et al.'s Indyref-Tweets dataset are realized as SHITE; more than twice the rate of Scottish variant use for any other variable), and for many users **SHIT** is the

---

[1] A *variable* is any linguistic item than can be produced in different ways; the *variants* are the different realizations.

Variable	Scottish variants	Std variants
DONT	DEH, DINI , DINNY	DONT, DO NOT
FOOTBALL	FITBA	FOOTBALL
MYSELF	MASEL, MASELF	MYSELF
SOMETHING	SUHIN	SOMETHING
TO	TAE	TO, TOO

Table 1: Examples of lexical variables.

only variable for which any Scottish variant use is observed. This suggests that SHITE is less marked as 'distinctively Scottish' than the Scottish-specific variants of the other 50 variables.

3.2 Dataset construction

We aim to study Scottish language use, but only a small proportion of Twitter users disclose their location, either by including it in their user profile or by opting to automatically tag their tweets with geographic coordinates when using a GPS-enabled device. Moreover, studies have indicated that those who do share their location are not representative of the wider Twitter user base (Pavalanathan and Eisenstein, 2015b; Sloan and Morgan, 2015).

To help assess the generalizability of our findings, we therefore consider two datasets, both covering the same time period but sampled from distinct (though slightly overlapping) populations: 'Scottish Geotag Users', who have tagged their tweets with locations in Scotland; and 'Indyref Hashtag Users', who have used hashtags relating to the 2014 Scottish Independence Referendum. As we will demonstrate, users in the two samples do differ in some aspects of their behaviour, emphasizing how biases implicit in the construction of datasets can affect results.

Our two groups of users are taken from the Geotagged-Scotland (GS) and Indyref-Tweets (IT) datasets collected by Shoemark et al. (2017). Both of these datasets were drawn from an archive of Twitter's 'Spritzer' stream, which provides a 1% sample of the public data flowing through Twitter, covering the period from September 2013 to September 2014. The GS dataset consists of tweets by users for whom the archive contained at least one tweet which was geotagged with a location in Scotland, while the IT dataset consists of users for whom it contained at least one tweet with a hashtag relating to the 2014 Scottish Independence referendum (see Table 3 in Shoemark et al. (2017) for a list of hashtags).

As a heuristic to filter out bots and spammers,

		IH Users	SG Users
(a)	N Users	14,572	17,942
	N Tweets	4,703,040	1,750,343
	N Variables	10,482,683	3,733,133
	% Scottish	0.5	1.8
(b)	N Users	12,101	11,307
	N Tweets	4,674,251	1,678,498
	N Variables	10,424,067	3,594,659
	% Scottish	0.5	1.8
(c)	N Users	10,786	10,103
	N Tweets	3,456,277	1,371,694
	N Variables	7,689,621	2,878,352
	% Scottish	0.7	2.3
(d)	N Users	10,784	10,103
	N Tweets	2,165,320	1,112,931
	N Variables	4,934,186	2,365,496
	% Scottish	0.8	2.3

Table 2: Dataset statistics for Indyref Hashtag Users and Scottish Geotag Users (a) after basic preprocessing, (b) after discarding users with $<$50 variable instances, (c) after discarding users for which there is strong evidence of non-use of Scottish variants and (d) after labelling audience & topic. '% Scottish' is the percentage of variables realized as the Scottish variant.

we computed the proportion of tweets for each user in the GS and IT datasets which contained URLs, and discarded users for whom this proportion was in the 90th percentile. For the remaining users, we then retrieved a more complete set of their tweets: for each user we attempted to retrieve all the tweets they posted in August, September, or October 2014 (excluding retweets), using Twitter's REST API. The API allows us to retrieve up to 3200 of a user's most recent tweets, so if a user had posted more than 3200 tweets since autumn 2014, we were unable to retrieve their tweet histories for this period. We obtained complete histories for at least one of the three months for a total of 18,370 Scottish Geotag (SG) Users, and 14,832 Indyref Hashtag (IH) Users. We then applied some simple ad-hoc text filters to remove tweets produced by apps which automatically share user's horoscopes or track users' follower counts, as well as some particularly prevalent types of marketing tweets. See Table 2a for summary statistics after this filtering step. Note that there are 363 users who are in both datasets.

Next, we removed all users for whom the total number of observed variable instances was less than 50 (see Table 2b), as with so few observations it would be difficult to make reliable inferences about these users' usage rates of distinctively Scottish variants.

Finally, since our population of interest is those who vary between Scottish and standard variants, we discard individuals for whom we had enough observed variable instances to conclude that they probably *never* used distinctively Scottish variants of any of our variables. For SG Users, we chose the threshold of 'enough observed variable instances' to be 298, since this is the smallest value n such that the cumulative binomial probability of seeing at least one Scottish variant in n variable instances is ≥ 0.99 (assuming a constant usage rate of Scottish variants of 0.0184, as listed in Table 2b). That is, if we assume that any user who does use Scottish variants will do so 1.84% of the time, then in 99% of cases where we have observed at least 298 variable instances from such a user, we would expect a Scottish variant to have been used in at least one of those instances. For IH Users, we assumed a constant usage rate of distinctively-Scottish variants of 0.05, and discarded all those for whom we had observed at least 870 variable instances and no Scottish variants. Table 2c provides summary statistics for the two resulting datasets.

When considering the differences in average rates of Scottish variant usage across the two groups, it is important to note that Shoemark et al. (2017) identified these Scottish variants using the GS dataset, i.e. the same dataset from which we drew our Scottish Geotag Users. It is therefore to be expected that that the Scottish Geotag Users would use these variants at a higher rate, and it is important to bear in mind that the Indyref Hashtag Users may be more frequent users of other distinctively Scottish variants.

4 Topic & Audience

4.1 Audience labelling

We follow Pavalanathan and Eisenstein (2015a) in assuming that tweets containing hashtags (any token prepended with the '#' character) typically have a wider audience than other tweets, since anyone interested in a particular topic or event can browse the stream of Tweets which contain associated hashtags. Conversely, tweets beginning with @-mentions typically have a narrow audience since by default they only appear in the feeds of the author, the mentionee, and users who follow both the author and the mentionee. Any user @-mentioned in a tweet (whether at the beginning, or elsewhere within the tweet) will by default receive a special

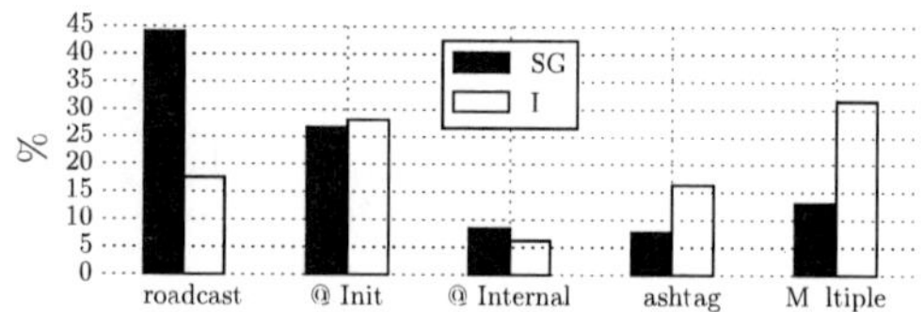

Figure 1: Distribution of tweets with each audience label in the two datasets.

notification drawing their attention to it.

Pavalanathan and Eisenstein hypothesise that both kinds of mention serve to narrow the intended audience, whilst hashtags serve to widen it, relative to broadcast tweets (i.e., those without hashtags or mentions, which appear on the feeds of all the author's followers). The grounds for hypothesising a narrowing function for tweet-internal mentions are less evident than those for tweet-initial mentions, since tweets which do not begin with a mention are *not* limited by default to the feeds of the author and mentionee's mutual followers.

We label each variable instance in our two datasets with three binary variables indicating whether or not they contain hashtags, initial mentions, and/or internal mentions. We then discard any tweets for which two or more of these indicators are activated, since we do not have intuitive a priori hypotheses about how combining more than one of these variables within a single tweet would affect its intended audience.

Figure 1 shows the proportion of tweets in each dataset which have each audience label (or which had multiple labels and were subsequently discarded), and reveals qualitative differences in the two groups' behaviour: SG Users post relatively more 'broadcast' tweets, whilst IH Users use relatively more hashtags (which is unsurprising given that they were selected on the basis of their hashtag use).

4.2 Topic labelling

We assign topics to tweets using a Latent Dirichlet Allocation (LDA) topic model (Blei et al., 2003) estimated with collapsed Gibbs sampling (Griffiths and Steyvers, 2004) from both datasets combined. Following Hong and Davison (2010) and others, we create 'documents' by concatenating together tweets by the same author. To account for possible topic drift within individuals over time, we group each user's tweets by month and model each per-user-per-month document as a distinct mixture of topics. We use the inferred topic model parameters to label each tweet with a topic, as described below.

The corpus was preprocessed as follows: tweets were tokenised using the Twokenize program[2], a tokeniser designed specifically for Twitter text, and all non-alphabetic tokens, except for those which begin with hashtags, were discarded. The vocabulary was then pruned to the 100,000 most frequent terms across the two datasets. We set the number of topics, T, to 30, and used symmetric Dirichlet priors of $\alpha = \frac{50}{T}$ and $\beta = 0.01$ on the multinomial distributions over topics and terms, respectively[3]. The Gibbs sampler was run for 750 iterations.

Upon inspection of the most probable words and documents for each topic, we deemed that twenty of the topics could be grouped into three broader themes, which we describe as 'chatter' , 'lifestyle' , and 'politics' . Later, we consider a different grouping, where we split off a 'sports' theme from the 'lifestyle' theme, and an 'indyref' theme from the 'politics' theme. Table 3 shows the most probable words (excluding stopwords) for each topic within these three/five themes. Of the ten topics that we did not assign to these themes, four could be described as spam topics, four as foreign language, and two as relating to purely stylistic dimensions as opposed to any particular topic of discussion: one for distinctively Scottish terms, and the other for 'netspeak'-style spellings and abbreviations.

To assign topic labels to individual tweets, we take a Gibbs sample and then for a given tweet, each topic t is assigned a weight, defined as

$$\text{weight}_t = \sum_{w \in \boldsymbol{w}} \hat{p}(t|w)$$

where $\boldsymbol{w}$ is the bag of words which occur in the tweet (excluding stopwords and any variant of any of our variables of interest), and $\hat{p}(t|w)$ is obtained by maximum likelihood estimation from the Gibbs-sampled topic-token assignments. Finally, we take the topic with the highest weight, and label the tweet with its broader theme. If the topic with the highest weight is one of the two 'stylistic' topics, we defer to the topic with the next highest weight. We discard tweets labelled as 'spam' or 'foreign language', as well as those for which the highest weight is not unique, if the topics which share this weight belong to different themes.

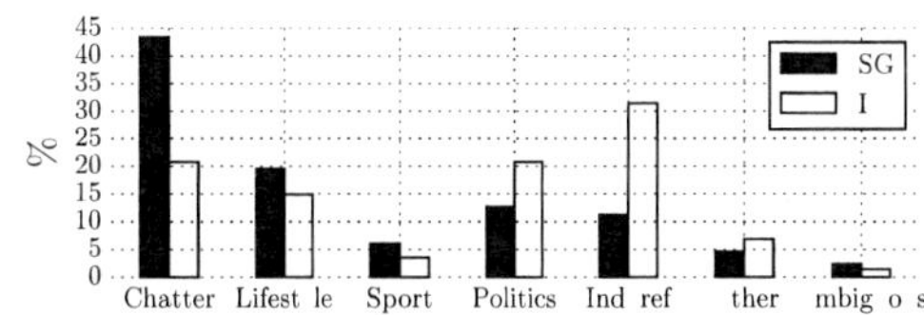

Figure 2: Distribution of tweets with each topic label in the two datasets.

Using this method, we obtain 2.3m broad-topic-labeled variable instances from SG Users, and 4.9m from IH Users. Figure 2 shows the distribution of topics in each data set, and Table 4 gives a breakdown of variable instances by audience-type and broad-topic-label. IH Users have a much larger proportion of tweets with 'indyref' or 'politics' labels than SG Users, which once again is unsurprising, given how these users were sampled.

5   Method

We use the glmer() function from the lme4 package (Bates et al., 2015) for R (R Core Team, 2013) to estimate mixed effects logistic regression models, predicting Scottish variant usage (yes = 1, no = 0) from the intended audience size and topic of the tweet in which a lexical variable occurs. Our four-level categorical audience factor (initial mention, internal mention, broadcast, hashtag) is dummy coded into three binary variables, with broadcasts as the reference level. Our tweet topic labels are also dummy coded, taking the 'chatter' topic as the reference level. By specifying random effects for users and variables, we control for the influence of different baseline rates of Scottish variant usage across different users and variables. Hence our models are of the form

$$\text{logit}\{E(\mathbf{y})\} = \mathbf{X}\beta + \mathbf{Z}\mathbf{u}, \mathbf{y} \sim Bernoulli$$

where $\mathbf{y}$ is the $n \times 1$ vector of responses from a Bernoulli distribution, $\mathbf{X}$ is an $n \times p$ design matrix for the fixed effects β, and $\mathbf{Z}$ is an $n \times q$ design matrix for the random effects $\mathbf{u}$. We do not include random slopes in our models, since we do not have enough observations per group to provide stable estimates of the variances. Our models are fit by Laplacian approximation to Maximum Likelihood estimation.

---

[2]https://github.com/myleott/ark-twokenize-py

[3]During development we experimented with values for T between 10 and 100, and α between 0.015 and 1.5, and saw little qualitative difference in the themes that emerged, based on manual inspection of topic keywords.

Topic theme	Keywords
Chatter	love feel life fucking fuck people shit actually hate omg school gonna time excited oh
	time yeah bit oh probably actually maybe seen lot pretty hope haha bad getting stuff
	lol love thank xx thanks hope day oh happy lovely xxx ha haha morning beautiful
	night happy birthday haha day wait tonight tomorrow hahaha bed getting wee weekend days week
Lifestyle	love song music album world amazing god top white black girl watch band ice looks baby life listen guy boys
	photo watching #xfactor #cbb day #scotland loving posted #gbbo life #glasgow #bbuk #love #edinburgh love
	video #auspol liked game awesome watch time apple iphone play app games phone buy facebook
	oh bit news ha twitter story brilliant bbc read book called tv look dear wonder
	day time morning night car run food bit nice week train getting tea eat days
	tonight day week time tomorrow night glasgow morning looking edinburgh forward coming weeks hear live
Sports	cup win ireland #glasgow2014 irish time team final match scottish round top games race live
	game celtic team football season league fans mate goal win play players club player haha
Politics	people read agree question thanks issue debate political article course mean change indeed etc politics
	news police pm russia minister russian via eu report ukraine president ebola court uk #ukraine #russia
	#ferguson rt obama #ukraine police #cdnpoli ukraine video via mt people news american time america
	labour uk ukip cameron party tory ed tax vote tories english mps miliband boris david
	people lol look tell money time stop wrong please believe mean job care saying talking
	israel #gaza war via isis gaza #isis world people children israeli #israel police hamas support
Indyref	#indyref scotland #voteyes #yes vote scottish independence #scotdecides #indyrefpic #bettertogether salmond #bbcindyref #the45 campaign debate
	scotland vote uk labour scottish snp scots union oil party wm country westminster voters voting

Table 3: Topic themes and the top 15 keywords for each topic within each theme

	Audience \ Topic	Chatter	Lifestyle	Politics	All
(a)	Broadcast	598,673 (2.7)	334,143 (2.3)	295,981 (1.8)	1,228,797 (2.4)
	Initial Mention	352,981 (3.0)	164,909 (2.9)	188,191 (1.9)	706,081 (2.7)
	Internal Mention	92,682 (1.8)	63,242 (1.5)	56,727 (1.2)	212,651 (1.6)
	Hashtag	67,630 (1.8)	69,833 (1.4)	80,504 (1.2)	217,967 (1.4)
	All	1,111,966 (2.7)	632,127 (2.3)	621,403 (1.7)	2,365,496 (2.3)
(b)	Broadcast	308,797 (1.3)	341,592 (0.9)	658,520 (0.8)	1,308,909 (1.0)
	Initial Mention	644,459 (1.1)	394,036 (1.0)	1,026,634 (0.6)	2,065,129 (0.8)
	Internal Mention	76,403 (0.6)	96,123 (0.5)	203,275 (0.4)	375,801 (0.5)
	Hashtag	124,333 (0.7)	197,925 (0.5)	862,089 (0.5)	1,184,347 (0.5)
	All	1,153,992 (1.1)	1,029,676 (0.8)	2,750,518 (0.6)	4,934,186 (0.8)

Table 4: Counts of variable instances in the (a) SG Users and (b) IH Users datasets, broken down by Topic and Audience. In each cell, the percentage of variable instances that are Scottish variants is given in parentheses.

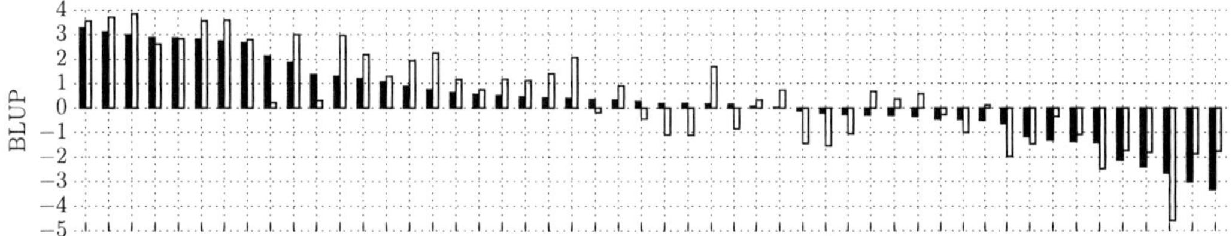

Figure 3: Barplots of by-variable BLUPs for SG Users (black bars) and for IH Users (white bars).

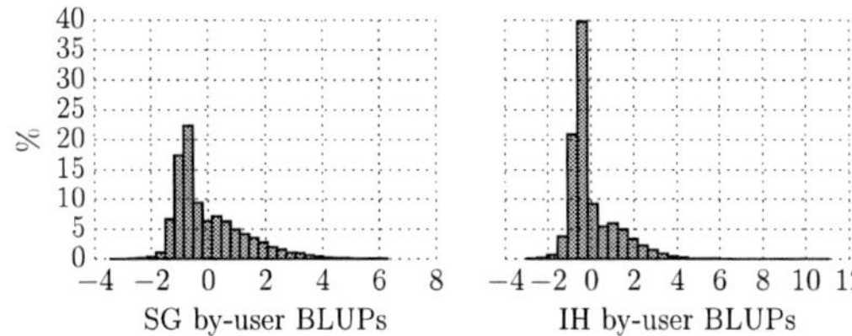

Figure 4: Histograms of by-user BLUPs.

6 Results and Discussion

6.1 Random Intercepts

We begin by constructing null models that predict the log odds of choosing a Scottish variant using only intercepts, which we allow to vary randomly by each user and by each lexical variable. The estimated variances of the by-user and by-variable adjustments to the intercept are given in Table 5a, for SG and IH Users, respectively.

The Best Linear Unbiased Predictors (BLUPs) of the by-variable random intercepts (i.e. the posterior estimates, given the data and model parameters, of the adjustment to the intercept for each variable) are shown in Figure 3. In both datasets, open class variables (e.g. **GRANDAD, BALLS, DOGS**) tend to have higher rates of Scottish variant usage than closed class variables (e.g. **WAS, OF, YOU**).

Figure 4 shows the distributions of by-user BLUPs. Although the models assume a normal distribution over the by-user intercepts, the BLUPs are positively skewed. We suspect the BLUPs reflect the fact that our datasets contain a mixture of two populations: Scottish speakers, who use Scottish variants at a range of rates, and non-Scottish speakers, who rarely if ever use Scottish variants. The non-Scottish speakers are responsible for the large number of users with slightly negative intercepts. Unfortunately there is no straightforward way to separate these groups (especially for users

with a relatively small number of observations). However, users with a constant near-zero rate of Scottish variant usage should, at worst, dilute any true effects of topic or audience on rates of usage, but should not change the direction of those effects.

6.2 Random Intercepts + Audience Effects

We now check whether Pavalanathan and Eisenstein's (2015a) reported effects of hashtags and mentions on the odds of using regional variants in US tweets, are replicated for distinctively Scottish variants in our two datasets.

We augment our null models with our dummy-coded audience factors as fixed effects. For each dataset, we assess the goodness-of-fit using chi-square tests on the log-likelihoods. Compared to the null models with only random effects, including fixed effects for audience significantly improves the fit on both datasets (SG: $\chi2(3) = 643.05$, p = $<2.2e\text{-}16$; IH: $\chi2(3) = 232.69$, p = $<2.2e\text{-}16$).

Parameters of the models with Audience effects are in Table 5b. Our results for SG Users largely accord with those of Pavalanathan and Eisenstein (2015a): Scottish variants are positively associated with tweet-initial mentions, and negatively associated with hashtags. Relative to broadcast tweets, the odds of seeing Scottish variants are about 28% higher in tweets with initial mentions, and about 17% lower in tweets with hashtags. However, while Pavalanathan and Eisenstein also found an association between the use of tweet-internal mentions and local/non-standard words in their data, our model does not show such a relationship in the SG dataset.

In the IH dataset, the audience effects in our model do not follow the pattern that Pavalanathan and Eisenstein observed in US tweets. Unlike for SG Users, there is no association between hashtags and Scottish variants, and the effects of mentions are in the opposite direction to those found by Pavalanathan and Eisenstein (2015a). Amongst

IH Users, initial mentions are *negatively* associated with Scottish variants, though the effect size is very small. Internal mentions are also negatively associated with Scottish variants, and in this case the effect is relatively large (in contrast with SG Users, for whom we found no effect). We discuss possible reasons for this result in Section 6.4.

6.3 Random Intercepts + Topic Effects

Next, we test for a relationship between the topic of a tweet and the odds of Scottish variant usage. For both datasets, models with fixed effects for topic significantly improve the fit over random-effects-only models (SG: $\chi2(2) = 570.48$, p = <2.2e-16; IH: $\chi2(2) = 1241$, p = <2.2e-16).

Parameters of the models are in Table 5c. The effects of tweet topic are qualitatively similar in each dataset: relative to 'chatter' tweets, tweeting about the 'lifestyle' topic reduces the odds of choosing Scottish variants by 11% for SG Users and 5% for IH Users, while tweeting about politics reduces them by 27% for SG Users, and 39% for IH Users.

6.4 Full Models

For each dataset, including fixed effects for audience and topic together significantly improves the model fit, both over the models with fixed effects for audience only (SG Users: $\chi2(2) = 508.67$, p = <2.2e-16; IH Users: $\chi2(2) = 1298.9$, p = <2.2e-16), and over the models with fixed effects for topic only (SG: $\chi2(3) = 581.25$, p = <2.2e-16; IH: $\chi2(3) = 290.6$, p = <2.2e-16).

Parameters of the full models are in Table 5d. When fixed effects for audience and topic are included together in the SG model, their effect sizes barely change. These results suggest that for SG Users, audience and topic have independent effects on Scottish usage, and that even after accounting for topic, the effects of audience size are as predicted by Pavalanathan and Eisenstein (2015a).

In the full IH model, while most of the fixed effect sizes are relatively unchanged, a positive association between the use of hashtags and Scottish variants emerges. Thus, the model reveals that the qualitative behavior of these users is very different from that of the SG Users. Although topic and audience are both significant factors in the models for each group, initial mentions and hashtags have the opposite effects for IH Users as for SG Users (and for Pavalanathan and Eisenstein's user sample).

Although they primarily interpret their findings in terms of audience size, Pavalanathan and Eisenstein acknowledge that mentions and hashtags can affect the composition of the audience in more nuanced ways than just its size. As an alternative explanation for the positive associations they found between mentions and local/non-standard words, they suggest that authors may use such words to express particular identities or stake claims to local authenticity, specifically when addressing users for whom such claims are meaningful.

In theory, this account could also apply to the positive association we find in the IH dataset between *hashtags* and local variants: while on the one hand, the indexing function of hashtags can be conceived of as broadening the audience of a tweet, on the other hand it could serve to narrow the tweet's intended audience, by explicitly targeting it at a circumscribed community. Hence, when using hashtags associated with communities for whom the notion of Scottish identity has strong currency (e.g. people with strong views on indyref, or supporters of a particular sports team), IH Users may use Scottish variants initiatively, in order to emphasise that part of their identity.

Suppose that authors tended to decrease their use of Scottish variants when discussing most political issues, but increase it when discussing Scottish independence—either to emphasise their own Scottish identity, or to accommodate towards an audience which is likely to contain many Scottish people. If this were the case, our models would be unable to account for this variation directly, since we have grouped indyref and other political issues together. However, since a large proportion (55%) of IH Users hashtag tweets are actually about indyref, one way the IH model could account for a difference between indyref and general politics is to increase the weight for hashtags. If this were the case, then including 'indyref' as a distinct topic should improve the model fit and alleviate the impact on the audience weights. To test this hypothesis, we performed a follow-up study where we split the topics into finer-grained categories.

6.5 Finer-grained topics

We added two topic categories, 'sport' and 'indyref', which we split off from the 'lifestyle' and 'politics' categories, respectively (see Table 3). Contrary to our hypothesis, re-defining the topic categories in this way made little difference to the model fit: the log-likelihoods for the new full model are -174169.4 for SG Users, and -121447.8

	Scottish Geotag Users	Indyref Hashtag Users
(a)	*Log-likelihood:* -174758.0 σ^2 *users:* 2.769 σ^2 *variables:* 2.477	*Log-likelihood:* -122240.2 σ^2 *users:* 3.058 σ^2 *variables:* 3.444

		Scottish Geotag Users				Indyref Hashtag Users			
(b)		*Log-likelihood:* -174436.4 σ^2 *users:* 2.750 σ^2 *variables:* 2.503				*Log-likelihood:* -122123.9 σ^2 *users:* 3.039 σ^2 *variables:* 3.443			
Fixed Ef.	*OR*	*95% CI*	*z*	*Pr (>|z|)*	*OR*	*95% CI*	*z*	*Pr (>|z|)*
@init	1.28	(1.25, 1.31)	21.2	<2e-16	0.96	(0.93, 0.99)	-2.8	0.005
@intrnl	0.96	(0.92, 1.00)	-1.9	0.052	0.62	(0.59, 0.67)	-15.4	<2e-16
hashtag	0.83	(0.80, 0.86)	-8.9	<2e-16	0.97	(0.93, 1.01)	-1.6	0.111
(c)	*Log-likelihood:* -174472.7 σ^2 *users:* 2.758 σ^2 *variables:* 2.472				*Log-likelihood:* -121619.7 σ^2 *users:* 3.069 σ^2 *variables:* 3.427			
Fixed Ef.	*OR*	*95% CI*	*z*	*Pr (>|z|)*	*OR*	*95% CI*	*z*	*Pr (>|z|)*
lifestyle	0.89	(0.87, 0.91)	-9.9	<2e-16	0.95	(0.92, 0.98)	-3.2	0.001
politics	0.73	(0.71, 0.75)	-24.2	<2e-16	0.61	(0.59, 0.63)	-33.6	<2e-16
(d)	*Log-likelihood:* -174182.1 σ^2 *users:* 2.742 σ^2 *variables:* 2.496				*Log-likelihood:* -121474.4 σ^2 *users:* 3.063 σ^2 *variables:* 3.416			
Fixed Ef.	*OR*	*95% CI*	*z*	*Pr (>|z|)*	*OR*	*95% CI*	*z*	*Pr (>|z|)*
@init	1.27	(1.24, 1.29)	20.6	<2e-16	0.93	(0.90, 0.95)	-5.04	<5e-07
@intrnl	0.96	(0.92, 1.00)	-1.9	0.052	0.63	(0.60, 0.67)	-15.3	<2e-16
hashtag	0.85	(0.82, 0.89)	-7.6	<3e-14	1.08	(1.04, 1.12)	3.9	<1e-04
lifestyle	0.90	(0.88, 0.92)	-8.7	<2e-16	0.95	(0.91, 0.98)	-3.4	<0.001
politics	0.74	(0.72, 0.76)	-22.9	<2e-16	0.60	(0.58, 0.61)	-34.3	<2e-16

Table 5: Summary of model parameters for the two datasets: (a) random intercepts only, (b) random intercepts + audience effects, (c) random intercepts + topic effects, (d) full model. σ^2 *users* and σ^2 *variables* are variance estimates for the random intercepts. *Fixed Ef.* tables show odds ratios (*OR*) derived from logit coefficients, with roughly estimated confidence intervals (using approximate standard errors), and results of Wald's z-tests.

for IH Users (c.f. Table 5d).

In general, the effect sizes and directions of the newly defined subtopics are similar to those of the broad topics from which they were isolated, and more importantly, changing the topic definitions has no effect on the audience coefficients for either user group. This provides some evidence that our results are not highly sensitive to the precise choice of topics.

7 Conclusion

This study examined how Twitter users shift their use of Scottish variants depending on the topic and audience. We looked at two groups of users with different overall rates of Scottish usage and found that both topic and audience affect usage in both groups. The qualitative effects of topic were similar across the two groups, demonstrating a clear relationship between the topic or genre of discussion and the odds of choosing Scottish variants. However, the sizes and directions of the audience affects are inconsistent across the two groups: for Scottish Geotag Users we found (as in a previous study) that local variants are used more in tweets with initial mentions and less in tweets with hashtags, but for Indyref Hashtag Users we found the opposite. The demographics and usage patterns of these two groups are very different, and one interesting possibility is that they might be using the affordances of mentions and hashtags in different ways and focusing on different aspects of how these affect their potential audience. In any case, our results underscore the need for caution when drawing broad conclusions from studies of social media data, until the results of those studies are shown to hold across a variety of user samples.

Acknowledgments

This work was supported in part by the EPSRC Centre for Doctoral Training in Data Science, funded by the UK Engineering and Physical Sciences Research Council (grant EP/L016427/1) and the University of Edinburgh.

References

David Bamman, Jacob Eisenstein, and Tyler Schnoebelen. 2014. Gender identity and lexical variation in social media. *Journal of Sociolinguistics* 18(2):135–160.

Douglas Bates, Martin Mächler, Ben Bolker, and Steve Walker. 2015. Fitting linear mixed-effects models using lme4. *Journal of Statistical Software* 67(1):1–48.

Allan Bell. 1984. Language style as audience design. *Language in society* 13(02):145–204.

David M Blei, Andrew Y Ng, and Michael I Jordan. 2003. Latent dirichlet allocation. *Journal of Machine Learning Research* 3(Jan):993–1022.

Jacob Eisenstein. 2015. Systematic patterning in phonologically-motivated orthographic variation. *Journal of Sociolinguistics* 19(2):161–188.

Jacob Eisenstein, Amr Ahmed, and Eric P. Xing. 2011. Sparse additive generative models of text. In *Proceedings of the International Conference on Machine Learning*. pages 1041–1048.

Thomas L Griffiths and Mark Steyvers. 2004. Finding scientific topics. *Proceedings of the National Academy of Sciences* 101(suppl 1):5228–5235.

Susan C Herring and John C Paolillo. 2006. Gender and genre variation in weblogs. *Journal of Sociolinguistics* 10(4):439–459.

Liangjie Hong and Brian D Davison. 2010. Empirical study of topic modeling in twitter. In *Proceedings of the first workshop on social media analytics*. ACM, pages 80–88.

Dirk Hovy. 2015. Demographic factors improve classification performance. In *Proceedings of the 53rd Annual Meeting of the Association for Computational Linguistics*. Association for Computational Linguistics, pages 752–762.

Fei Huang and Alexander Yates. 2014. Improving word alignment using linguistic code switching data. In *Proceedings of the 14th Conference of the European Chapter of the Association for Computational Linguistics*. Association for Computational Linguistics, Gothenburg, Sweden, pages 1–9.

Yuan Huang, Diansheng Guo, Alice Kasakoff, and Jack Grieve. 2016. Understanding U.S. regional linguistic variation with Twitter data analysis. *Computers, Environment and Urban Systems* 59:244 – 255.

Dong Nguyen, Dolf Trieschnigg, and Leonie Cornips. 2015. Audience and the use of minority languages on twitter. In *Proceedings of the Ninth International Conference on Web and Social Media*. pages 666–669.

Umashanthi Pavalanathan and Jacob Eisenstein. 2015a. Audience-modulated variation in online social media. *American Speech* 90(2):187–213.

Umashanthi Pavalanathan and Jacob Eisenstein. 2015b. Confounds and consequences in geotagged Twitter data. In *Proceedings of the 2015 Conference on Empirical Methods in Natural Language Processing*. Association for Computational Linguistics, pages 2138–2148.

R Core Team. 2013. *R: A Language and Environment for Statistical Computing*. R Foundation for Statistical Computing, Vienna, Austria. http://www.R-project.org/.

John R Rickford and Faye McNair-Knox. 1994. Addressee-and topic-influenced style shift: A quantitative sociolinguistic study. *Sociolinguistic perspectives on register* pages 235–276.

Philippa Shoemark, Debnil Sur, Luke Shrimpton, Iain Murray, and Sharon Goldwater. 2017. Aye or naw, whit dae ye hink? Scottish independence and linguistic identity on social media. In *Proceedings of the 15th Conference of the European Chapter of the Association for Computational Linguistics: Volume 1, Long Papers*. Association for Computational Linguistics, pages 1239–1248.

Luke Sloan and Jeffrey Morgan. 2015. Who tweets with their location? Understanding the relationship between demographic characteristics and the use of geoservices and geotagging on Twitter. *PloS one* 10(11):e0142209.

Wessel Stoop and Antal van den Bosch. 2014. Using idiolects and sociolects to improve word prediction. In *Proceedings of the 14th Conference of the European Chapter of the Association for Computational Linguistics*. Association for Computational Linguistics, Gothenburg, Sweden, pages 318–327.

Yogarshi Vyas, Spandana Gella, Jatin Sharma, Kalika Bali, and Monojit Choudhury. 2014. POS tagging of English-Hindi code-mixed social media content. In *Proceedings of the 2014 Conference on Empirical Methods in Natural Language Processing*. volume 14, pages 974–979.

Differences in type-token ratio and part-of-speech frequencies in male and female Russian written texts

Tatiana Litvinova[1,2], **Pavel Seredin**[1,2,3], **Olga Litvinova**[1,3] **Olga Zagorovskaya**[1,4]

[1]RusProfiling Lab, Voronezh, Russia
[2]The Kurchatov Institute, Moscow, Russia
[3]Voronezh State University, Voronezh, Russia
[4]Voronezh State Pedagogical University, Voronezh, Russia
centr_rus_yaz@mail.ru

Abstract

The differences in the frequencies of some parts of speech (POS), particularly function words, and lexical diversity in male and female speech have been pointed out in a number of papers. The classifiers using exclusively context-independent parameters have proved to be highly effective. However, there are still issues that have to be addressed as a lot of studies are performed for English and the genre and topic of texts is sometimes neglected. The aim of this paper is to investigate the association between context-independent parameters of Russian written texts and the gender of their authors and to design predictive regression models. A number of correlations were found. The obtained data is in good agreement with the results obtained for other languages. The model based on 5 parameters with the highest correlation coefficients was designed.

1 Introduction

Differences in male and female speech have long been of linguists' interest. However, they used to be investigated by means of the qualitative methods and were largely descriptive, whereas these days the quantitative analysis methods are being employed and the goal of the ongoing paper to identify the gender of text authors using numerical values of text parameters. The fundamental paper in the field is the one called "Automatically Categorizing Written Texts by Author Gender" (Koppel et al., 2002). The text parameters were morphological, i.e. context-independent (405 common function words, i.e. pronouns, articles, prepositions, and conjunctions, POS n-grams,

n=1,2,3). It was found that even if the number of parameters is reduced to 8 most frequent function words (FW), the classifier shows the accuracy of 80 %. Usefulness of morphological features in gender identification was shown in studies for different European languages (Argamon et al., 2003; Bortolato, 2016; Mikros, 2013; Newman et al., 2008; Rangel and Rosso, 2013; Sarawgi et al., 2011; Schler et al., 2006).

As NLP tools are being employed a lot these days, the list of the text parameters used to identify the gender of text authors has been largely expanded (see Rangel et al. (2016) for review). However, as correctly noted by Company and Wanner (2014), «nearly all state-of-the-art works in the area still very much depend on the datasets they were trained and tested on, since they heavily draw on content feature». We think that in order to continue improving the gender profiling methods, especially those ones which can be applied in for forensic settings, it is necessary to further explore the associations between text author gender and context independent parameters in different languages, not only Western European ones.

Slavic languages have been underrepresented in authorship profiling studies until now, but recently the problem of gender identification in Slavic languages has been raised. For example, in a recent paper by Sboev et al. (2016) it was shown that using topic independent features gives 86 % accuracy of gender identification, however the paper presents no analysis of the differences between male and female texts.

The aim of this paper is to study the association between topic independent parameters of Russian written texts and the gender of the authors and to design predictive regression models. It should be noted that we deliberately avoid parameters directly indicating author gender (some forms of verbs, etc.) since they are easily imitated.

69

Proceedings of the Workshop on Stylistic Variation, pages 69–73
Copenhagen, Denmark, September 7–11, 2017. ©2017 Association for Computational Linguistics

2 Methods

2.1 Corpus

This study utilised a specially designed corpus designed for authorship profiling studies, *RusPersonality*, which contained, aside from the texts themselves, metadata with information about the authors (gender, age, education, psychological testing data, etc.). All of the texts in the corpus were written in the presence of the researchers in order to prevent borrowings. The texts were manually written and then converted into the digital format preserving the original style. These are all samples of what is called natural written speech. All of the texts contained an average of 130-160 words. The texts are short, which makes the task more daunting, since most stylometric features exhibit authorship quantitative patterns in larger texts (Mikros, 2013) but makes it more similar to those in forensic settings.

Each author was instructed to write one or two texts choosing among topics "A Letter to a Friend", "Description of a Picture", "How I Spent Yesterday", "Why I Am Perfect for this Position (any)", etc. We selected only those authors who chose to write two texts.

All the authors are students of Russia's largest universities and they are all native speakers of Russian. So, it is assumed that participants have similar social and educational background.

Each text from a male author with specific topic and genre should be matched by a text in the same topic and genre from a female author. The total number of texts was 1112 with 112 chosen for testing the models and 1000 for designing them. Then 1000 texts were used to design two subcorpora. In the first one ("joined") made up by texts written by the same author, they were both joined into one and processed as one text (500 texts in total). In the second subcorpus ("separate") each text was processed individually (1000 texts in total). Both subcorpora were processed individually.

2.2 Text processing

All of the texts were processed using morphological analyzer for the Russian language pymorphy2 (https://pymorphy2.readthedocs.org/en/latest/) able to normalize, decline and conjugate words, provide analyses or give predictions for unknown word. Also all of the texts were processed using an online service *istio.com*. The text parameters were only those that were not consciously controlled: indicators of lexical diversity of a text, POS (17 broad categories, see https://pymorphy2.readthedocs.io/en/latest/user/grammemes.html for tagset), different ratios of POS (a total of 78 parameters). While choosing the parameters we stuck to the criteria set forth by Oakes (2014) Firstly, the parameter should be frequent enough so that the results are statistically reliable (we chose only the parameters with the frequency more than 0 in no less than 50 % of the texts). Secondly, the parameter needs to be objectively countable.

2.3 Mathematical analysis

To estimate the association between gender and text parameters, we calculated Pearson's correlation coefficient r (t-tailed) using SPSS Statistics software.

3 Results

A large number of the parameters of the texts were correlated with the gender of their authors with r in the range 0.25-0.39 (p < 0.05; they are not presented due to lack of space). We have chosen only the parameters that were shown to correlate with the gender of authors in the joined and separate subcorpora and then 5 of them that had the highest averaged r were selected.

1. Type-token ratio (TTR). This is the most commonly used index of lexical diversity of a text (Hardie and McEnery, 2006). Given a text t, let Nt be the number of tokens in t and Vt be the number of types in t, then the simplest measure for the TTR of the text t is:

$$TTRt = Vt / Nt \qquad (1)$$

Note that the measure in eq. (1) is a number defined in [0, 1], since for any text results $1 \leq Vt \leq Nt$.

Since the texts in subcorpora were of a different length, we calculated TTR in the first one hundred words of each text. Indeed, TTR-value is known to depend on the length of the analysed text and therefore the comparison of values makes sense at the same number of tokens (Caruso et al., 2014: 139).

The index was calculated using *istio.com*. The averaged correlation coefficient r = 0.39.

2. Percentage of the 100 most frequent Russian words divided by text length in words (averaged r = -0.322). The list of the words was taken from Lyashevskaya, Sharov, 2009.

3. The index of formality. It was calculated using the following formula (Nini, 2014):

$$F = (noun + adjective + preposition - pronoun - verbs - participles - adverbs - interjections + 100)/2 \quad (2)$$

Averaged r = 0.315.

4. The index of the lexical density. It was calculated as a ratio of function words to content words multiplied by 100 % in a text. It is also known as an index of functional density (Nini, 2014), averaged r= -0.295.

5. Percentage of prepositions and modifiers (so called pronoun-like adjectives, i.e. такой "such", какой "what", всякий "any", мой "my", наш "our", ваш "your", тот "that", этот "this", etc.) (averaged r = 0.243).

For each text parameter a linear regression model was designed. In order to properly estimate the obtained result, let us determine the average arithmetic values from the solution of the five equations:

$$GENDER = \frac{\sum_{i=1}^{5} GENDER_i}{5} \quad (3)$$

Let us assume that a design value in the range [0; 0.499] indicates that the author of a text is female and in the range [0.500; 1] shows that they are male. According to our experiments, this approach proved to be more accurate than using single linear regression model over all of the features in combination.

Let us determine the accuracy of the model. Accuracy, in this context, is the ratio of the number of texts that were correctly classified according to the author gender to the total number of texts. The calculations suggest that gender was correctly identified in 65% of women and 63% of men. Thus, the accuracy of the approach was 64% (averaged accuracy for "joined" and "separate" subcorpora).

4 Discussion

The analysis showed that in Russian written texts by men compared to those by women, the index of lexical diversity and the proportion of prepositions and modifiers are higher; their texts are more formal (see Figure 1 for details).

Overall, the data are in good agreement with the results obtained for other languages.

A high degree of lexical diversity in male texts was pointed out by Argamon et al. (2003) as well as significantly higher mean word lengths, which

was also identified in the study performed by Oschepkova (2003) using Russian texts by different social groups (students and prisoners). Fewer clichés were also found in Russian male speech. We argue that a higher index of lexical diversity in texts by men is due to the above differences: in "male" texts there are fewer most frequent words, the majority of which are function words.

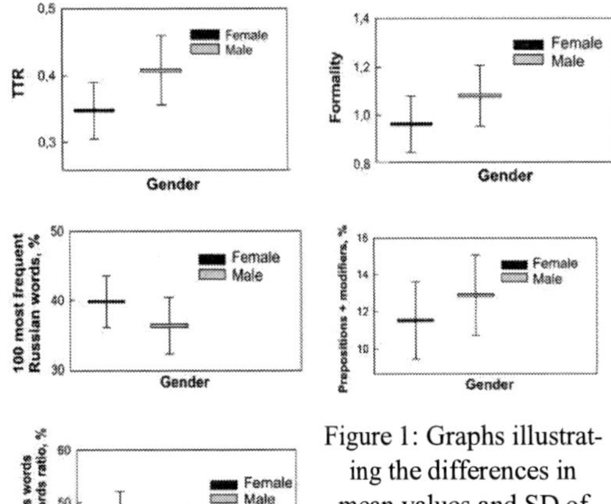

Figure 1: Graphs illustrating the differences in mean values and SD of the selected parameters for texts by women and men

Argamon et al. (2003) found that males use the informational features attributive adjectives and prepositions significantly more often and had significantly higher mean word lengths in nonfiction texts. In fiction texts, men used significantly more nouns and prepositions.

Rangel and Rosso (2013) also observed male preference for prepositions and female preference for pronouns and interjections. A high level of "formality" in male texts was also reported in a large number of studies (see a detailed review in Nini, 2014). According to the literature, this is indicative of profound cognitive differences in the linguistic profiles of men and women: reporting is more important for men while rapport is more significant for women; therefore, texts by men seem more "formal" and those by women more "contextual" (see Heylighen and Dewaele (2002) for more detail). It is interesting to compare this with the paper by Säily et al. (2011), which shows that the prevalence of nouns in texts by men as opposed to pronouns in those by women was common in personal letters written in English from 1415 to 1681. Indeed, this shows that the above gender differences seem to be universal (see also Johannsen et. al., 2015).

In a paper by Nini (2014) it was shown that "the more personal a text becomes the less likely it is to show a gender pattern of the rapport/report type. In other words, in a register in which individuals are already pressed to be Involved and person-centred then there is no room for variation between rapport and report discourse, thus blocking the gender pattern from emerging" (p. 132). However, this effect is retained in Russian personal texts such as letters to a friend.

As for the ratio of function and content words, it is not commonly employed in studies related to gender identification but is used in other sorts of analysis (García and Martín, 2007). E.g., it was shown to be significant in distinguishing Alzheimer's patients and healthy individuals, i.e. it is indicative of some personal cognitive features (Kernot et al., 2017). As far as gender identification is concerned, using Italian literary texts Bortolato (2016) showed that this parameter is more informative than frequencies of function words (particularly, conjunctions and pronouns) individually.

5   Conclusions

In this paper we have proved that there are differences between male and female texts in a number of morphological indices and TTR level. Some of these differences are in agreement with the previous findings for other languages, which suggests that they are universal. We argue that it is necessary that a list of context-independent text parameters is expanded and Russian texts of other genres are explored.

There are currently plans to account for the relations between the text parameters selected for analysis as well as to apply other methods of statistical analysis.

It is also essential that the parameters that are easily to imitate while pretending to be someone of the opposite sex are investigated. Therefore we have collected a text corpus named Russian Gender Imitation Corpus. Each author was instructed to write three texts on the same topic (out of a list of five) in their natural style, as someone of the opposite sex, someone else of the same sex. Studies of the corpus would enable us to identify which parameters changed while taking on the role of the other gender and which ones persist even during conscious imitation.

In addition, it is essential to analyse the gender characteristics of authors of texts with respect to their personality traits and femininity/masculinity, laterality, etc. As correctly pointed out by Nini

(2014, p. 34), it can be assumed that "the real differences in the linguistic patterns adopted by people depend on their personality and/or hormone levels and that genders are different to the extent that on average different genders are prone to different personality orientations and/or hormone levels". Taking this into account, in future it will be useful to treat gender as non-binary category.

This analysis to be conducted during further research would allow one to develop a more current and deeper insight into the way gender is manifested in written texts and to develop more accurate methods of identifying the gender of individuals based on the quantitative parameters of their texts for forensic settings.

Acknowledgments. This work was supported by the grant of the Russian Science Foundation, project No 16-18-10050 "Identifying the Gender and Age of Online Chatters Using Formal Parameters of their Texts".

The authors would like to thank four anonymous reviewers for their valuable comments and suggestions to improve the quality of the paper.

References

Aleksandr Sboev, Tatiana Litvinova, Dmitry Gudovskikh, Roman Rybka, Ivan Moloshnikov. 2016. Machine Learning Models of Text Categorization by Author Gender Using Topic-independent Features. *Procedia Computer Science*, 101, 135-142. https://doi.org/10.1016/j.procs.2016.11.017

Anders Johannsen, Dirk Hovy, and Anders Søgaard. 2015. Variation in noun and pronoun frequencies in a sociohistorical corpus of English. *Literary and Linguistic Computing*, 26(2): 167-188. https://doi.org/10.1093/llc/fqr004

Andrea Nini. 2014. *Authorship Profiling in a Forensic Context.* PhD thesis. Aston Uni. http://publications.aston.ac.uk/25337/1/Nini_Andrea _2015.pdf

Andrew Hardie, Tony McEnery. 2006. Statistics. In: BROWN K. (ed.). *Encyclopedia of Language and Linguistics, 2nd edition.* Amsterdam: Elsevier, pp. 138-146.

Antonio M. García, Javier C. Martín. 2007. Function words in authorship attribution studies. *Literary and Linguistic Computing*, 22(1): 49-66. https://doi.org/10.1093/llc/fql048

Assunta Caruso, Antonietta Folino, Francesca Parisi, Roberto Trunfio. 2014. A statistical method for minimum corpus size determination. In *Proceedings of Proceedings of the Twelfth International Conference on Textual Data Statistical Analysis (JADT 2014)*. JADT.org, pages 135-146.

Claudia Bortolato. 2016. Intertextual Distance of Function Words as a Tool to Detect an Author's Gender: A Corpus-Based Study on Contemporary Italian Literature. *Glottometrics*, 34: 28-43.

David Kernot, Terry Bossomaier, Roger Bradbury. 2017. The Impact of Depression and Apathy on Sensory Language. *Open Journal of Modern Linguistics*, 7: 8-32. https://doi.org/10.4236/ojml.2017.71002

Ekaterina S. Oschepkova. 2003. Written Text Author Identification: Lexicogrammatical aspect. PhD thesis. Moscow State Linguistic Uni. (in Russian).

Francis Heylighen, Jean-Marc Dewaele. 2002. Variation in the contextuality of language: an empirical measure. *Foundations of Science*, 7: 293-340. doi:10.1023/A:1019661126744

Francisco Rangel, Paolo Rosso, Ben Verhoeven, Walter Daelemans, Martin Potthast, Benno Stein. 2016. 4th Author Profiling Task at PAN 2016: Cross-Genre Evaluations. In Proceedings of CLEF (Working Notes), ceur-ws.org, pages 750-784. Available at: http://www.clips.ua.ac.be/~walter/papers/2016/rrvdps16.pdf

Francisco Rangel, Paolo Rosso. 2013. Use of language and author profiling: identification of gender and age. In *Proceeding of the 10th workshop on natural language processing and cognitive science* (NLPCS 2013). Marseille, France. Available at: http://users.dsic.upv.es/~prosso/resources/RangelRosso_NLPCS13.pdf

George K. Mikros. 2013. Systematic stylometric differences in men and women authors: a corpus-based study. In Köhler, R. and Altmann, G. (eds.), *Issues in Quantitative Linguistics*, 3, pages 206-223. Lüdenscheid: RAM – Verlag. http://users.uoa.gr/~gmikros/Pdf/Systematic%20stylometric%20differences%20in%20men%20and%20women%20authors.pdf

Jonathan Schler, Moshe Koppel, Shlomo Argamon, James W. Pennebaker. 2006. Effects of Age and Gender on Blogging. In *AAAI Spring Symposium: Computational Approaches to Analyzing Weblogs*, pages 199-205.

Juan S. Company, Leo Wanner. 2014. How to Use Less Features and Reach Better Performance in Author Gender Identification. In *Proceedings of the 9th International Conference on Language Resources and Evaluation (LREC)*, Reykjavik, Iceland, pages 1315-1319.

Matthew L. Newman, Carla J. Groom, Lori D. Handelman, James W. Pennebaker. 2008. Gender differences in language use: An analysis of 14.000 text samples. *Discourse Processes*, 45(3): 211–236. http://dx.doi.org/10.1080/01638530802073712

Michael P. Oakes. 2014. *Literary Detective Work on the Computer.* Amsterdam/Philadelphia: John Benjamins Publishing.

Morphological analyzer pymorphy2. URL: https://pymorphy2.readthedocs.io/en/latest/ (in Russian)

Moshe Koppel, Shlomo Argamon, Anat R. Shimoni. 2002. Automatically categorizing written texts by author gender. Lit Linguist Computing, 17(4): 401-412. https://doi.org/10.1093/llc/17.4.401

Olga Lyashevskaya, Sergei Sharov. 2009. *Frequency Dictionary of Modern Russian language (on materials of the Russian National Corpus)*. Moscow, Azbukovnik. URL: http://dict.ruslang.ru/freq.php (in Russian).

Ruchita Sarawgi, Kailash Gajulapalli, Yejin Choi. 2011. Gender attribution: tracing stylometric evidence beyond topic and genre. In *Proceedings of the fifteenth conference on computational natural language learning (CoNLL '11)*, Association for Computational Linguistics, pages 78-86.

Shlomo Argamon, Moshe Koppel, Jonathan Fine, Anat R. Shimoni. 2003. Gender, genre, and writing style in formal written texts. *Interdisciplinary Journal for the Study of Discourse,* 23(3): 321–346. https://doi.org/10.1515/text.2003.014

Tanja Säily, Terttu Nevalainen, Harri Siirtola. 2011. Variation in noun and pronoun frequencies in a sociohistorical corpus of English. *Literary and Linguistic Computing*, 26(2): 167-188. https://doi.org/10.1093/llc/fqr004

Modeling Communicative Purpose with Functional Style:
Corpus and Features for German Genre and Register Analysis

Thomas Haider
Max Planck Institute for Empirical Aesthetics
Frankfurt am Main, Germany
thomas.haider@ae.mpg.de

Alexis Palmer
University of North Texas
Denton, Texas, USA
alexis.palmer@unt.edu

Abstract

While there is wide acknowledgement in NLP of the utility of document characterization by genre, it is quite difficult to determine a definitive set of features or even a comprehensive list of genres. This paper addresses both issues. First, with prototype semantics, we develop a hierarchical taxonomy of discourse functions. We implement the taxonomy by developing a new text genre corpus of contemporary German to perform a text based comparative register analysis. Second, we extract a host of style features, both deep and shallow, aiming beyond linguistically motivated features at situational correlates in texts. The feature sets are used for supervised text genre classification, on which our models achieve high accuracy. The combination of the corpus typology and feature sets allows us to characterize types of communicative purpose in a comparative setup, by qualitative interpretation of style feature loadings of a regularized discriminant analysis. Finally, to determine the dependence of genre on topics (which are arguably the distinguishing factor of sub-genre), we compare and combine our style models with Latent Dirichlet Allocation features across different corpus settings with unstable topics.

1 Introduction

Language users exhibit a high degree of variability at all levels of the linguistic system and language use. In this paper, we focus on variation at the level of text (or discourse). Texts vary along numerous parameters such as *medium* (spoken, written), *topic / domain* (e.g. art, science, religion, government), *rhetorical mode* (e.g. narration, argumentation, description, exposition), or *communicative purpose* (e.g. persuade, report, entertain, edify, instruct, express opinion).

Such variational aspects, captured under the terms *register* and *genre*, have been central to previous investigations of discourse and textual variation. Both terms have been used to refer to language variety associated with particular situations of use and, lacking a clear differentiation between the two terms, many studies simply adopt one and disregard the other (cf. Biber et al., 2007, 1.4).

For Biber and Conrad (2009), though, *genre*, *register* and *style* are different perspectives on a single text. Each dimension can describe the others, e.g. a *commentary* voices an *opinion* that is *inclusive*, *angry* and *aloof* – it refers to non-specific entities, but avoids deixis and possession.

The cornerstone of our approach is to model textual variation via stylistic features, which we argue is the level at which both genre and register variation can be convincingly modeled.

Following Lee (2001), we consider *register* as variation according to use in broad societal situations. It describes a functional adaptation to the immediate situational parameters of contextual use, as different situations 'require' appropriate configurations of language. *Genre* views text by consensus within a culture, as artifacts categorized by purposive goals, distinguished by conventionally recognized criteria and hence subject to change as conventions are challenged and revised over time. In short (see table 1): *genre* is described by a **conventional label**, while *register* is described through its **pervasive features** (cf. Biber and Conrad, 2009).

A comprehensive typology of texts at the same level of generality is a research prerequisite for any comparative register analysis. Because current multi-genre text corpora do not easily ad-

74

Proceedings of the Workshop on Stylistic Variation, pages 74–84
Copenhagen, Denmark, September 7–11, 2017. ©2017 Association for Computational Linguistics

Genre	Purpose / Function
scientific texts	inform
advertising	persuade
legal texts	instruct
...	...

Table 1: Sample genres, with dominant purpose.

mit to functional analysis of types (Section 2), we turn instead to the theoretical framework of Steen (1999), which promises a general taxonomy of discourse. We operationalize the core of Steen's theory for corpus design, modeling register variation top-down with prototype semantics to develop a comparative genre taxonomy (Section 3.1). The taxonomy is then implemented in a general genre/register corpus of contemporary German. (Section 3.2).

We employ a wide range of stylistic features for the classification of text, (Section 3.3), going beyond previous computational stylometric genre analysis, that has often relied on shallow lexico-syntactic patterns such as function words, surface forms, character / part-of-speech n-grams, etc., (Karlgren and Cutting, 1994; Stamatatos et al., 2000a,b; Koppel et al., 2003; Gries and Shaoul, 2011; Sharoff, 2007; Kanaris and Stamatatos, 2007), extending beyond linguistically motivated features (Biber and Conrad, 2009; Santini, 2005) with a fine-grained morphology, psycholinguistic word norms, and topic models. With these feature sets and corpus, we perform supervised genre classification (Section 4), showing that results remain high and stable across shifting sets of categories.

A major problem with relying on surface level features - particularly lexical features - is that they tend to capture topical information. Petrenz and Webber (2011) make a strong case that a genre classification system should not be susceptible to changes in topic/domain. We therefore test topic distributions learned with Latent Dirichlet Allocation (LDA) (Blei et al., 2003) against lexico-syntactic features in such a scenario (Section 4.4). Finally, we identify functional dimensions for characterizing communicative function (register) by examining the features most prominently associated with different communicative purposes. (Section 5).

2   Selected related work

There are a number of genre-aware corpora for English, but none for contemporary German that go

beyond web-genre, or are freely available. Early examples for English include the Brown corpus (Francis and Kučera, 1964/79) and the Lancaster-Oslo/Bergen (LOB) corpus (Johansson et al., 1978). Both were sampled according to library classification systems and contain relatively small numbers of samples distributed over various genre classes of different granularity. MASC[1] (Ide, 2008) also balances genre classes over number of tokens. To analyze the variety across texts, one needs to arbitrarily split its documents (to 2000 tokens, as done by Passonneau (2014)). There is an extensive collection of web-genre corpora (Santini, 2007; Meyer zu Eißen and Stein, 2004; Rehm et al., 2008; Santini et al., 2010). See Sharoff and Markert (2010) for an overview and the success of Char-4-bin features (later found to be unstable by Petrenz and Webber (2011)). *GECCo* is a bilingual (English-German) corpus for investigating cohesion across register (Lapshinova-Koltunski et al., 2012). It is not freely available. The DWDS 'Kernkorpus' for super-genre of 20th century texts is also not available.[2]

The Hierarchical Genre Corpus (HGC) (Stubbe and Ringlstetter, 2007) and the British National Corpus (BNC) [3] are designed to offer representative samples across different genres in a hierarchical fashion. However, the categories of HGC are not clear-cut and focus on web-genre. The BNC is highly imbalanced.

Some additional related work uses features from systemic functional grammar in the tradition of Halliday for text genre classification (Argamon and Koppel, 2010; Argamon et al., 2003; Argamon and Koppel, 2012; Argamon et al., 2007).

3   Method

We present a methodology for corpus driven analysis of situated language use. We achieve this by: 1) building a corpus, and 2) classifying and characterizing situationally-defined text categories, aiming at a comparative register analysis.

3.1   A taxonomy for discourse

Genre follows a categorical paradigm, such that it assigns labels to text. A problem with genre labels is that they can have many different levels of generality, e.g. the genre "academic discourse" is very

---

[1]Manually Annotated Sub-Corpus of American English
[2]http://194.95.188.16/ressourcen/
kernkorpus/
[3]http://www.natcorp.ox.ac.uk/

broad, and texts within such a high-level genre category will show considerable internal variation in their use of language, as Biber (1989) has shown. On a lower level, different genres can be based on many different criteria (domain, topic, participants, setting, form, etc.), e.g. 'Western' vs. 'Romance' novels[4] or 'Elegy' vs. 'Ballad'.[5]

Steen (1999) develops a solution for this by applying prototype theory (Rosch, 1973) to the conceptualization of genre (and hence to the formalisation of a taxonomy of discourse). A prototype is the most typical instance of a more encompassing and varied, fuzzy conceptual category – some instances are more central than others – e.g. the basic-level concept *chair* is a prototypical instance of the superordinate concept *furniture*. Functionally, basic-level concepts are maximally informative (easily recognized, remembered, and learned), whereas subordinate concepts are less richly differentiated from their respective alternatives (e.g. *dentist chair* vs. *recliner*).[6] Taylor (1995) finds that "terms above the basic level are sometimes deviant in some way (e.g. furniture is morphosyntactically unusual in that it is uncountable, i.e. one cannot say 'a furniture' or 'furnitures')".

Steen proposes that we can recognize genres by their cognitive basic-level status: True genres, being basic-level, are maximally distinct from one another. He analyzes the distance of genres in terms of specific attributes (parameters). Biber (1993, table 1) introduces situational parameters as sampling strata for corpora, which we combine with the parameters of Steen (1999).

For our corpus design, we use the following parameters, that our features aim to cover, to distinguish genre: **medium / discourse channel** (written, spoken, scripted), **factuality** (imaginative), **purpose / discourse function** (persuade, entertain, report, edify, inform, instruct, explain, keep records, reveal self, express attitudes, opinions, etc.), **rhetorical mode / discourse type** (narration, argumentation, description, exposition), **participants** (plurality, interactiveness, shared knowledge, demographic), **topic / domain** (art, science, religion, government, etc.), **content** (topics, themes, keywords). We do not use **setting, formality, format, form**.

3.2 Corpus Design

Genre corpora are faced with the problem of finding an operationalizable definition for each genre and avoiding meaningless miscellaneous categories, i.e. choosing the right granularity of classes. The multitude of possible genre categories makes it impractical to determine a fixed set of classes for a corpus that is representative for all genre. However, for a corpus to be useful for analysis, it needs to include a representative range of classes. We focus on written language that allows us to model types of communicative function through genre.

We design our genre corpus in a top-down hierarchical fashion as a taxonomy, where super-genre categories are based on the *broad social embedding* of text. The four super-level categories for written language are taken from the DTA (Deutsches Textarchiv) (Geyken et al., 2011): *Wissenschaft (science), Belletristik (literature), Zeitung (press)* and *Gebrauchstext (operative text)*. We add a *Gesprochen (spoken)* variety to also test our model on a different medium of communication.

We subdivide each super-category into functionally dichotomous basic-categories, i.e. maximally distinct prototypical instances, mainly relying on *communicative purpose/function* as the distinctive attribute for written language. Then we assign a basic level-genre to each function, as found in DeReKo[7] (Kupietz et al., 2010). The genre annotation in DeReKo was delivered by the publishers and is not evaluated on annotators, consequently only being a 'silver standard'. Table 2 illustrates our taxonomy.

To measure human agreement on assigning these categories, we randomly selected 20% of the test set of our 8-way typology for written basic-genre (10 documents per class) for manual annotation. The three raters were (under)graduate students, native speakers of German, with backgrounds in linguistics (R1,R3) and psychology (R1,R2), employed at the MPIEA[8]. They were given minimal instruction on text genre, communicative functions and the purpose of the study. The first eight texts covered all types to make them familiar with the variety.

Inter-rater agreement is measured with Cohens κ and shown in table 4. We compare each rater to

---

[4]Distinguised by topic, protagonists, and purpose.
[5]Distinguished by topic, form, and purpose.
[6]Steen (1999) also claims superordinates to be less differentiated.

[7]Deutscher Referenzkorpus: German Reference Corpus
[8]Max Planck Institute for Empirical Aesthetics

Super-Genre	**Genre**	Dominant purpose	Ger. label	Comment
Science	Academic	research	Wissensch.	Linguistik Online crawl
	Popular science	educate	Pop. Wiss.	Spektrum d. Wiss.
Literature	Novel (epic)	narrate	Roman	
	Drama	perform	Drama	
Press	Report	report	Bericht	
	Commentary	opinion	Kommentar	
	Reportage	coverage	Reportage	
Operative Text	Advertising	persuade	Anzeigen	From newspapers
	Pharma leaflets	instruct	Pack.beilage	Rote Liste crawl
Spoken	Speech	asymmetric	Rede	German Bundestag
	Interview	symmetric	Interview	

Table 2: DeGeKo Genre Taxonomy translated to English

	advertising	report	novel	commentary	leaflets	pop.sci.	reportage	academic
document_length	486.7	736.6	1404.4*	788.4	2689.4	933.4	2042.4	3631.6**
avg_sentence_length	12.70	18.77	27.25	19.22	19.04	21.41	17.80	15.83
avg_word_length	5.25	5.38	4.98	5.29	5.66	5.48	4.91	5.24
type_token_ratio	0.317	0.265	0.230	0.270	0.269	0.240	0.219	0.294

Table 3: DeGeKo written document stats

	R1	R2	R3	Silver
R1	-	.79	.62	.84
R2		-	.58	.78
R3			-	.61

Table 4: Inter-rater agreement, 8-way typology (κ)

the others, and to the silver standard. R1 and R2 show a high level of agreement with each other (κ of .79) and with the silver standard (κ of .84 and .78, respectively). R3 shows lower agreement, often confusing academic writing with popular science.[9] A common difficulty for all raters was to distinguish among the press varieties (report, commentary, coverage), as we will also encounter in our experiments.

We propose that a fine-grained topic annotation at document level acts as viable proxy for sub-genre distinction, e.g. advertising text can be sub-categorized to *Leisure_Entertainment:Travel* ads or *Economy_Finance:Banking* ads. Topic annotation in DeReKo was assigned by a Naive-Bayes classifier trained on the opendirectory[10] taxonomy as described by Weiß (2005). Where this annotation is not consistent, we use the existing domain annotation to examine genre-internal variation.[11]

In the press genres, some topics were overly represented in the original population (e.g. re-ports on sports clubs). While it can be argued that those are the most prototypical instances of a given genre, we balance those topics in the population to achieve a more 'natural' topic distribution through sampling, so there is no bias towards certain content. The target is the mean size of topic classes plus one standard deviation.

Table 2 illustrates our taxonomy. For classes with insufficient material in DeReKo to satisfy our sampling criteria (below), we crawl the web (academic & leaflets). Where we still did not retrieve enough documents (academic & drama), we employ an *upsampling* technique: we chop documents evenly by three-sentence chunks and disperse them according to their original position in the document (i.e., beginning, middle and end are still intact). Due to this upsampling, we cannot use document length as a feature for classification.

Genre collections are often relatively small and / or imbalanced. We implement a modular corpus balancer tool able to fine tune the selection of documents. In line with our focus on 'register by genre', we balance the corpus by documents, attaining 500 documents for each of the eleven genre classes, randomly split to 400 docs for training, 50 for development and 50 for testing. With synchronic analysis in mind, we take no documents published before 1950. To retrieve a prototypical size of the documents, we restricted the max_doc_size to one standard deviation over the mean. For min_doc_size, we used $\frac{mean\_size}{2}$ or 120 tokens, as they would be too small for stylistic

---

[9] R3 complained of having had a stressful day.
[10] http://dmoztools.net/
[11] Domain here is equivalent to the newspaper section in which the text originally appeared (ger.: *ressort*).

analysis otherwise. Biber (1989, 1993) argues that a text 'sample' should be 2000 tokens large. This is not an issue in our setup, as each class is itself as large as the whole LOB corpus.

As you can see in table 3, on average, advertisements are the shortest documents and academic articles (*wissenschaft*) are the longest. Superscript ** documents have been upsampled. Also * signifies that the size for novels is not entirely trustworthy, because this category includes both shortened novels and short stories, skewing the document length distribution. Still, novels have the longest sentences by far. Reports (*berichte*) dominate in average word length. Advertising (*anzeigen*) has the highest type-token ratio.

3.3 Feature Design

We model style features that are (a) able to distinguish particular usage situations, and (b) based on sufficiently robust linguistic annotation tools. Therefore, we focus on the engineering of fine grained morpho-syntactic features, linguistic lexicons, word norms and surface forms. To test the topic sensitivity of genre, we also generate topic distributions for documents with Latent Dirichlet Allocation (LDA). Our feature-groups are organized as a nested hierarchy, shown in Table 5. Individual features are described below. We implemented our feature extraction pipeline in python. Each feature is normalized relative to its own individual group (e.g. pos with pos) per text. Before classification, we use the sklearn StandardScaler.

Preprocessing for feature extraction. We use the Julie Lab Segmenter (Tokenization, Sentences) (Hahn et al., 2016) and the RF-Tagger (Lemmatization, STTS pos-tags, SMOR morphological tags) (Schmid and Laws, 2008).

Part-of-Speech Tags We use the Stuttgart-Tübingen Tagset (STTS)[12] with 47 tags.

Verb Classes German verb classes are retrieved from GermaNet (Hamp et al., 1997; Henrich and Hinrichs, 2010). The GermaNet scheme contains 9,382 unique verbs (including particles and affixes) across 15 groups, where a verb can be a member of several groups, totaling 15,327 tokens. For each verb token that we detect, we count every relevant class with equal weight.

Surface Cues This is a heterogenous feature-group of linguistic surface cues.

1. *Avg. word length* in # of characters.
2. *Avg. sentence length* in # of words.
3. *Type-Token-ratio*: The ratio of unique types and tokens thereof. Always between 0 and 1.
4. *Alliteration*: Two subsequent words share the same first character (**bitter butter**).
5. *Assonance*: Two subsequent words share the same first vowel (*loose goose*).
6. *Repetition*: Minimum four character words recur within a 20 word context. + variant without proper names to exclude speaker roles in drama.

We do not use document length, as we want to learn linguistic information only.

Morphology RF-Tagger (Schmid and Laws, 2008) annotates very fine-grained (767) morphological tags according to SMOR (Schmid et al., 2004). One such feature would be "VFIN.Full.2.Pl.Pres.Ind" for a *full finite verb in second person plural present indicative*.

WWN word norms Lahl et al. (2009) crowd-sourced ratings for *concreteness, valency* and *arousal* for 2,654 German nouns. We draw the mean for each dimension (0 - 10) per document.

LIWC - word norms The English Linguistic Inquiry and Word Count (Tausczik and Pennebaker, 2010; Pennebaker et al., 2015) contains 6400 words and stems (and select emoticons). The German version (Wolf et al., 2008) includes 7510 entries. It provides a hierarchical annotation of 68 linguistic and psychological categories, e.g. the word *cried* is part of five categories: *sadness, negative emotion, overall affect, verbs* and *past focus*. Hence, all five will be counted for the document.

Connectives The *HDK* list of 312 discourse connectives is described in (Versley, 2010). We match connectives by iterating over word n-grams. For connectives with a gap ("entweder ... oder"), we look ahead 20 words. If the right side element returns a match, we include the whole (gapped) connective, otherwise we only count the left side.

Stopwords Our German stopword list is by so-lariz,[13] containing 996 inflected wordforms (of which 4 do not occur in the corpus).

---

[12]`http://www.ims.uni-stuttgart.de/forschung/ressourcen/lexika/TagSets/stts-table.html`

[13]`https://solariz.de/de/deutsche_stopwords.htm`

Feat.set	Features
POS	Part-of-speech tags (47)
BASIC	POS + verb classes (15), surface cues (7)
SELECT	BASIC + SMOR morphology (767), LIWC (62), WWN (3), connectives (231)
FULL	SELECT + POS-bigrams (1822), morph-single (81), stopwords (992), punctuation (13)
POS3	POS-trigrams (51473)
LDA200	LDA topics (200), trained on whole corpus
	- CONTENT: only content words - STOP: only stopwords

Table 5: Nested hierarchy of feature sets; numbers quantify individual features.

Latent Dirichlet Allocation - LDA   We train gensim (Řehůřek and Sojka, 2010) LDA (Blei et al., 2003) models on word lemmas, to model semantic domain. We train on the whole corpus (incl. the test set) and derive the topic distribution for each document (as probabilities). We experimented with 50, 100 and 200 topic dimensions, the latter giving best results. For feature generation, a relatively large number of topics is preferred.

3.4 Classification algorithms

For classification, we use Linear Discriminant Analysis (LinDA), a Naive Bayes Multinomial classifier, Random Forest ensemble classifiers (FOREST) and Support Vector Machines (SVM). We train one SVM on 10 dimensions (ordered by explained covariance) of a Principal Component Analysis (PCA), one SVM vanilla version, and lastly, with a feature selection based on ANOVA, selecting the (3-20 percentile) best performing features. All models were optimized for several parameters with a grid search.[14] We used the API of scikit-learn 0.18 (Pedregosa et al., 2011). The algorithms were selected based on their success in the related literature on genre classification. The use of Random Forests and LDA is novel however.

3.5 Characterization algorithms

For the characterization of communicative functions, we work with a Linear Discriminant Analysis (LinDA) and a Stochastic Gradient Descent (SGD). A linear model allows us to easily interpret feature loadings for each class, as each class is characterized by the linear combination of its feature weights. Also, it can be easily evaluated with a F1 score or a confusion matrix. The general form (1) means that it is easy to see the relative importance and contribution of each feature and to sanity check the model. The equation is solved by calculating a Bayesian objective, i.e. fitting a Gaussian density distribution.

$$C_k = C_{k0} + C_{k1}X_1 + C_{k2}X_2 + ... + C_{kn}X_n \quad (1)$$

where C_k is the classification score for group k and C_{kn} are the coefficients for the features X_n.

The main problem of a linear model is posed by strongly collinear features from different feature groups (PTKZU vs. Part.ZU) that consequently dominate the objective function (they become important for many classes). So we need to apply regularization techniques that allow a noise-free interpretation. But penalizing (e.g. setting variables to zero) with L1 or L2 makes the model less interpretable. This may ignore relevant information from the dataset. Consequently, we regularize LinDA with a PCA (with 150 dimensions), so that we "align" (near) identical features that load into opposing directions by their covariance. A side-effect is that this also avoids overfitting.[15]

4   Experiments

This section presents supervised classification experiments for labeling texts with communicative function, as construed in our corpus by genre labels. First, we classify basic-level genre for written language only (Section 4.1). Second, we add spoken varieties to the set of genres, changing the range of variation (Section 4.2). The third experiment changes the granularity of classification, instead targeting super-genre classes (Section 4.3). Finally, to ensure that our models learn genre rather than simply capturing differences in topics, we create an expanded sub-corpus of press documents, allowing us to keep the set of topics present in training data distinct from those represented in the test data (Section 4.4). Details of models and settings appear in Sections 3.4 and 3.5.

---

[14]Most notably for SVM: C and kernel method. For Forest: Number of trees and their depth.

[15]SGD with an ElasticNet consistently delivers somewhat similar results, but due to its nature it only "approximates" results, making it less preferable. On a small dataset (which ours arguably is), the closed-form-solution LinDA is to be preferred, as it delivers more consistent results.

Featureset	POS	BASIC	FULL	POS3	SELECT.	LDA200 STOP	LDA200 CONTENT	SELECT.+LDA200
	F1 score	F1 score	F1 score	F1 score	F1 score	F1 score	F1 score	F1 score
$LinDA$	.70	.77	.30	.28	.80	.73	.79	.86
$BAYES_{multinom}$	?	.73	.75	.51	.76	.73	.78	.81
$FOREST_{entropy}$	.74	.81	.86	.80	**.88**	.81	**.90**	**.92**
$FOREST_{gini}$	.75	.81	**.88**	.82	**.87**	.82	**.89**	**.92**
SVM_{PCA10}	.68	.75	.85	.55	.82	.77	.86	time
$SVM_{VANILLA}$	time	.79	.83	.72	.83	time	**.92**	.88
SVM_{ANOVA}	time	.70	**.88**	.77	.86	.	.	.

Table 6: Supervised classification on DeGeKo's eight written classes.

4.1 Written Basic-Level

In our corpus, the basic-level written genres are academic, popular science, novel, report, commentary, reportage, advertising, and leaflets.

Table 6 shows the classification results for written genres. Results shown are for the test set; performance is similar ($\pm$ 2 points) for the dev set. 'time' means that the classifier did not finish in a reasonable time frame (a day).

For all classifiers, SELECTED and LDA200CONTENT feature sets show the best results. The FOREST classifiers appear to be the most robust to changing the feature set. Overall, the best result is obtained by a vanilla SVM on LDA200CONTENT, on par with FOREST on SELECTED+LDA200CONTENT. Also, the smaller SELECTED set compares well to the larger FULL set, making it the best model for a characterization of communicative function (FULL contains POS2-grams).[16] The main confusion between classes is caused by the press varieties, mostly because reports and commentaries are confused for each other, and commentaries confused with many other classes.

Most strikingly, LDA200CONTENT outperforms SELECTED by 2 - 4 points. This raises the important question of how strongly the genre of a document is influenced by its topics. Petrenz and Webber (2011) show that some genre classification models suffer heavily when the topics present in a given genre during testing are different from those seen in training.

4.2 Including Spoken Classes

Next, we enrich the written basic-genre classes with the spoken varieties *symmetric speech, asymmetric interviews*, and *drama*, which is written to be spoken. The main difference is that *drama*

---

[16]The bad performance of LinDA_POS3, LinDA_Full, Bayes_POS3 and SVMPCA10_POS3 is likely attributable to a skewed distribution of pos-n-grams.

does not contain spontaneous speech, indicated by monologues. It is also arguable that political speeches – as used here – were prepared in written form to be performed in spoken form.

Experiment	Written+Spoken		Super-Level	
Feature set	BASIC	SEL.	BASIC	SEL.
	F1: test	F1: test	F1: test	F1: test
$LinDA$	.74	.80	.89	.91
$BAYES$	.68	.76	.83	.89
$FOREST_{ent}$	**.78**	.85	.91	**.96**
$FOREST_{gini}$	.77	**.86**	.91	.95
SVM_{PCA10}	.	.82	.86	.94
SVM_{VAN}	.	.80	.91	.94

Table 7: Written+spoken (L), Super-genres (R).

The left-hand side of Table 7 shows classification results for the BASIC and the SELECTED feature sets. The richer feature set clearly outperforms the simpler one. Interestingly, even though we added three classes of spoken material, we do not lose any accuracy over the corpus with only written varieties.

4.3 Written Super-Level

Next, written-language classes are mapped to four coarse-grained super-genres: *Presse, Wissenschaft, Belletristik* and *Gebrauchstext*.

The right-hand side of Table 7 shows these results. We see that basic-level genre classes are quite robust concerning their super-class. The score improves somewhat over basic-genre, partly because the task is simplified from 8 classes to 4. Prototype theory (and consequently Steen (1999)) would hypothesize that super-genre cannot be as richly distinguished as basic-genre. However, given the machine learning context of fewer classes and more data, the results are what you would expect. In a production system, this coarse set of classes can be used to predict text genre with a fair amount of certainty with most classifiers.

Topic Class		Politik	Freizeit_Unterh.	Kultur	Sport	Wirtsch._Finanz.	Staat_Gesell.	Wissensch.
Bericht	train	147	65	88	-	-	-	-
Kommentar	train	95	-	180	25	-	-	-
Reportage	train	176	-	-	-	-	118	6
Bericht	test	-	-	-	31	19	50	-
Kommentar	test	-	19	-	-	14	67	-
Reportage	test	-	89	8	3	-	-	-

Table 8: DeGeKo Presse Topic Distinct Set # of documents

...	Featureset	**Basic**	**Full**	**Selected**	**LDA Cont retrain**	**LDA Stop full**	**LDA Cont full**
	Classifier	F1 score	F1 score	F1 score	F1 score	F1 score	F1 score
original	$LinDA$	.68	.65	.54	.56	.67	.56
	$FOREST_{entropy}$	.75	.78	**.79**	**.70**	**.69**	**.82**
	$SVM_{vanilla}$	time	.70	.73	.68	.70	.79
distinct	$LinDA$	.63	.61	.48	.37	.63	.65
	$FOREST_{entropy}$	.68	.69	**.68**	.54	**.68**	**.70**
	$SVM_{vanilla}$	.63	.65	.65	**.61**	.66	.69

Table 9: DeGeKo Topic Stability Compared Results

4.4 Topic Distinct Set

Theoretically, a text from any given genre can be about any given topic, yet it is clear that co-variances exist between genre and topic, with some genre/topic combinations more likely than others. Because both exploit low-level features to make predictions, a feature indicative of topic benefits a genre classifier through correlations in the training corpus. However, if the topics addressed in a genre can change unpredictably over time, such correlated features can harm performance. Petrenz and Webber (2011) found that neither character-4-grams nor bag-of-words models actually learn genre, but drop from 98% F1 to 38% (with char4) on three classes when topic is not held stable.

To test whether LDA topics are stable over a changing topic distribution, we create a subcorpus with the three press genre, where the topic annotations in our corpus are most reliable. Crucially, the distributions of topics for training data vs. test data are distinct. This yields two corpora: *Original & Distinct*. See Table 8 for distribution of documents over topics and genre. See Table 9 for classification results over changing topics.

We retrain LDA on the subcorpora and compare classification results to LDA trained on the full corpus, and against our style features. We find that each model compares unfavorably in the unstable topic setting, e.g. the FOREST&SELECTED model loses 11 F1 points. In the unlikely case that we have a huge genre corpus available for training LDA, the model is comparable to the style feature set (which would be theoretically possible if we feed new documents to our gensim model). The retrained LDA model compares badly for all models. This shows that (a) LDA needs as much training data as it can get, and (b) LDA is not robust against changing topics.

5 Characterizing register

A major advantage of our corpus is that we do not need sophisticated covariance metrics for the analysis of stylistic variation. In our setup, we can interpret class feature loadings, and we can validate our linear classifier with a simple F1 metric. We achieve .81 F1 score. The error stems mostly from press variety. The details of our register characterization approach are described in Section 3.5.

For each class, we retrieve the 80 features with the largest coefficient (40 negative & 40 positive) and use them for a qualitative analysis based on hypotheses formed on prior investigations (Breuer and Eroms, 2009) and to identify feature agglomerations that are apparent in a comparative setup (e.g. scientific text uses lots of connectives, particularly contrastive connectives). Figures 1 and 2 show such coefficient plots for advertising and academic writing. We next discuss, for four representative registers, the features most strongly associated, according to the method just described.

Gebrauchstext / Advertising (persuasion)
Advertising often features *repetition, named entities, proper nouns* with the according *compositional parts* and *adjectives, plural pronouns of first and third person*, and also *attributive possessive pronouns*. We rarely find verbs or articles. So ads feature *object reference* and *blunt language* (nom-

inal style but rarely articles). We find a *simple syntax, but lexical diversity* (high type/token ratio, short sentences, no sub. conj.) and *overt persuasion* (Positive sentiment, Certainty).

Presse / Bericht (report) Reports feature most prominently *present tense, passive voice, indirect speech* (subjunctive), *facts* (indicative) and *information* (num., art., NN, NE, ADJ). Also, by a positive loading of *prepositions, adverbs, reflexive pronouns* and negative loading of sub. conj., we conjecture a *balanced, compact style*.

Literature / Novel (storytelling) Storytelling stands out through the use of the *past tense and the third person (V.3.past, 'damals')*. We also find quite *long sentences* (almost 30 words on average), consequently many commas, and an aesthetic feature: *alliteration*.

Wissenschaft / Academic texts (Linguistik

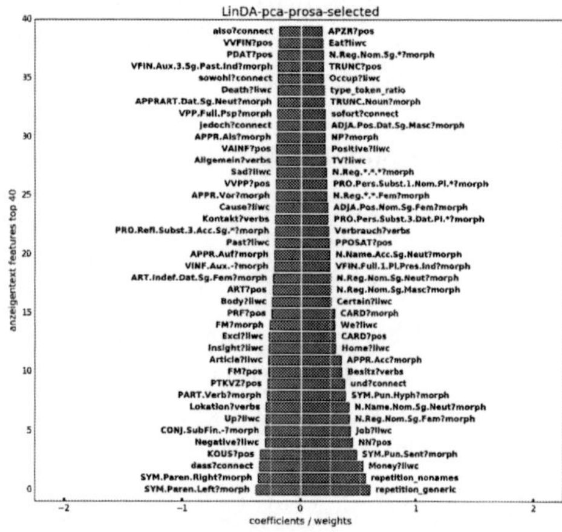

Figure 1: Feature loading for advertising

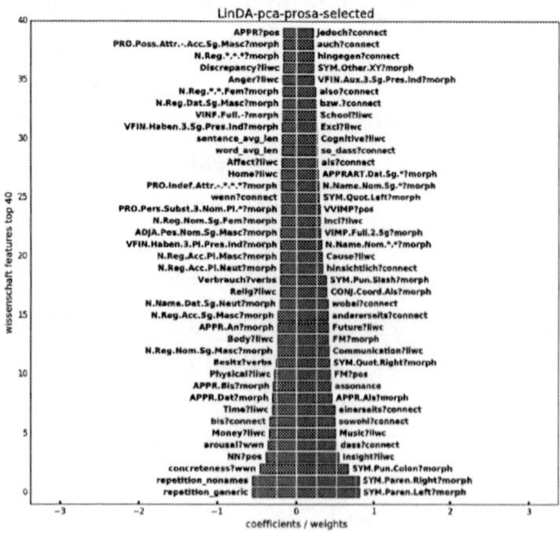

Figure 2: Feature loading for academic text

online) Academic writing (unsurprisingly) shows *complex exposition* and *argumentation* with many *(contrastive) connectives* (dass, sowohl, einerseits, hinsichtlich, bzw., also), *diverse punctuation* (parentheses, slashes) and the LIWC classes *insight, causation, communication*. Furthermore, this text genre uses fairly *abstract language*, as we find no concreteness and no arousal. We find a lot of *foreign material* (we use linguistics papers), and a prominent *focus on the future* (liwc). Apparently, academic writing is assonant.

6 Conclusion

We have developed a genre taxonomy (for German) based on prototype semantics that can be used for a comparative register analysis, modelling a central aspect of situative text use: communicative purpose of text.

We find that fine grained morphology, surface cues and psycholinguistic word norms allow us to reason about situational text embedding, while – given enough training data – Latent Dirichlet Allocation can approximate genre distinctions, seeing that certain topics are prevalent in most genre categories. However, LDA is not stable over changing topic distributions under constant genre.

Future work should look at the communicative/situative function of constituency tree features, as they have proven to be useful e.g. for authorship attribution or deception detection. Also, the dimension of aesthetic style features (foregrounding) has typically been ignored in register research, as those are not necessarily functional. Given the abundance of material, we should look at press variety only. We have seen that report, commentary and reportage are prone to be confused, particularly by linear models. As humans also have a problem here, we have to conclude that they are not as clearly distinguished as other genre. Furthermore, press includes genre categories that are not as prototypical as the ones selected here (Dossier, Portrait, Feuilleton, Leitartikel). There are promising results (Sharoff, 2016) to view genre as topology, not as typology.

Finally, future research might benefit from word embeddings and particularly morphological embeddings to model stylistic variation.

Acknowledgements

The bulk of this work was conducted while the first author was a Master's student at the University of

Heidelberg, with support of the Leibniz Science Campus (LiMo). We thank Yannick Versley, Katja Markert, Josef Ruppenhofer and Stefan Blohm for helpful discussions and our annotators Elena Vaporova, Sebastien Nicolay and Christian Dueck. Thanks also to the anonymous reviewers for helpful comments.

References

Shlomo Argamon and Moshe Koppel. 2010. The rest of the story: Finding meaning in stylistic variation. In *The Structure of Style*, Springer, pages 79–112.

Shlomo Argamon and Moshe Koppel. 2012. Systemic functional approach to automated authorship analysis, a. In *JL & Pol'y 21*, page 299.

Shlomo Argamon, Moshe Koppel, Jonathan Fine, and Anat Rachel Shimoni. 2003. Gender, genre, and writing style in formal written texts. WALTER DE GRUYTER & CO, volume 23, pages 321–346.

Shlomo Argamon, Casey Whitelaw, Paul Chase, Sobhan Raj Hota, Navendu Garg, and Shlomo Levitan. 2007. Stylistic text classification using functional lexical features. *Journal of the American Society for Information Science and Technology* 58(6):802–822.

Douglas Biber. 1989. A typology of english texts. *Linguistics 27.1* pages 3–44.

Douglas Biber. 1993. Representativeness in corpus design. *Literary and linguistic computing* 8(4):243–257.

Douglas Biber, Ulla Connor, and Thomas A Upton. 2007. *Discourse on the move: Using corpus analysis to describe discourse structure*, volume 28. John Benjamins Publishing.

Douglas Biber and Susan Conrad. 2009. *Register, genre, and style*. Cambridge University Press.

David M Blei, Andrew Y Ng, and Michael I Jordan. 2003. Latent dirichlet allocation. *the Journal of machine Learning research* 3:993–1022.

Ulrich Breuer and Hans-Werner Eroms. 2009. *Stil und Stilistik. Eine Einführung*. Grundlagen der Germanistik 45.

Winthrop Nelson Francis and Henry Kučera. 1964/79. *Manual of information to accompany a standard corpus of present-day edited American English, for use with digital computers*. Brown University, Department of Lingustics.

Alexander Geyken, Susanne Haaf, Bryan Jurish, Matthias Schulz, Jakob Steinmann, Christian Thomas, and Frank Wiegand. 2011. Das deutsche textarchiv: Vom historischen korpus zum aktiven archiv. *Digitale Wissenschaft. Stand und Entwicklung digital vernetzter Forschung in Deutschland, 20./21. September 2010, Köln. Beiträge der Tagung, 2., ergänzte Fassung* pages 157–161.

Stefan Th John Newman Gries and Cyrus Shaoul. 2011. N-grams and the clustering of registers. *Empirical Language Research Journal 5.1* .

Udo Hahn, Franz Matthies, Erik Faessler, and Johannes Hellrich. 2016. Uima-based jcore 2.0 goes github and maven central — state-of-the-art software resource engineering and distribution of nlp pipelines.

Birgit Hamp, Helmut Feldweg, et al. 1997. Germanet-a lexical-semantic net for german. In *Proceedings of ACL workshop Automatic Information Extraction and Building of Lexical Semantic Resources for NLP Applications*. pages 9–15.

Verena Henrich and Erhard W Hinrichs. 2010. Gernedit-the germanet editing tool. In *ACL (System Demonstrations)*. Citeseer, pages 19–24.

Nancy et al. Ide. 2008. Masc: The manually annotated sub-corpus of american english. In *In Proceedings of the Sixth International Conference on Language Resources and Evaluation (LREC)*.

S Johansson, G Leech, and H Goodluck. 1978. Manual of information to accompany the lancaster-olso/bergen corpus of british english, for use with digital computers .

Ioannis Kanaris and Efstathios Stamatatos. 2007. Webpage genre identification using variable-length character n-grams. In *Tools with Artificial Intelligence, 2007. ICTAI 2007. 19th IEEE International Conference on. Vol. 2*. IEEE.

J. Karlgren and D. Cutting. 1994. Recognizing text genres with simple metrics using discriminant analysis. In *In Proc. of the 15th. International Conference on Computational Linguistics (COLING 94)*. Kyoto, Japan, page 1071 – 1075.

Moshe Koppel, Navot Akiva, and Ido Dagan. 2003. A corpus-independent feature set for style-based text categorization. In *IJCAI-2003 Workshop on Computational Approaches to Text Style and Synthesis, Acapulco, Mexico*.

Marc Kupietz, Cyril Belica, Holger Keibel, and Andreas Witt. 2010. The german reference corpus dereko: A primordial sample for linguistic research. In *LREC*.

Olaf Lahl, Anja S Göritz, Reinhard Pietrowsky, and Jessica Rosenberg. 2009. Using the world-wide web to obtain large-scale word norms: 190,212 ratings on a set of 2,654 german nouns. *Behavior Research Methods* 41(1):13–19.

Ekaterina Lapshinova-Koltunski, Kerstin Kunz, and Marilisa Amoia. 2012. Compiling a multilingual spoken corpus. In *Proceedings of the VIIth GSCP*

International Conference: Speech and Corpora. Firenze: Firenze University Press.

D. Lee. 2001. Genres, registers, text types, domains, and styles: clarifying the concepts and navigating a path through the bnc jungle. In *Language Learning and Technology*, page 5(3):37–72.

Sven Meyer zu Eißen and Benno Stein. 2004. Genre Classification of Web Pages: User Study and Feasibility Analysis. In Susanne Biundo, Thom Frühwirth, and Günther Palm, editors, *Advances in Artificial Intelligence. 27th Annual German Conference on AI (KI 04)*. Springer, Berlin Heidelberg New York, volume 3228 LNAI of *Lecture Notes in Artificial Intelligence*, pages 256–269.

R. J. Ide N. Su S. an Stuart J. Passonneau. 2014. Biber redux: Reconsidering dimensions of variation in american english. In COLING, pages (pp. 565–576).

F. Pedregosa, G. Varoquaux, A. Gramfort, V. Michel, B. Thirion, O. Grisel, M. Blondel, P. Prettenhofer, R. Weiss, V. Dubourg, J. Vanderplas, A. Passos, D. Cournapeau, M. Brucher, M. Perrot, and E. Duchesnay. 2011. Scikit-learn: Machine learning in Python. *Journal of Machine Learning Research* 12:2825–2830.

James W Pennebaker, Ryan L Boyd, Kayla Jordan, and Kate Blackburn. 2015. The development and psychometric properties of liwc2015. *UT Faculty/Researcher Works* .

Philipp Petrenz and Bonnie Webber. 2011. Stable classification of text genres. In *Computational Linguistics 37.2.* pages 385–393.

Georg Rehm, Marina Santini, Alexander Mehler, Pavel Braslavski, Rüdiger Gleim, Andrea Stubbe, Svetlana Symonenko, Mirko Tavosanis, and Vedrana Vidulin. 2008. Towards a reference corpus of web genres for the evaluation of genre identification systems. In *LREC*.

Radim Řehůřek and Petr Sojka. 2010. Software Framework for Topic Modelling with Large Corpora. In *Proceedings of the LREC 2010 Workshop on New Challenges for NLP Frameworks*. ELRA, Valletta, Malta, pages 45–50. `http://is.muni.cz/publication/884893/en`.

Eleanor H Rosch. 1973. Natural categories. *Cognitive psychology* 4(3):328–350.

Marina Santini. 2005. Itri-05-02 linguistic facets for genre and text type identification: A description of linguistically-motivated .

Marina Santini. 2007. Automatic identification of genre in web pages. diss. .

Marina Santini, Alexander Mehler, and Serge Sharoff. 2010. Riding the rough waves of genre on the web. In *Genres on the Web. Springer Netherlands*, pages 3–30.

Helmut Schmid, Arne Fitschen, and Ulrich Heid. 2004. Smor: A german computational morphology covering derivation, composition and inflection. In *LREC*.

Helmut Schmid and Florian Laws. 2008. Estimation of conditional probabilities with decision trees and an application to fine-grained pos tagging.

Serge Sharoff. 2007. Classifying web corpora into domain and genre using automatic feature identification. In *Proceedings of the 3rd Web as Corpus Workshop*.

Serge Sharoff. 2016. Functional text dimensions for annotation of web corpora .

Serge Zhili Wu Sharoff and Katja Markert. 2010. The web library of babel: evaluating genre collections. In *LREC*.

Efstathios Stamatatos, Nikos Fakotakis, and George Kokkinakis. 2000a. Automatic text categorization in terms of genre and author. In *Computational linguistics 26.4*, pages 471–495.

Efstathios Stamatatos, Nikos Fakotakis, and George Kokkinakis. 2000b. Text genre detection using common word frequencies. In *Proceedings of the 18th conference on Computational linguistics-Volume 2. Association for Computational Linguistics*.

Gerard Steen. 1999. Genres of discourse and the definition of literature. *Discourse Processes* 28(2):109–120.

A. Stubbe and C. Ringlstetter. 2007. Recognizing genres. In *In Santini, M. and Sharoff, S., editors, Proc. Towards a Reference Corpus of Web Genres*.

Yla R Tausczik and James W Pennebaker. 2010. The psychological meaning of words: Liwc and computerized text analysis methods. *Journal of language and social psychology* 29(1):24–54.

John Taylor. 1995. Linguistic categorization: Prototypes in linguistic theory. *and Categorization, JR Linguistic Clarendon: Oxford University Press* .

Yannick Versley. 2010. Discovery of ambiguous and unambiguous discourse connectives via annotation projection. In *Proceedings of Workshop on Annotation and Exploitation of Parallel Corpora (AEPC)*. pages 83–82.

Christian Weiß. 2005. Die thematische erschließung von sprachkorpora. *Mannheim: Institut für Deutsche Sprache.(= OPAL-Online publizierte Arbeiten zur Linguistik, 1/2005)* .

Markus Wolf, Andrea B Horn, Matthias R Mehl, Severin Haug, James W Pennebaker, and Hans Kordy. 2008. Computergestützte quantitative textanalyse: Äquivalenz und robustheit der deutschen version des linguistic inquiry and word count. *Diagnostica* 54(2):85–98.

Stylistic Variation in Television Dialogue for Natural Language Generation

Grace I. Lin and **Marilyn A. Walker**

Natural Language and Dialogue Systems Lab
University of California, Santa Cruz
{glin5,mawwalker}@ucsc.edu

Abstract

Conversation is a critical component of storytelling, where key information is often revealed by what/how a character says it. We focus on the issue of character voice and build stylistic models with linguistic features related to natural language generation decisions. Using a dialogue corpus of the television series, *The Big Bang Theory*, we apply content analysis to extract relevant linguistic features to build character-based stylistic models, and we test the model-fit through an user perceptual experiment with Amazon's Mechanical Turk. The results are encouraging in that human subjects tend to perceive the generated utterances as being more similar to the character they are modeled on, than to another random character.

1 Introduction

Conversation is an essential component of social behavior, one of the primary means by which humans express emotions, moods, attitudes, and personality. Conversation is also critical to storytelling, where key information is often revealed by what a character says, how s/he says it, and how s/he reacts to what other characters say. Here we focus on the issue of character voice. One way to produce believable, dramatic dialogue is to build stylistic models with linguistic features related to natural language generation (NLG) decisions. Television dialogue are exemplars of many different linguistic styles that were designed to express dramatic characters. Thus we construct a corpus of television character dialogue from *The Big Bang Theory* (BBT) and apply content analysis and language modeling techniques to extract relevant linguistic features to build character-based stylistic

models. We test the model-fit of character models through a generation experiment to test user perceptions of characters.

Our work can be applied to storytelling applications such as video games, interactive narrative, chatbots, or education systems where dialogue with personalities may improve user experience.

2 Related Work

Research from corpus linguistics include Bednarek's work on using *Gilmore Girls* to compare the genre dramedy to other types (Bednarek, 2011a), and Quaglio's work on using *Friends* with unscripted conversations (Quaglio, 2009). Other related research focuses on characterization through dialogue. For example, Bubel explored the friendship among characters in the *Sex and the City* (Bubel, 2005), and Bednarek analyzed linguistic stylistics shifts from characters from the *Gilmore Girls* (Bednarek, 2011b) and *The Big Bang Theory* (Bednarek, 2012).

Research from computational stylistics (or stylometry) focuses on the use of quantitative methods to study writing styles to characterize authors, which can be applied to many applications such as classical literary text, modern forensic text, and online reviews, just to name a few (Stamatatos, 2009). Principal component analysis is used to analyze the variations in words, focusing on the challenge of relating features and meanings in text, which is not fixed depending on the context (Schreibman et al., 2008).

There is an extensive amount of research in story generation (narrative content), which tends to focus on plots and character development to achieve narrative goals. One source of creating stories comes from crowd participants writing detailed descriptions for events, going into details

85

Proceedings of the Workshop on Stylistic Variation, pages 85–93
Copenhagen, Denmark, September 7–11, 2017. ©2017 Association for Computational Linguistics

with characters' intentions, facial expressions, and actions (Li et al., 2014). In addition, they used the Google N-Gram Corpus and Project Gutenberg to help select different types of sentences (most/least probable, most fictional, most interesting details) and different sentiments (most positive/negative). Our work is also related to character modeling from film dialogue for NLG (Lin and Walker, 2011; Walker et al., 2011), except that we focused on TV series because they offered more dialogue.

Despite overlaps, our work differs in that we: 1) extract linguistic stylistic features based on personality studies from psychology; 2) focus on features that can be generated given our current system; 3) find significant features and use them as building blocks to 4) create models using techniques such as standard scores and classification; and 5) apply the models to applications such as natural language generation.

Natural Language Generation Engine

PYPER (Bowden et al., 2016) is a spin-off implementation of PERSONAGE (Mairesse and Walker, 2007) in Python that provides new controls for expressive NLG. It is currently part of the M2D Monolog-to-Dialogue generation (Bowden et al., 2016) framework, which we briefly describe the architecture below (Figure 1).

The EST framework (Rishes et al., 2013) produces a story annotated by SCHEHERAZADE (Elson and McKeown, 2009) as a list of sentences represented as Deep Syntactic Structures (DsyntS). DSyntS is therefore a dependency-tree structure with nodes containing lexical information about words. This is the input format for the surface realizer RealPro (). M2D converts the story (list of DsyntS) into two-speaker dialogue by accepting input parameters that control the allocation of content, pragmatic markers, etc.

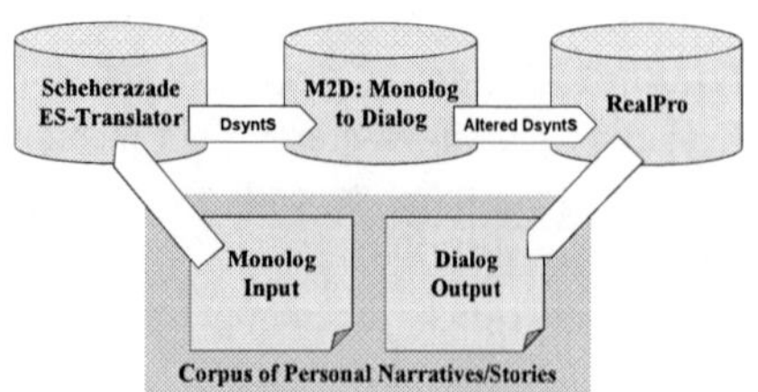

Figure 1: M2D Monolog-to-Dialogue Generation (Bowden et al., 2016)

3 Corpus

We parsed fan-transcribed BBT scripts, seasons 1-4 and partial season 5, to obtain scenes, speakers, and utterances. The series centers around 5 characters, 4 of them (all male) are scientists/engineers working at Caltech, and 1 (Penny) is a waitress. The comedy's theme focuses on the contrast between the geekiness of the male characters and Penny's social skills. Two additional female characters, both scientists, were introduced as love interests to two main male characters, and have since became main characters themselves.

4 Stylistic Features Extraction

After extracting dialogic utterances from transcripts, we extract features reflecting particular linguistic behaviors for each character. Table 1 describes major feature sets, which include sentiment polarity, dialogue act, passive voice, word categories from LIWC (Pennebaker et al., 2001), tag questions, etc.

Character Stylistic Models

We calculate a standard score (z-value) for each feature to measure the differences between main characters: Leonard, Sheldon, Penny, Howard, Raj, Bernadette, and Amy. A better measurement could be used due to the small population and normal assumption, however we reviewed the results and they seem to capture enough relative differences among characters. Character models are composed of significant features with $|z| \geq 1$. While using features with $|z| \geq 2$ might be a better choice, our NLG engine can manipulate many features under $|z| \geq 1$.

The number and examples of significant features for each character are shown in Table 2. We see that for $|z| \geq 1$, Sheldon, Penny, Bernadette and Amy have over 200 significant features. Sheldon, more specifically, has close to 400 significant features. When we narrow them down to $z \geq 2$, significant features for Bernadette and Amy decreased by over 85%, Leonard, Penny, Howard, and Raj decreased by 70%, and Sheldon decreased by 54%.

5 Generating Expressive Utterances

The workflow for generation is to 1) annotate stories using SCHEHERAZADE; 2) use EST to automatically translate annotated stories to deep syntactic structures (DSyntS); 3) PYPER reads

Table 1: Automatically Annotated Linguistic Features for TV Dialogue

Feature Set and Description
1. Basic. Tokens per sentence, tokens per utterance, etc., plus words from different types of emotion and other psychological categories from the Nodebox English Linguistics library.
2. Sentiment Polarity. Overall polarity, polarity of sentences, etc., using SENTIWORDNET[1] to calculate positive, negative, and neutral score.
3. Dialogue Act. Train Naive Bayes classifier with NPS Chat Corpus' 15 dialogue act types using simple features. We also determine "First Dialogue Act", where we look at the dialogue act of the first sentence of each turn.
4. Merge Ratio. Use regular expression to detect the merging of subject and verb of two propositions.
5. Passive Voice. Using a third party software (see text) to detect passive sentences.
6. Concession Polarity. Look for concession cues, then calculate polarity of concession portion.
7. LIWC Categories. Word categories from the Linguistic Inquiry and Word Count (LIWC) text analysis software.
8. Markers - PERSONAGE. collect words used in PERSONAGE for generation, which where selected based on psychological studies to identify pragmatic markers of personality that affect the utterance.
9. Tag Questions. Use regular expression to capture tag questions.
10. Verb Strength. Averaged sentiment values of verbs.
11. Content Words Length. Find the average length of content words.
12. Markers - Others. Inspired by PERSONAGE words. Extended set.
13. Hedges. Collect words from a list of pre-defined hedges and their categories. LACKOFF hedges.
14. Repeating Verbs. Find verbs that are repeated used in a turn.
15. BIGRAMs. Top 10 bigrams.
16. Part-of-Speech BIGRAMs. Top 10 POS bigrams.

Table 2: Number and Examples of Significant Features for *The Big Bang Theory* Characters

Speaker	$\|z\| \geq 1$	$\|z\| \geq 2$	Example Features for $z \geq 1$ (i.e., positive z-values only)
Leonard	172	54	words:[*even if, nevertheless, whereas, even though*], Dialogue Act–{Greet, Bye}, LIWC-{Causation, Impersonal Pronouns}, hedges per sentence, connect words, concept words
Sheldon	394	180	words: [*all the same, although, despite, however, nevertheless, on the other hand, whereas, more or less, though, all, yet*], passive-ratio, important words per utt/sent, LIWC-{Inhibition, Prepositions, Number, Quantifiers}
Penny	232	68	words:[*nevertheless, even if, while, even though, on the other hand, yet*], connect words, emotional words, Dialogue Act–{Greet, Bye}, swear/near swear words, LIWC–{Adverbs, Present Tense, Dictionary Words}
Howard	133	41	words:[*although, even if, whereas*], LIWC–{Hear, See, Third Person Singular}, concept words, in-group words, hedges-per-sent
Raj	179	51	words:[*on the other hand, however, despite, though, also, even though, but*], in-group words, LIWC–{Conjunctions, Third Person Plural, See}, hedges per sentence
Bernadette	283	43	persuasive words, emotional words, conceptual words, words:[*even though, yet, while*], Dialogue Act–emphasis, LIWC–{Personal Pronouns, Second person, Auxiliary Verbs, Function Words, Past Tense}
Amy	246	43	LIWC–{Quantifiers, UniqueWords, FutureTense, Causation}, RID Emotion words, Dialogue Act - Continuer, opinion words, words:[*though, but*]

and manipulates DSyntS to add expressive elements, and 4) send "expressive" DSyntS to Real-Pro (Lavoie and Rambow, 1997) (a sentence realizer) for generation. We focus on operation 3 where we use our learned character stylistic models to add expressive elements to generic sentences.

5.1 Mapping Stylistic Features to NLG Decisions

The re-written and better-controlled PYPER allows for more useful mapping of character models for NLG. For example, hedge insertion patterns are kept in a library where new additions can be easily added. As an example, a partial mapping for LIWC categories are shown in Table 3. For multiple features mapped to the same PYPER parameter, we calculate a weighted average of the features.

5.2 Narrative Content

Our narrative content comes from fables and stories: 1 fable (*The Fox and the Crow*) and 6 blog stories about garden, protest, squirrel, bug, employer, and storm (Gordon et al., 2007). We use *The Fox and the Crow* fable as an example to describe our process shown in Figure 2.

Some phrases are highlighted to show how they

Table 3: Partial Mapping of LIWC Categories to Expressive NLG Parameters

PYPER **Parameter**	LIWC Category	PYPER **Parameter**	LIWC Category
near-expletives	swear, anger	low-expletives	swear, anger
emph-actually	certain	emph-exclamation	excl
emph-really	certain	emph-great	assent
emph-you-know	filler	emph-particularly	certain
emph-technically	certain	emph-literally	certain
emph-quintessential	certain	emph-essentially	certain, i
emph-somewhat	tentat	emph-very	certain
emph-especially	certain	emph-roughly	tentat
in-group-marker	family, friends, we, incl	init-reject	tentat

were annotated and translated. Many complicated sentences have been broken down into shorter ones. Note that some additional descriptions (adjectives) were added in order to provide enough search space for PYPER to exercise enough expressive parameters, so that characters' personalities will come through in different variations of the story.

The final, expressive version of the story shows different stylistic features such as converting a statement to a question and adding character dialogue inspired expressions such as *Typical*.

6 Evaluation with User Perceptual Experiment

We used Mechanical Turk to get user feedback on the generated dialogue. The PYPER generated output dialogue were post-processed to get rid of typos and minor grammatical issues. Referring to the MTurk survey (one HIT) in Figure 3, we first show some information about the character in interest (Sheldon, in this case), followed by two sets of dialogue: one by Sheldon and the other by a different random character. The worker does not know which one was modeled by Sheldon. S/he was asked to pick the dialogue that sounded most similar to Sheldon, along with providing reasons.

Referring to results in Table 5, we used three participants per pair of characters comparison per story. The character on the left-most column indicates the modeled character, and the compared-to character was the "other random character" in the survey. Each circle (empty or filled) indicates a worker's choice. A filled circle (●) means the worker picked the "matched" generated dialogue to the intended character, otherwise an empty circle (○) is shown.

The probability that at least two out of three participants agree on the right character is > 50% (Table 4), while all three participants agree on the right character is 31.3%, which is higher than

chance (12.5%).

Table 4: Participants Agreement

Choose the right character	# HITs (out of 294)	%
● ● ● (3 out of 3)	92	**31.3**
● ● ○ (2 out of 3)	57	**20.4**
● ○ ○ (1 out of 3)	122	41.5
○ ○ ○ (0 out of 3)	23	7.8

Overall the 7 characters over all 7 stories were recognized about 65.5% of the time (out of 882 ratings). Per character-wise over all 7 stories, Penny was recognized the most with 82.5% of the time, followed by Leonard (78.6%), Bernadette (66.7%), Amy and Sheldon (both 61.9%), Howard (57.9%), and finally Raj, who was recognized the least with 49.2% of the time.

Certain character pairs were easier to distinguish than others. For example, Leonard-Penny and vise-versa (95.2%), Sheldon-Penny and vise-versa (85.7%, 90.5%), and Amy-Bernadette and vise-versa (85.7%). On the other hand, these were among the pairs harder to distinguish: Amy-Leonard and vise-versa (47.6%, 57.1%), Bernadette-Penny and vise-versa (33.3%, 57.1%), and Sheldon-Howard and vise-versa (47.6%, 57.1%).

7 Character Analysis

In this section we provide some insights to the results, including with participants' comments about their perception of characters through the generated dialogue.

We found the following pairs of characters most distinguishable from each other (Table 6): Amy vs. Bernadette, Bernadette vs. Howard, Howard, Leonard, Sheldon vs. Penny, Penny vs. Leonard, and Raj vs. Sheldon. On the other hand, we found the most similar pairs of characters to be Amy-Leonard, Bernadette-Penny, Howard-Leonard, Leonard-amy, Penny-Bernadette, Raj-

The Fox and the Crow Partial (Original)
A Crow was sitting on a branch of a tree with a piece of cheese in her beak when a Fox observed her and set his wits to work to discover some way of getting the cheese.
SCHEHERAZADE & EST
The crow sat on the tall tree's branch. The crow has elegant talons. The crow has a good beak. The crow has ugly wings. The crow has bad eyes. The delicious cheese was in the crow's beak. The hungry fox observed the crow. The fox has good claws. The fox has bad teeth. The fox tried to discover for the fox to get the cheese.
PYPER: **Monologue to Dialogue**
Speaker 1: The crow sat on the tall tree's branch. The crow has elegant talons, and a good beak. The crow has ugly wings, and bad eyes.   **Speaker 2:** The delicious cheese was in the crow's beak. The hungry fox observed the crow. The fox has good claws, but bad teeth.   **Speaker 1:** The fox tried to discover for the fox to get the cheese. The fox came and stood under the tall tree. The fox looked toward the crow.   **Speaker 2:** The fox said the fox saw the crow. The fox said the crow's beauty was incomparable. The fox said the crow's plumage's hue was exquisite.
PYPER: **M2D + Stylistic Parameters**
Speaker 1: She sat on the tall tree's branch. She has elegant talons, and a good beak. She has ugly wings, and bad eyes.   **Speaker 2:** He has good claws, but bad teeth.   **Speaker 1:** What was in her beak?   **Speaker 2:** The delicious cheese was, i see, in her beak. Typical. Really ok, I do not remember what happened next? Do you want to know more about that?

Figure 2: The *Fox and the Crow* Story Transformation

Leonard, and Sheldon-Howard/Leonard. Note that the comparison is not symmetrical because in the survey we gave a "known" (reference) character, which is the first column in the table.

It is not surprising to see Penny being different from most of the male characters, as it is the premise of BBT. Raj is an exception, mainly due to his lack of (expressive) dialogue, though he is definitely different from Sheldon. It is also believable that Leonard is similar to many characters, as he is the most "normal" character out of the group.

We further explore a few characters below.

7.1 Penny

7.1.1 Perception of Penny in comparison to Leonard (most distinguishable)

Penny is one of the best expressed character in the experiment, missing only by one selection in comparison to Leonard (95.2%), and missing by two in comparison to Sheldon (90.5%). Here we take a look at the comparison with Leonard, where 20 (out of 21) Penny-modeled generated dialogue were rated more similar to Penny, and only 1 (out of 21) Leonard-modeled generated dialogue were rated more similar to Penny.

Overall, participants' perception of **Penny-modeled generated dialogue** seem to agree with Penny's personality, capturing her "bubbly, cheerfulness", as mentioned by one worker. Some no-

table descriptions include:

- talkative, randomness, random pauses, better wording, more personality   - seek feedback from others, lots of questions, not always sure of what she's saying, hesitation   - good mix of colloquialisms and Penny-like filler, some brief, fairly simple statements   - stand-out word choices: *magic, huh?, mhmm, let's see, that..., the crow needed what?, oh gosh, I mean, damn yeah*

Participants perceived **Leonard-modeled generated dialogue** as not suitable for Penny, mostly because of his bland language. Here are some notable descriptions:

- too simple, monotone, boring, direct, bare, straightforward, matter-of-fact, boxy, bland, not enough questioning for Penny   - too much adverb usage on precision or intellect for Penny   - not like Penny to use complex words and phrases   - not like Penny to use: *technically, darn*   - too rude for her to use, since she wants people to like her: *everybody knows that, obviously*

The MTurk worker of the one missed selection cited Penny being a very simple speaker, implying that her dialogue would contain brief and simple statements. While this is true, she also uses quite a bit of fillers and questions around her "simple" dialogue to sound chatty.

7.1.2 Perception of Penny in comparison to Bernadette (least distinguishable)

It is not surprising to see Penny being the least distinguishable with Bernadette (57.1%). Bernadette was introduced in the series as Penny's friend and coworker working as a waitress. Her role on the show seemed to be more similar to Penny (friendly

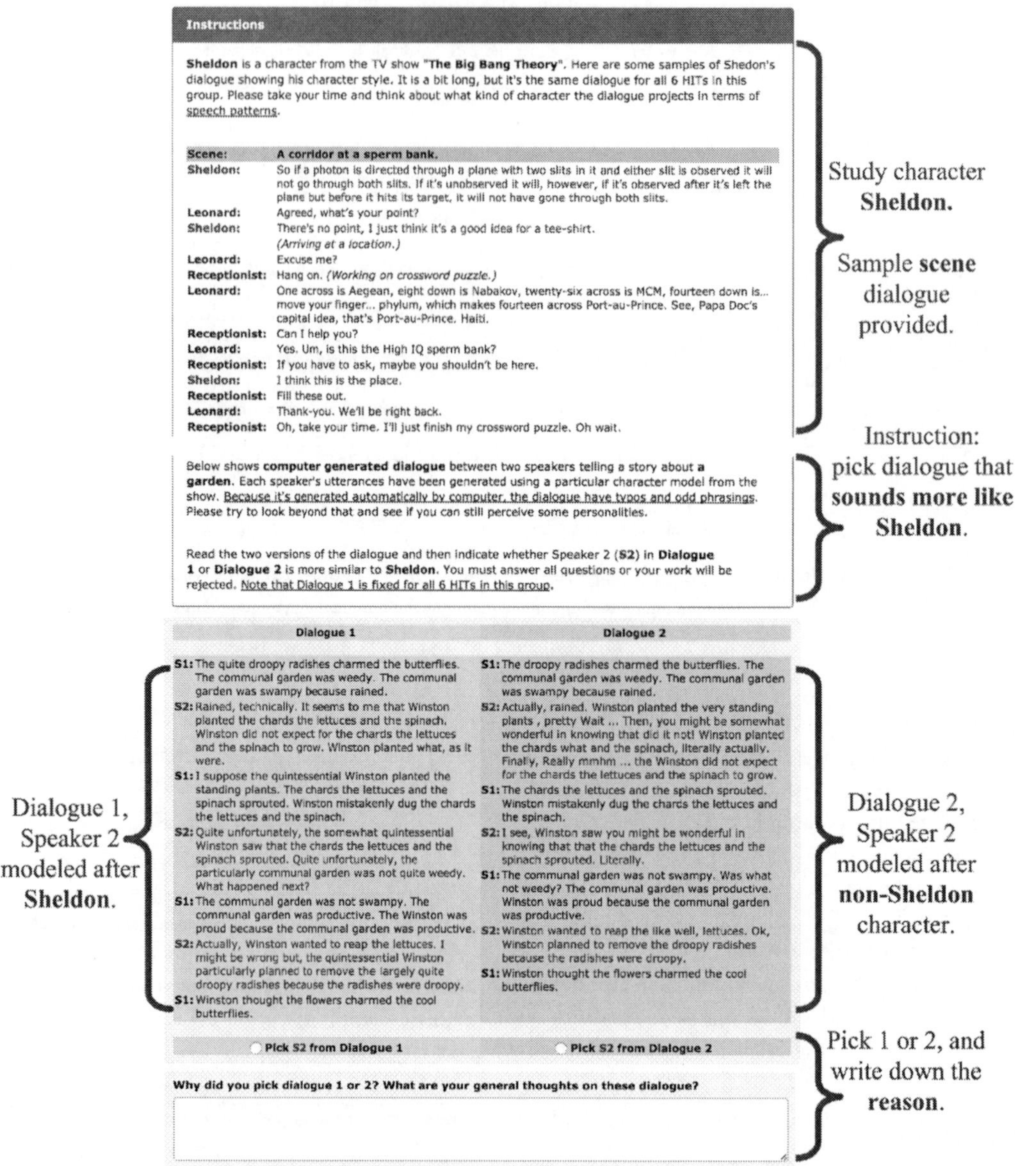

Figure 3: Amazon Mechanical Turk Survey (One HIT) Example

and sociable) than everyone else (nerdy and socially awkward), despite that she became a scientist eventually.

While the Bernadette-model contain chatty word choices (similar to Penny's), it also contains "intellect" word choices. However due to the randomness of the generated dialogue, where not all features are expressed/activated, some dialogue/story might not show enough of her nerdy side. For example, precise adverbs such as *essentially, particularly* are more likely to be used by a scientist/engineer (Bernadette) but not by Penny.

In terms of stories, Bug and Garden did the best at distinguished the character pair, while Employer and Storm did the worst (none of the Penny-modeled dialogue sounded like Penny).

7.2 Sheldon

7.2.1 Perception of Sheldon in comparison to Penny (most distinguishable)

With Sheldon differs the most with Penny (85.7%), we focus on comments by participants

Table 5: Characters and Stories MTurk Results by HITs

Each HIT had 3 participants, each indicated by a circle (○).
A solid circle (●) indicates the worker picked the "matched" generated dialogue to the original character.
Characters are listed in alphabetical order; circles are sorted by ● then ○
blue: best result; red: worst result

Character	compared-to	Bug	Employer	FoxCrow	Garden	Protest	Squirrel	Storm	#/% similar (out of 21)
Amy	Bernadette	●●●	●●●	●●○	●●●	●●●	●●●	●○○	18 / 85.7
	Howard	●○○	●●○	●●○	●●○	●●○	●●○	●○○	12 / 57.1
	Leonard	○○○	●●○	○○○	●●●	●●○	●●○	●○○	10 / 47.6
	Penny	●○○	●●○	●●○	●●○	●●○	●●○	●●○	13 / 61.9
	Raj	●○○	●●●	○○○	●●○	●●○	●●○	●●○	12 / 57.1
	Sheldon	●●○	●●○	●●●	●●●	●○○	●●○	○○○	13 / 61.9
	#/% similar (out of 18)	8 / 44.4	14 / 77.8	9 / 50.0	15 / 83.3	12 / 66.7	13 / 72.2	7 / 38.9	**78 / 61.9** (out of 126)
Bernadette	Amy	●●●	●●●	●●●	●●○	●●○	●●○	●●●	18 / 85.7
	Howard	●●●	●●●	●●○	●●●	●●○	●●○	●●●	18 / 85.7
	Leonard	●●○	●●○	●○○	●●●	●○○	●●○	●●○	13 / 61.9
	Penny	●●○	●○○	○○○	●○○	●●●	○○○	○○○	7 / 33.3
	Raj	●●○	●●●	●●●	○○○	●●○	●○○	●●●	14 / 66.7
	Sheldon	●●○	●●○	●○○	●●○	●●○	●●○	●●●	14 / 66.7
	#/% similar	14 / 77.8	14 / 77.8	10 / 55.6	11 / 61.1	12 / 66.7	9 / 50.0	14 / 77.8	**84 / 66.7**
Howard	Amy	●●○	●●○	●○○	●●○	●○○	●●○	●●○	12 / 57.1
	Bernadette	●●○	●●○	○○○	●●○	●○○	●●○	●●○	11 / 52.4
	Leonard	●●○	●●○	●○○	○○○	●○○	●●○	●●○	10 / 47.6
	Penny	●●●	●○○	●●○	●○○	●●●	●●○	●●●	15 / 71.4
	Raj	●●○	●●●	●○○	●○○	●●○	●●●	●○○	13 / 61.9
	Sheldon	●●○	●●○	●●●	●○○	●○○	●●○	●○○	12 / 57.1
	#/% similar	13 / 72.2	12 / 66.7	8 / 44.4	7 / 38.9	9 / 50.0	13 / 72.2	11 / 61.1	**73 / 57.9**
Leonard	Amy	●●○	●●○	●●○	●●○	●○○	○○○	●●●	12 / 57.1
	Bernadette	●○○	●●○	●●●	●●●	●○○	●●○	●●●	15 / 71.4
	Howard	●●○	●●●	●●●	●●●	●●●	●●○	●●●	19 / 90.5
	Penny	●●○	●●●	●●●	●●●	●●●	●●●	●●●	20 / 95.2
	Raj	●○○	●●●	●●○	●●●	●●○	●●●	●●○	16 / 76.2
	Sheldon	●●●	●●●	●●○	●●○	●●○	●●○	●●●	17 / 81.0
	#/% similar	11 / 61.1	16 / 88.9	15 / 83.3	16 / 88.9	12 / 66.7	12 / 66.7	17 / 94.4	**99 / 78.6**
Penny	Amy	●●●	●●●	●●●	●●●	●●●	●●●	○○○	18 / 85.7
	Bernadette	●●●	○○○	●●○	●●●	●●○	●●○	○○○	12 / 57.1
	Howard	●●●	●●●	●●○	●●●	●●●	●○○	●●○	17 / 81.0
	Leonard	●●●	●●●	●●○	●●●	●●●	●●●	●●●	20 / 95.2
	Raj	●●●	●●●	●●○	●●●	●●●	●●○	●●○	18 / 85.7
	Sheldon	●●●	●●●	●●○	●●●	●●●	●●●	●●○	19 / 90.5
	#/% similar	18 / 100	15 / 83.3	13 / 72.2	18 / 100	17 / 94.4	14 / 77.8	9 / 50.0	**104 / 82.5**
Raj	Amy	●●○	●○○	●●○	●○○	●○○	●○○	●○○	9 / 42.9
	Bernadette	●●○	●○○	●●○	●○○	●○○	●○○	●●○	10 / 47.6
	Howard	●○○	●○○	●●○	●●●	●●●	●○○	●●○	13 / 61.9
	Leonard	○○○	○○○	●●○	●●○	●○○	○○○	●○○	6 / 28.6
	Penny	●○○	●●○	●○○	○○○	●●○	●○○	●●●	10 / 47.6
	Sheldon	●●●	●●○	●●○	●●●	●○○	●●○	●○○	14 / 66.7
	#/% similar	9 / 50.0	7 / 38.9	11 / 61.1	10 / 55.6	9 / 50.0	6 / 33.3	10 / 55.6	**62 / 49.2**
Sheldon	Amy	●●●	●○○	○○○	●●●	●○○	●●○	●●●	13 / 61.9
	Bernadette	●●○	●●○	●●○	●●●	●●●	●●○	●●○	16 / 76.2
	Howard	●●○	●○○	●●○	●●●	●○○	●○○	○○○	10 / 47.6
	Leonard	●●○	●○○	●○○	●●●	●●○	●○○	○○○	10 / 47.6
	Penny	●●○	●●○	●●●	●●●	●●●	●●○	●●●	18 / 85.7
	Raj	●●●	●●○	●●○	●●○	○○○	●●○	○○○	11 / 52.4
	#/% similar	14 / 77.8	9 / 50.0	10 / 55.6	17 / 94.4	10 / 55.6	10 / 55.6	8 / 44.4	**78 / 61.9**
	#/% similar (out of 126)	87 / 69.0	87 / 69.0	76 / 60.3	94 / 74.6	81 / 64.3	77 / 61.1	76 / 60.3	**578 / 65.5** (out of 882)

Table 6: Most/Least Distinguishable Characters

Ref. Char	Most distinguishable with	Least distinguishable with
Amy	Bernadette (85.7%)	**Leonard** (47.6%)
Bernadette	Amy, Howard (85.7%)	Penny (33.3%)
Howard	**Penny** (71.4%)	**Leonard** (47.6%)
Leonard	**Penny** (95.2%)	Amy (57.1%)
Penny	Leonard (95.2%)	Bernadette (57.1%)
Raj	Sheldon (66.7%)	**Leonard** (28.6%)
Sheldon	**Penny** (85.7%)	Howard, **Leonard** (47.6%)

who confused the two characters. It turns out that certain phrases intended for Penny were perceived as "arrogant" when spoken by Sheldon. Here are the actual comments by participants:

- *"mmhm..."* I can picture coming from Sheldon in an irritated manner. *"...you are kidding, right"* would be said by Sheldon in an arrogant and condescending manner.
- *"You might be interested in knowing..."* sounds like an arrogant Sheldon line, followed by the *"Oh God..."* I can actually picture Sheldon saying this line.
- *"You might be interested in knowing..."* is used twice in Dialogue 2, and would be something Sheldon might say to make another person feel inferior.

91

7.2.2 Perception of Sheldon in comparison to Leonard (least distinguishable)

As roommates and colleague at work, their similarity is understandable. Here are summarized comments by participants describing the dialogue:

```
- matter-of-fact, straightforward
- clear, unhesitant
- shorter, more direct sentences; to the point
- use "technically"
- do not use a long string of adjectives
```

7.3 Leonard

For Leonard, Penny is considered the most distinguishable. Even though Leonard is considered less nerdy than other male characters, his language is still very different from Penny's.

Amy being the least distinguishable for Leonard is also believable. Amy, despite her language closely resembles Sheldon, is also interested in relationships and friendship (e.g., with Penny and Bernadette).

Here are some participants' comments on perceiving Amy's dialogue as Leonard's dialogue:

```
- intelligently spoken but also have a natural tone to them
- quick and to the point without over complicating things
- "I mean..." sounds like Leonard in his somewhat whiny manner
- Leonard sometimes smooths things over for Sheldon so he doesn't get
upset. I think he would soften some things he says when he uses "I
think" or "I mean"
- intelligent yet normal way of speaking
- both dialogue work okay really
```

7.4 Other Observations

Leonard and Penny represent the opposite-attracts couple. The biggest differentiating factor is that Penny's dialogue are perceived as being more emotional than Leonard's.

A general theme for Leonard's dialogue is that his speech pattern is "normal", implying that everyone else has a more stylized dialogue. This is an interesting observation because Leonard is not "normal" relative to the general population; he is being characterized as a typical nerd. Yet he is "normal" relative to his friends and therefore easier to identify on many cases.

According to (Brooks and Hébert, 2006), individual's social identities are largely shaped by the popular media: what it means to be white, black, male, female, heterosexual, homosexual, etc. Since characters are expressed through language and therefore connected to characters' identity as an individual and as part of a community (Hurst, 2011), the media such as television often provides the first (and sometimes the only) impression of certain groups of people.

In the context of BBT and the significant features we used to represent characters, it seems that Penny's language represents the typical female as identified by Lackoff (Lakoff, 1973): hedging, emotional emphasis, adjectives, etc. This is in contrast with the male characters as scientists, who tend to be more matter-of-fact.

Do scientists talk differently from the general population? Our results answer with a "yes" in that Penny's language is mostly in contrast with male scientists' language. Such contrast is also reflected in the real world (e.g., % of scientists versus. U.S. population believe in climate change).

What makes the show interesting is the "in-between" characters: female scientists Amy and Bernadette. The perception of the dialogue showed that the Penny-Bernadette, and Leonard-Amy pairs shared some similar language. With the right intention and scripts, the media can help narrow the perception and narrative gap between scientists and the general public.

8 Conclusion and Future Work

We explored character voice from the TV show BBT by building stylistic models relating character dialogue's linguistic features to natural language generation decisions. These models are then used to manipulate an expressive NLG to transform regular sentences into an expressive version. The generated, expressive dialogue are then used in a perceptual experiment to see how users perceive expressed personalities. Our results were encouraging in that people were able to perceive differences among characters, though some better than others. For the ones that were hard to distinguish, participants' comments provided great insight into how to better express the extracted features through NLG.

One possible future work is to use people's blogs as a source to create speaker-specific models. Another possible future work is to use character models to drive the monologue-to-dialogue process that created the stories used in our experiment. For example, if the character sounds mostly negative, the process can try to allocate all negative sentences to a story character's dialogue.

We believe our work can be applied to storytelling applications, such as video games, interactive narrative, chatbots, or education systems where dialogue with personalities may improve user experience, in a more controllable way (than using a neural network for generation, for example).

References

Monika Bednarek. 2011a. The language of fictional television: a case study of the dramedy gilmore girls. *English Text Construction* 4(1):54–83.

Monika Bednarek. 2011b. The stability of the televisual character: A corpus stylistic case study. *R. Piazza, M* .

Monika Bednarek. 2012. Constructing "nerdiness": Characterisation in the big bang theory. *Multilingua* 31(2-3):199–229.

Kevin K Bowden, Grace I Lin, Lena I Reed, Jean E Fox Tree, and Marilyn A Walker. 2016. M2d: Monolog to dialog generation for conversational story telling. In *Interactive Storytelling: 9th International Conference on Interactive Digital Storytelling, ICIDS 2016, Los Angeles, CA, USA, November 15–18, 2016, Proceedings 9*. Springer, pages 12–24.

Dwight E Brooks and Lisa P Hébert. 2006. Gender, race, and media representation. *Handbook of gender and communication* 16:297–317.

Claudia Bubel. 2005. *The linguistic construction of character relations in TV drama: Doing friendship in Sex and the City*. Ph.D. thesis, Universität des Saarlandes.

D.K. Elson and K.R. McKeown. 2009. A tool for deep semantic encoding of narrative texts. In *Proceedings of the ACL-IJCNLP 2009 Software Demonstrations*. Association for Computational Linguistics, pages 9–12.

Andrew S Gordon, Qun Cao, and Reid Swanson. 2007. Automated story capture from internet weblogs. In *Proceedings of the 4th international conference on Knowledge capture*. ACM, pages 167–168.

M Hurst. 2011. *Language, Gender, and Community in Late Twentieth-century Fiction: American Voices and American Identities*. Springer.

Robin Lakoff. 1973. Language and woman's place. *Language in society* 2(1):45–79.

Benoit Lavoie and Owen Rambow. 1997. A fast and portable realizer for text generation systems. In *Proceedings of the fifth conference on Applied natural language processing*. Association for Computational Linguistics, pages 265–268.

Boyang Li, Mohini Thakkar, Yijie Wang, and Mark O Riedl. 2014. Data-driven alibi story telling for social believability. In *Proceedings of the FDG 2014 Social Believability in Games Workshop*. Citeseer.

G.I. Lin and M.A. Walker. 2011. All the world's a stage: Learning character models from film. In *Proceedings of the Seventh AI and Interactive Digital Entertainment Conference, AIIDE*. volume 11.

François Mairesse and Marilyn Walker. 2007. Personage: Personality generation for dialogue. In *Annual Meeting-Association For Computational Linguistics*. volume 45, page 496.

James W Pennebaker, Martha E Francis, and Roger J Booth. 2001. Linguistic inquiry and word count: Liwc 2001. *Mahway: Lawrence Erlbaum Associates* 71:2001.

Paulo Quaglio. 2009. *Television Dialogue: The sitcom Friends vs. natural conversation.*. John Benjamins Publishing Company.

Elena Rishes, Stephanie M Lukin, David K Elson, and Marilyn A Walker. 2013. Generating different story tellings from semantic representations of narrative. In *Interactive Storytelling*, Springer, pages 192–204.

Susan Schreibman, Ray Siemens, and John Unsworth. 2008. *A companion to digital humanities*. John Wiley & Sons.

Efstathios Stamatatos. 2009. A survey of modern authorship attribution methods. *Journal of the American Society for information Science and Technology* 60(3):538–556.

M.A. Walker, R. Grant, J. Sawyer, G.I. Lin, N. Wardrip-Fruin, and M. Buell. 2011. Perceived or not perceived: Film character models for expressive nlg. *International Conference on Interactive Digital Storytelling* .

Controlling Linguistic Style Aspects in Neural Language Generation

Jessica Ficler and **Yoav Goldberg**
Computer Science Department
Bar-Ilan University
Israel
{jessica.ficler, yoav.goldberg}@gmail.com

Abstract

Most work on neural natural language generation (NNLG) focus on controlling the content of the generated text. We experiment with controlling several stylistic aspects of the generated text, in addition to its content. The method is based on conditioned RNN language model, where the desired content as well as the stylistic parameters serve as conditioning contexts. We demonstrate the approach on the movie reviews domain and show that it is successful in generating coherent sentences corresponding to the required linguistic style and content.

1 Introduction

The same message (e.g. expressing a positive sentiment towards the plot of a movie) can be conveyed in different ways. It can be long or short, written in a professional or colloquial style, written in a personal or impersonal voice, and can make use of many adjectives or only few.

Consider for example the following to sentences:

(1) *"A genuinely unique, full-on sensory experience that treads its own path between narrative clarity and pure visual expression."*
(2) *"OMG... This movie actually made me cry a little bit because I laughed so hard at some parts lol."*

They are both of medium length, but the first appears to be written by a professional critic, and uses impersonal voice and many adjectives; while the second is written in a colloquial style, using a personal voice and few adjectives.

In a text generation system, it is desirable to have control over such stylistic aspects of the text: style variations are used to express the social meanings of a message, and controlling the style of a text is necessary for appropriately conveying a message in a way that is adequate to the social context (Biber and Conrad, 2009; Niederhoffer and Pennebaker, 2002). This work focuses on generating text while allowing control of its stylistic properties.

The recent introduction of recurrent neural language models and recurrent sequence-to-sequence architectures to NLP brought with it a surge of work on natural language generation. Most of these research efforts focus on controlling the *content* of the generated text (Lipton et al., 2015; Kiddon et al., 2016; Lebret et al., 2016; Kiddon et al., 2016; Tang et al., 2016; Radford et al., 2017), while a few model more stylistic aspects of the generated text such as the identity of the speaker in a dialog setting (Li et al., 2016); the politeness of the generated text or the text length in a machine-translation setting (Sennrich et al., 2016; Kikuchi et al., 2016); or the tense in generated movie reviews (Hu et al., 2017). Each of these works targets a single, focused stylistic aspect of the text. *Can we achieve finer-grained control over the generated outcome, controlling several stylistic aspects simultaneously?*

We explore a simple neural natural-language generation (NNLG) framework that allows for high-level control on the generated content (similar to previous work) as well as control over multiple stylistic properties of the generated text. We show that we can indeed achieve control over each of the individual properties.

As most recent efforts, our model (section 3) is based on a conditioned language model, in which the generated text is conditioned on a context vector.[1] In our case, the context vector encodes a set

---

[1] See (Hoang et al., 2016) for other conditioning models.

Proceedings of the Workshop on Stylistic Variation, pages 94–104
Copenhagen, Denmark, September 7–11, 2017. ©2017 Association for Computational Linguistics

of desired properties that we want to be present in the generated text.[2] At training time, we work in a fully supervised setup, in which each sentence is labeled with a set of linguistic properties we want to condition on. These are encoded into the context vector, and the model is trained to generate the sentence based on them. At test time, we can set the values of the individual properties to get the desired response. As we show in section 6.3, the model generalizes fairly well, allowing the generation of text with property combinations that were not seen during training.

The main challenge we face is thus obtaining the needed annotations for training time. In section 4 we show how such annotations can be obtained from meta-data or using specialized text-based heuristics.

Recent work (Hu et al., 2017) tackles a similar goal to ours. They propose a novel generative model combining variational auto-encoders and holistic attribute discriminators, in order to achieve individual control on different aspects of the generated text. Their experiments condition on two aspects of the text (sentiment and tense), and train and evaluate on sentences of up to 16 words. In contrast, we propose a much simpler model and focus on its application in a realistic setting: we use all naturally occurring sentence lengths, and generate text according to two content-based parameters (sentiment score and topic) and four stylistic parameters (the length of the text, whether it is descriptive, whether it is written in a personal voice, and whether it is written in professional style). Our model is based on a well-established technology - conditioned language models that are based on Long Short-Term Memory (LSTM), which was proven as strong and effective sequence model.

We perform an extensive evaluation, and verify that the model indeed learns to associate the different parameters with the correct aspects of the text, and is in many cases able to generate sentences that correspond to the requested parameter values. We also show that conditioning on the given properties in a conditioned language model indeed achieve better perplexity scores compared to an unconditioned language model trained on the entire dataset, and also compared to unconditioned models that are trained on subsets of the data that

correspond to a particular conditioning set. Finally, we show that the model is able to generalize, i.e., to generate sentences for combinations that were not observed in training.

2 Task Description and Definition

Our goal is to generate natural language text that conforms to a set of content-based and stylistic properties. The generated text should convey the information requested by the content properties, while conforming to the style requirements posed by the style properties.

For example in the movie reviews domain, `theme` is a content parameter indicating the topical aspect which the review refers to (i.e. the plot, the acting, and so on); and `descriptive` is a style parameter that indicates whether the review text uses many adjectives. The sentence *"A wholly original, well-acted, romantic comedy that's elevated by the modest talents of a lesser known cast."* corresponds to `theme:acting` and `descriptive:true`, as it includes many descriptions and refers to the acting, while the sentence *"In the end, there are some holes in the story, but it's an exciting and tender film."* corresponds to `theme:plot` and `descriptive:false`.

More formally, we assume a set of k parameters $\{p_1, \ldots, p_k\}$, each parameter p_i with a set of possible values $\{v_1, \ldots, v_{p_i}\}$. Then, given a specific assignment to these values our goal is to generate a text that is compatible with the parameters values. Table 1 lists the full set of parameters and values we consider in this work, all in the movie reviews domain. In section 4 we discuss in detail the different parameters and how we obtain their values for the texts in our reviews corpus.

To give a taste of the complete task, we provide two examples of possible value assignments and sentences corresponding to them:

Type	Parameter	Value (1)	Value (2)
Content	Theme	Acting	Other
Content	Sentiment	Positive	Negative
Style	Professional	True	False
Style	Personal	False	True
Style	Length	21-40 words	11-20 words
Style	Descriptive	False	True

<u>Sentences for value set 1:</u>

- "This movie is excellent, the actors aren't all over the place ,but the movie has a lot of fun, exploring the lesson in a way that they can hold their own lives."

---

[2] Another view is that of an encoder-decoder model, in which the encoder component encodes the set of desired properties.

	Parameter	Description	Source	Possible values	Examples
Style	Professional	Whether the review is written in the style of a professional critic or not	meta-data	False	"So glad to see this movie !!"
				True	"This is a breath of fresh air, it's a welcome return to the franchise's brand of satirical humor."
	Personal	Whether the review describes subjective experience (written in personal voice) or not	content derived	False	"Very similar to the book."
				True	"I could see the movie again, "The Kid With Me" is a very good film."
	Length	Number of words	content derived	$\leq$ 10 words / 11-20 words / 21-40 words / > 40 words	
	Descriptive	Whether the review is in descriptive style or not	content derived	True	"Such a hilarious and funny romantic comedy."
				False	"A definite must see for fans of anime fans, pop culture references and animation with a good laugh too."
Content	Sentiment	The score that the reviewer gave the movie	meta-data	Positive	"In other words: "The Four" is so much to keep you on the edge of your seat."
				Neutral	"While the film doesn't quite reach the level of sugar fluctuations, it's beautifully animated."
				Negative	"At its core ,it's a very low-budget movie that just seems to be a bunch of fluff."
	Theme	Whether the sentence's content is about the *Plot, Acting, Production, Effects* or none of these (*Other*)	content derived	Plot	"The characters were great and the storyline had me laughing out loud at the beginning of the movie."
				Acting	"The only saving grace is that the rest of the cast are all excellent and the pacing is absolutely flawless."
				Production	"If you're a Yorkshire fan, you won't be disappointed, and the director's magical."
				Effects	"Only saving grace is the sound effects."
				Other	"I'm afraid that the movie is aimed at kids and adults weren't sure what to say about it."

Table 1: Parameters and possible values in the movie-reviews domain.

- "It's a realistic and deeply committed performance from the opening shot, the movie gives an excellent showcase for the final act, and the visuals are bold and daring."

Sentences for value set 2:

- "My biggest gripe is that the whole movie is pretty absurd and I thought it was a little too predictable."
- "The first half is pretty good and I was hoping for a few funny moments but not funny at all."

3 Conditioned Language Model

Like in previous neural language-generation work (Lipton et al., 2015; Tang et al., 2016), our model is also a conditioned language model. In a regular language model (LM), each token w_t is conditioned on the previous tokens, and the probability of a sentence $w_1, ..., w_n$ is given by:

$$P(w_1, ..., w_n) = \Pi_{t=1}^n P(w_t | w_1, \ldots w_{t-1}) \quad (1)$$

In a conditioned language model, we add an additional conditioning context, c:

$$P(w_1, ..., w_n | c) = \Pi_{t=1}^n P(w_t | w_1, \ldots w_{t-1}, c) \quad (2)$$

Each token in the sentence is conditioned on the previous ones, as well the additional context c.

A conditioned language model can be implemented using an recurrent neural network language model (RNN-LM, (Mikolov et al., 2010)), where the context **c** is a vector that is concatenated to the input vector at each time step.

Conditioned language models were shown to be effective for natural language generation. We differ from previous work by the choice of conditioning contexts, and by conditioning on many parameters simultaneously.

In our case, the condition vector **c** encodes the desired textual properties. Each parameter value is associated with an embedding vector, and **c** is a concatenation of these embedding vectors. The vector **c** is fed into the RNN at each step, concatenated to the previous word in the sequence.

Technical Details We use an LSTM-based language model (Hochreiter and Schmidhuber, 1997), and encode the vocabulary using Byte Pair Encoding (BPE), which allows representation of an open vocabulary through a fixed-size vocabulary by splitting rare words into subword units, providing a convenient way of dealing with rare words. Further details regarding layer sizes, training regime, vocabulary size and so on are provided in the supplementary material.

4 Data-set Collection and Annotation

For training the model, we need a dataset of review texts, each annotated with a value assignment to each of the style and the content parameters. We obtain these values from two sources: (1) We derive it from meta-data associated with the review, when available. (2) We extract it from the review text using a heuristic. We use three kinds of heuristics: based on lists of content-words; based on the existence of certain function words; and based on the distribution on part-of-speech tags. These annotations may contain noise, and indeed some of our heuristics are not very tight. We demonstrate that we can achieve good performance despite the noise. Naturally, improving the heuristics is likely to results in improved performance.

Our reviews corpus is based on the Rotten-Tomatoes website.[3] We collected 1,002,625 movie reviews for 7,500 movies and split them into sentences. Each sentence is then annotated according to four style parameters (`professional`, `personal`, `descriptive` and `length`) and two content parameters (`sentiment` and `theme`). The meanings of these properties and how we obtain values for them are described below.

4.1 Annotations Based on Meta-data

Professional indicates whether the review is written in a professional (`true`) or a colloquial (`false`) style. We label sentences as `professional:true` if it is written by either (1) a reviewer that is a professional critic; (2) a reviewer that is marked as a "super-reviewer" on the RottenTomatoes website (a title given to reviewers who write high-quality reviews). Other sentences are labeled as `professional:false`.

Sentiment reflects the grade that was given by the review writer. Possible values for grade are: `positive`, `neutral`, `negative` or `none`. In audience reviews the movies are rated by the reviewer on a scale of 0 to 5 stars. In critic reviews, the score was taken from the original review (which is external to the rotten-tomatoes website). We normalized the critics scores to be on 0-5 scale. We then consider reviews with grade 0-2 as `negative`, 3 as `neutral` and 4-5 as `positive`. Cases where no score information was available are labeled as `none`.[4]

4.2 Annotations Derived from Text

Length We count the number of tokens in the sentence and associate each sentence to one of four bins: $\leq$10, 11-20, 21-40, >40.

Personal whether the sentence is written in a personal voice, indicating a subjective point of view (*"I thought it was a good movie."*, *"Just not my cup of tea."*) or not (*"Overall, it is definitely worth watching."*, *"The movie doesn't bring anything new."*), We label sentences that include the personal pronoun or possessive (*"I"*, *"my"*) as `personal:true` and others as `personal:false`.

Theme the aspect of the movie that the sentence refers to. The possible values are `plot`, `acting`, `production` and `effects`. We assign a category to a sentence using word lists. We went over the frequent words in the corpus, and looked for words that we believe are indicative of the different aspects (i.e., for `plot` this includes words such as *sciprt, story, subplots*. The complete word lists are available in the supplementary material). Each sentence was labeled with the category that has the most words in the sentence. Sentences that do not include any words from our lists are labeled as `other`.

Descriptive whether the sentence is descriptive (*"A warm and sweet, funny movie."*) or not (*"It's one of the worst movies of the year, but it's not a total waste of time."*), Our (somewhat simplistic) heuristic is based on the premise that descriptive texts make heavy use of adjectives. We labeled a sentence as `descriptive:true` if at least

[4]Note that while the sentiment scores are assigned to a complete review, we associate them here with individual sentences. This is a deficiency in the heuristic, which may explain some of the failures observed in section 6.1.

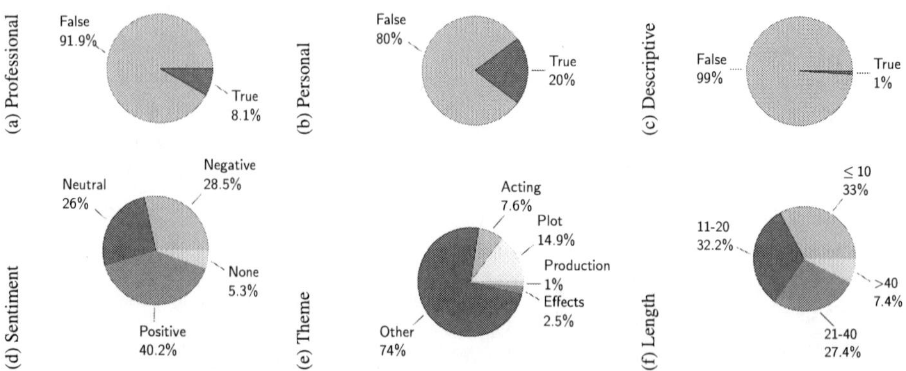

Figure 1: Movie reviews data-set statistics.

35% of its part-of-speech sequence tags are adjectives (JJ). All other sentences were considered as non-descriptive.

4.3 Dataset Statistics

Our final data-set includes 2,773,435 sentences where each sentence is labeled with the 6 parameters. We randomly divided the data-set to training (#2,769,138), development (#2,139) and test (#2,158) sets. Figure 1 shows the distribution of the different properties in the dataset.

5 Evaluating Language Model Quality

In our first set of experiments, we measure the quality of the conditioned language model in terms of test-set perplexity.

5.1 Conditioned vs. Unconditioned

Our model is a language model that is conditioned on various parameters. As a sanity check, we verify that knowing the parameters indeed helps in achieving better language modeling results. We compare the dev-set and test-set perplexities of our conditioned language model to an unconditioned (regular) language model trained on the same data. The results, summarized in the following table, show that knowing the correct parameter values indeed results in better perplexity.

	dev	test
Not-conditioned	25.8	24.4
Conditioned	**24.8**	**23.3**

Table 2: Conditioned and not-conditioned language model perplexities on the development and test sets.

5.2 Conditioned vs. Dedicated LMs

A second natural baseline to the conditioned LM is to train a separate unconditioned LM on a subset of the data. For example, if we are interested in generating sentences with the properties `personal:false`, `sentiment:pos`, `professional:false`, `theme:other` and `length:≤10`, we will train a dedicated LM on just the sentences that fit these characteristics.

We hypothesize that the conditioned LM trained on all the data will be more effective than a dedicated LM, as it will be able to generalize across properties-combinations, and share data between the different settings. In this set of experiment, we verify this hypothesis.

For a set of parameters and values $\{p_1, p_2, \cdots p_n\}$, we train n sub-models where each sub-model m_i is trained on the subset of sentences that match parameters $\{p_1, p_2, \cdots p_i\}$. For example, given the set of parameters values as above, we train 5 sub-models: the first on data with `personal:false` only, the second on data with `persoal:false` and `sentiment:positive`, etc. As we add parameters, the size of the training set of the sub-model decreases.

For each dedicated sub-model, we measure its perplexity on the test-set sentences that match the criteria, and compare it to a conditioned LM with these criteria, and to an unconditioned language model. We do this for 4 different parameter-sets. Figure 2 presents the results.

The results indicate that when only few conditioning parameters are needed, and if the coverage of the parameter combination in the training set is large enough, the dedicated LM approach in-

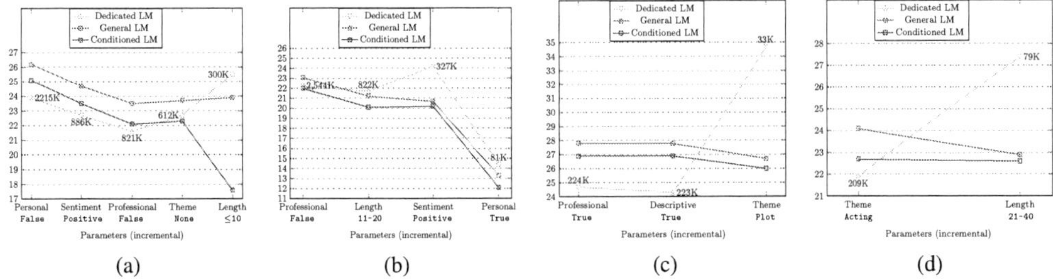

Figure 2: Perplexities of conditioned, unconditioned and dedicated language models for various parameter combinations. The numbers on the dedicated-model line indicates the number of sentences that the sub-model was trained on.

deed outperforms the conditioned LM. This is the case in the first three sub-models in 2a, and the first two sub-models in 2c. With few conditioning criteria, the dedicated LM approach is effective. However, it is not scalable. As we increase the number of conditioning factors, the amount of available training data to the dedicated model drops, and so does the modeling quality. In contrast, the conditioned model manages to generalize from sentences with different sets of properties, and is effective also with large number of conditioning factors. We thus conclude that for our use case, in which we need to condition on many different aspects of the generated sentence, the conditioned LM is far more suitable than the dedicated LM.

5.3 Conditioned vs. Flipped Conditioning

The previous experiments show that a conditioned model outperforms an unconditioned one. Here, we focus on the effect of the individual conditioning parameters. We compare the perplexity when using the correct conditioning values to the perplexity achieved when flipping the parameter value to an incorrect one. We do that for parameters that have opposing values: `personal`, `professional`, `sentiment` and `descriptive`. The following table summarizes the results:

Correct Value	23.3
Replacing Descriptive with non-Descriptive	27.2
Replacing Personal	27.5
Replacing Professional	25
Replacing Sentiment `Pos` with `Neg`	24.3

Table 3: Test-set perplexities when supplying the correct parameter values and when supplying the opposite values.

There is a substantial drop in quality (increase in perplexity) when flipping the parameter values. The drop is smallest for sentiment, and largest for descriptiveness and personal voice. We conclude that the model distinguishes descriptive text and personal voice better than it distinguishes sentiment and professional text.

6   Evaluating the Generated Sentences

In section 5.3 we verified the effectiveness of the conditioned model by showing that flipping a conditioning parameter value results in worse perplexity. However, we still need to verify that the model indeed associates each parameter with the correct behavior. In this set of experiments, we use the model to generate random sentences with different conditioning properties, and measure how well they match the requested behavior.

We generated 3,285 sentences according to the following protocol: for each property-combination attested in the development set, we generated 1,000 random sentences conditioned on these properties. We then sorted the generated sentences according to their probability, and chose the top $k = (c_f/m_f) * 100$ sentences, where c_f is the frequency of the property-combination in the dev set and m_f is the frequency of the most frequent property-combination in the dev set.

This process resulted in 3,285 high-scoring but diverse sentences, with properties that are distributed according to the properties distribution in the development set.

6.1   Capturing Individual Properties

Length   We measure the average, minimum and maximum lengths, and deviation of the sentences that were generated for a requested length value. The following table summarizes the results:

Requested Length	Avg	Min	Max	Deviation$_{m=2}$
<=10	7.6	1	21	0.2 %
11-20	20.6	5	25	2.6 %
21-40	34	7	49	0.6 %

Table 4: Average, minimum and maximum lengths of the sentences generated according to the correspond length value; as well as deviation percentage with margin (m) of 2.

The average length fits the required range for each of the values and the percentage of sentences that exceed the limits with margin 2 is between 0.2% to 2.6%.

Descriptive We measure the percentage of sentences that are considered as descriptive (containing >35% adjectives) when requesting `descriptive:true`, and when requesting `descriptive:false`. When requesting descriptive text, **85.7%** of the generated sentences fit the descriptiveness criteria. When requesting non-descriptive text, **96%** of the generated sentences are non-descriptive according to our criteria.

Personal Voice We measure the percentage of sentences that are considered as personal voice (containing the pronouns *I* or *my*) when requesting `personal:true`, and when requesting `personal:false`. **100%** of the sentence for which we requested personal voice were indeed in personal voice. When requesting non-personal text, **99.85%** of the sentences are indeed non-personal.

Theme For each of the possible theme values, we compute the proportion of the sentences that were generated with the corresponding value. The confusion matrix in the following table

shows that the vast majority of sentences are generated according to the requested theme.

Requested value	% Plot	% Acting	% Prod	% Effects	% Other
Plot	98.7	0.8	0	0.2	0.3
Acting	2.5	95.3	0	0.6	1.6
Production	0	0	97.4	2.6	0
Effects	0	5.9	0	91.7	2.4
Other	0.04	0.03	0	0.03	99.9

Table 5: Percentage of generated sentences from each theme, when requesting a given theme value.

Professional The `professional` property of the generated sentences could not be evaluated au-

tomatically, and we thus performed manual evaluation using Mechanical Turk. We randomly created 1000 sentence-pairs where one is generated with `professional:true` and the other with `professional:false` (the rest of the property values were chosen randomly). For example in the following sentence-pair the first is generated with `professional:true` and the second with `professional:false`:

(t) *"This film has a certain sense of imagination and a sobering look at the clandestine indictment."*
(f) *"I know it's a little bit too long, but it's a great movie to watch !!!!"*

The annotators were asked to determine which of the sentences was written by a professional critic. Each of the pairs was annotated by 5 different annotators. When taking a majority vote among the annotators, they were able to tell apart the professional from non-professional sentences generated sentences in **72.1%** of the cases.

When examining the cases where the annotators failed to recognise the desired writing style, we saw that in a few cases the sentence that was generated for `professional:true` was indeed not professional enough (e.g. *"Looking forward to the trailer."*, and that in many cases, both sentences could indeed be considered as either professional or not, as in the following examples:

(t) *"This is a cute movie with some funny moments, and some of the jokes are funny and entertaining."*
(f) *"Absolutely amazing story of bravery and dedication."*

(t) *"A good film for those who have no idea what's going on, but it's a fun adventure."*
(f) *"An insult to the audience's intelligence."*

Sentiment To measure `sentiment` generation quality, we again perform manual annotations using Mechanical Turk. We randomly created 300 pairs of generated sentences for each of the following settings: `positive/negative`, `positive/neutral` and `negative/neutral`. The annotators were asked to mark which of the reviewers liked the movie more than the other. Each of the pairs was annotated by 5 different annotators and we choose by a majority vote. The annotators correctly identified **86.3%** of the sentence in the Positive/Negative case, **63%** of the sentences in the Positive/Neutral case, and **69.7%** of the sentences in the `negative/neutral` case.

Below are some examples for cases where the annotators failed to recognize the intended sentiment:

(Pos) *"It's a shame that this film is not as good as the previous film, but it still delivers."*
(Neg) *"The premise is great, the acting is not bad, but the special effects are so bad."*

(Pos) *"The story line is a bit predictable but it's a nice one, sweet and hilarious in its own right."*
(Neg) *"It's a welcome return to form an episode of Snow White, and it turns in a great way."*

6.2 Examples of Generated Sentences

All of the examples throughout the paper were generated by the conditioned LM. Additional examples are available in the supplementary material.

6.3 Generalization Ability

Finally, we test the ability of the model to generalize: can it generate sentences for parameter combinations it has not seen in training? To this end, we removed from the training set the 75,421 sentences which were labeled as `theme:plot` and `personal:true`, and re-trained a conditioned LM. The trained model did see 336,567 examples of `theme:plot` and 477,738 examples of `personal:true`, but has never seen examples where both conditions hold together. We then asked the trained model to generate sentences with these parameter values. **100%** of the generated sentences indeed contained personal pronouns, and **82.4%** of them fit the `theme:plot` criteria (in comparison, a conditioned model trained on *all* the training data managed to fit the `theme:plot` criteria in **97.8%** of the cases). Some generated sentence examples are:

"Some parts weren't as good as I thought it would be and the acting and script were amazing."

"I had a few laughs and the plot was great, but the movie was very predictable."

"I really liked the story and the performances were likable and the chemistry between the two leads is great."

"I've never been a fan of the story, but this movie is a great film that is a solid performance from Brie Larson and Jacob Tremblay."

7 Related Work

In neural-network based models for language generation, most work focus on content that need to be conveyed in the generated text. Similar to our modeling approach, (Lipton et al., 2015; Tang et al., 2016) generates reviews conditioned on parameters such as category, and numeric rating scores. Some work in neural generation for dialog (Wen et al., 2015; Dušek and Jurcicek, 2016b,a) condition on a dialog act ("request", "inform") and a set of key,value pairs of information to be conveyed ("price=low, food=italian, near=citycenter"). The conditioning context is encoded either similarly to our approach, or by encoding the desired information as a string and using sequence-to-seqeunce modeling with attention. Mei et al. (2016) condition the content on a set of key,value pairs using an encoder-decoder architecture with a coarse-to-fine attention mechanism. Kiddon et al. (2016) attempt to generate a recipe given a list of ingredients that should be mentioned in the text, tracking the ingredients that were already mentioned to avoid repetitions. Lebret et al. (2016) condition on structured information in Wikipedia infoboxes for generating textual biographies. [5] These work attempt to control the content of the generated text, but not its style.

In other works, the conditioning context correspond to a specific writer or a group of writers. In generation of conversational dialog, Li et al. (2016) condition the text on the speaker's identity. While the conditioning is meant for improving the factual consistency of the utterances (i.e., keeping track of age, gender, location), it can be considered as conditioning on stylistic factors (capturing personal style and dialect). A recent work that explicitly controls the style of the generated text was introduced by Sennrich et al. (2016) in the context of Machine Translation. Their model translates English to German with a feature that encodes whether the generated text (in German) should express politeness. All these works, with the exception of Sennrich et al condition on parameters that were extracted from meta-data or some database, while Sennrich et al heuristically extracts the politeness information from the training data. Our

---

[5]Recent work by Radford et al. (2017) trained an unconditioned LSTM language model on movie reviews, and found in a post-hoc analysis a single hidden-layer dimension that allows controling the sentiment of the generated reviews by fixing its value. While intriguuing, it is not a reliable method of deriving controllable generation models.

work is similar to the approach of Sennrich et al but extends it by departing from machine translation, conditioning on numerous stylistic aspects of the generated text, and incorporating both metadata and heuristically derived properties.

The work of Hu et al. (2017) features a VAE based method coupled with a discriminator network that tackles the same problem as ours: conditioning on multiple aspects of the generated text. The Variational component allows for easy sampling of examples from the resulting model, and the discriminator network directs the training process to associate the desired behavior with the conditioning parameters. Compared to our work, the VAE component is indeed a more elegant solution to generating a diverse set of sentences. However, the approach does not seem to be scalable: Hu et al. (2017) restrict themselves to sentences of up to length 16, and only two conditioning aspects (sentiment and tense). We demonstrate that our conditioned LSTM-LM appraoch easily scales to naturally-occuring sentence lengths, and allows control of 6 individual aspects of the generated text, without requiring a dedicated discriminator network. The incorporation of a variational component is an interesting avenue for future work.

In Pre-neural Text Generation The incorporation of stylistic aspects was discussed from very early on (McDonald and Pustejovsky, 1985). Some works tackling stylistic control of text produced in a rule-based generation system include the works of Power et al. (2003); Reiter and Williams (2010); Hovy (1987); Bateman and Paris (1989) (see (Mairesse and Walker, 2011) for a comprehensive review). Among these, the work of Power et al. (2003), like ours, allows the user to control various stylistic aspects of the generated text. This works by introducing soft and hard constraints in a rule-based system. The work of Mairesse and Walker (2011) introduce statistics into the stylistic generation process, resulting in a system that allows a user to specify 5 personality traits that influence the generated language.

More recent statistical generation works tackling style include Xu et al. (2012) who attempt to paraphrase text into a different style. They learn to paraphrase text in Shakespeare's style to modern English using MT techniques, relying on the modern translations of William Shakespeare plays. Abu Sheikha and Inkpen (2011) generate texts with different formality levels by using lists of formal and informal words.

Finally, our work relies on heuristically extracting stylistic properties from text. Computational modeling of stylistic properties has been the focus of several lines of study, i.e. (Pavlick and Tetreault, 2016; Yang and Nenkova, 2014; Pavlick and Nenkova, 2015). Such methods are natural companions for our conditioned generation approach.

8 Conclusions

We proposed a framework for NNLG allowing for relatively fine-grained control on different stylistic aspects of the generated sentence, and demonstrated its effectiveness with an initial case study in the movie-reviews domain. A remaining challenge is providing finer-grained control on the generated *content* (allowing the user to specify either almost complete sentences or a set of structured facts) while still allowing the model to control the style of the generated sentence.

Acknowledgements The research was supported by the Israeli Science Foundation (grant number 1555/15) and the German Research Foundation via the German-Israeli Project Cooperation (DIP, grant DA 1600/1-1).

References

Fadi Abu Sheikha and Diana Inkpen. 2011. Generation of formal and informal sentences. In *Proceedings of the 13th European Workshop on Natural Language Generation*. Association for Computational Linguistics, Nancy, France, pages 187–193. http://www.aclweb.org/anthology/W11-2826.

John A Bateman and Cecile Paris. 1989. Phrasing a text in terms the user can understand. In *IJCAI*. pages 1511–1517.

Douglas Biber and Susan Conrad. 2009. *Register, genre, and style*. Cambridge University Press.

Ondřej Dušek and Filip Jurcicek. 2016a. A context-aware natural language generator for dialogue systems. In *Proceedings of the 17th Annual Meeting of the Special Interest Group on Discourse and Dialogue*. Association for Computational Linguistics, Los Angeles, pages 185–190. http://www.aclweb.org/anthology/W16-3622.

Ondřej Dušek and Filip Jurcicek. 2016b. Sequence-to-sequence generation for spoken dialogue via deep syntax trees and strings. In *Proceedings of the 54th Annual Meeting of the Association for Computational Linguistics (Volume*

2: Short Papers). Association for Computational Linguistics, Berlin, Germany, pages 45–51. http://anthology.aclweb.org/P16-2008.

Cong Duy Vu Hoang, Gholamreza Haffari, and Trevor Cohn. 2016. Incorporating side information into recurrent neural network language models. In *Proceedings of NAACL-HLT*. pages 1250–1255.

Sepp Hochreiter and Jürgen Schmidhuber. 1997. Long short-term memory. MIT Press, volume 9, pages 1735–1780.

Eduard Hovy. 1987. Generating natural language under pragmatic constraints. Journal of Pragmatics, volume 11, pages 689–719.

Zhiting Hu, Zichao Yang, Xiaodan Liang, Ruslan Salakhutdinov, and Eric P Xing. 2017. Controllable text generation. In *Proc. of ICML*.

Chloé Kiddon, Luke Zettlemoyer, and Yejin Choi. 2016. Globally coherent text generation with neural checklist models. In *Proceedings of the 2016 Conference on Empirical Methods in Natural Language Processing*. Association for Computational Linguistics, Austin, Texas, pages 329–339. https://aclweb.org/anthology/D16-1032.

Yuta Kikuchi, Graham Neubig, Ryohei Sasano, Hiroya Takamura, and Manabu Okumura. 2016. Controlling output length in neural encoder-decoders. In *Proceedings of the 2016 Conference on Empirical Methods in Natural Language Processing*. Association for Computational Linguistics, Austin, Texas, pages 1328–1338. https://aclweb.org/anthology/D16-1140.

Rémi Lebret, David Grangier, and Michael Auli. 2016. Neural text generation from structured data with application to the biography domain. In *Proceedings of the 2016 Conference on Empirical Methods in Natural Language Processing*. Association for Computational Linguistics, Austin, Texas, pages 1203–1213. https://aclweb.org/anthology/D16-1128.

Jiwei Li, Michel Galley, Chris Brockett, Georgios Spithourakis, Jianfeng Gao, and Bill Dolan. 2016. A persona-based neural conversation model. In *Proceedings of the 54th Annual Meeting of the Association for Computational Linguistics (Volume 1: Long Papers)*. Association for Computational Linguistics, Berlin, Germany, pages 994–1003. http://www.aclweb.org/anthology/P16-1094.

Zachary C Lipton, Sharad Vikram, and Julian McAuley. 2015. Capturing meaning in product reviews with character-level generative text models. arXiv preprint arXiv:1511.03683.

François Mairesse and Marilyn A Walker. 2011. Controlling user perceptions of linguistic style: Trainable generation of personality traits. MIT Press, volume 37, pages 455–488.

David D McDonald and James D Pustejovsky. 1985. A computational theory of prose style for natural language generation. In *Proceedings of the second conference on European chapter of the Association for Computational Linguistics*. Association for Computational Linguistics, pages 187–193.

Hongyuan Mei, Mohit Bansal, and Matthew R. Walter. 2016. What to talk about and how? selective generation using lstms with coarse-to-fine alignment. In *Proceedings of the 2016 Conference of the North American Chapter of the Association for Computational Linguistics: Human Language Technologies*. Association for Computational Linguistics, San Diego, California, pages 720–730. http://www.aclweb.org/anthology/N16-1086.

Tomas Mikolov, Martin Karafiát, Lukas Burget, Jan Cernockỳ, and Sanjeev Khudanpur. 2010. Recurrent neural network based language model. In *Interspeech*. volume 2, page 3.

Kate G Niederhoffer and James W Pennebaker. 2002. Linguistic style matching in social interaction. Journal of Language and Social Psychology, volume 21, pages 337–360.

Ellie Pavlick and Ani Nenkova. 2015. Inducing lexical style properties for paraphrase and genre differentiation. In *Proceedings of the 2015 Conference of the North American Chapter of the Association for Computational Linguistics: Human Language Technologies*. Association for Computational Linguistics, Denver, Colorado, pages 218–224. http://www.aclweb.org/anthology/N15-1023.

Ellie Pavlick and Joel Tetreault. 2016. An empirical analysis of formality in online communication. Transactions of the Association for Computational Linguistics, volume 4, pages 61–74.

Richard Power, Donia Scott, and Nadjet Bouayad-Agha. 2003. Generating texts with style. In *Proc. of CiCLING*. Springer, pages 444–452.

Alec Radford, Rafal Jozefowicz, and Ilya Sutskever. 2017. Learning to generate reviews and discovering sentiment. arXiv preprint arXiv:1704.01444.

Ehud Reiter and Sandra Williams. 2010. Generating texts in different styles. In *The Structure of Style*, Springer, pages 59–75.

Rico Sennrich, Barry Haddow, and Alexandra Birch. 2016. Controlling politeness in neural machine translation via side constraints. In *Proceedings of NAACL-HLT*. pages 35–40.

Jian Tang, Yifan Yang, Sam Carton, Ming Zhang, and Qiaozhu Mei. 2016. Context-aware natural language generation with recurrent neural networks. arXiv preprint arXiv:1611.09900.

Tsung-Hsien Wen, Milica Gasic, Nikola Mrkšić, Pei-Hao Su, David Vandyke, and Steve Young.

2015. Semantically conditioned lstm-based natural language generation for spoken dialogue systems. In *Proceedings of the 2015 Conference on Empirical Methods in Natural Language Processing*. Association for Computational Linguistics, Lisbon, Portugal, pages 1711–1721. http://aclweb.org/anthology/D15-1199.

Wei Xu, Alan Ritter, Bill Dolan, Ralph Grishman, and Colin Cherry. 2012. Paraphrasing for style. In *Proceedings of COLING 2012*. The COLING 2012 Organizing Committee, Mumbai, India, pages 2899–2914. http://www.aclweb.org/anthology/C12-1177.

Yinfei Yang and Ani Nenkova. 2014. Detecting information-dense texts in multiple news domains. In *AAAI*. pages 1650–1656.

Approximating Style by N-gram-based Annotation

Melanie Andresen and **Heike Zinsmeister**
Universität Hamburg
Institute for German Language and Literature
Germany
{melanie.andresen, heike.zinsmeister}@uni-hamburg.de

Abstract

The concept of style is much debated in theoretical as well as empirical terms. From an empirical perspective, the key question is how to operationalize style and thus make it accessible for annotation and quantification. In authorship attribution, many different approaches have successfully resolved this issue at the cost of linguistic interpretability: The resulting algorithms may be able to distinguish one language variety from the other, but do not give us much information on their distinctive linguistic properties. We approach the issue of interpreting stylistic features by extracting linear and syntactic n-grams that are distinctive for a language variety. We present a study that exemplifies this process by a comparison of the German academic languages of linguistics and literary studies. Overall, our findings show that distinctive n-grams can be related to linguistic categories. The results suggest that the style of German literary studies is characterized by nominal structures and the style of linguistics by verbal ones.

1 Introduction

The concept of style is hotly debated in theoretical as well as empirical terms. From an empirical perspective, the key question is how to operationalize style and thus make it accessible for annotation and quantification. Many recent definitions of style focus on this aspect, resulting in very general definitions:

> Style is a property of texts constituted by an ensemble of formal features which can be observed quantitatively or qualitatively. (Herrmann et al., 2015)

This is a good starting point and for many studies focusing on applications such as authorship attribution or author profiling, this concept of style is perfectly sufficient. However, when the aim of investigation is interpretation rather than application, these 'formal features' need to meet additional requirements.

Most importantly, the features need to be interpretable by human readers, which is not strictly true for features like character-n-grams. Also token-based n-grams can be difficult to interpret, as they do not necessarily correspond to an actual phrase. To give a meaningful description of a language variety's style, we need to map the features to linguistic categories and, if possible, also offer independent, non-linguistic explanations. For the former purpose, we suggest an annotation task with multiple annotators that ensures a certain degree of intersubjectivity.

In the present study, this process is exemplified by a comparison of the German academic languages of linguistics and literary studies. It is part of a bigger research project that aims at describing the stylistic differences between the two disciplines. We consider this research question relevant because the two disciplines are often subsumed under one study program (e. g. *German Studies*). While this suggests a very close relationship between linguistics and literary studies, they differ in many respects.

Our analysis is based on features that are not initially linguistically motivated, but widely used: n-grams based on tokens and part-of-speech (pos) annotation. We complement them by more linguistically informed syntactic n-grams (Sidorov et al., 2012; Goldberg and Orwant, 2013). The core of our study is the following annotation experiment: After determining distinctive n-grams automatically based on frequencies, we give the most distinctive 260 token n-grams and 160 pos

Proceedings of the Workshop on Stylistic Variation, pages 105–115
Copenhagen, Denmark, September 7–11, 2017. ©2017 Association for Computational Linguistics

n-grams to three annotators. They annotated whether they found the n-grams to be interpretable and, if yes, what kind of linguistic category they could derive from the n-grams.

The paper is structured as follows: Section 2 gives an overview of work in computational stylistics relevant to our study. Section 3 gives a short overview of linguistic as well as non-linguistic properties of linguistics and literary studies to which we will relate our results. We present the study's setup in section 4 by describing our data and how n-grams were generated (section 4.1) and ranked (section 4.2). Section 4.3 gives a detailed account of the annotation scheme and process. In section 5, we present the results of the annotation experiment and relate them to non-linguistic properties of the two disciplines. Section 6 discusses our study's implications.

2 Related Work

In this section we give an overview of studies in computational stylistics, focusing on those interested in linguistically interpretable features.

Boukhaled et al. (2015) differentiate between two methodological types of computational stylistics: 1) the *classification approach* that uses linguistic features to confirm or question a grouping of texts based on non-linguistic features, e. g. author or genre, and 2) the *hermeneutic approach*[1] identifying relevant linguistic features that serve as a data-driven starting point for human interpretation.

Most work has been done adopting the first approach, dominated by studies on the task of authorship attribution as described in the survey by Stamatatos (2009). The huge variety of features presented here refers to all kinds of language aspects that are meaningful to a greater or lesser extent, seen from a linguistic point of view. The use of a character-based data compression model is an extreme case of a linguistically uninformative method. Especially syntactic features, on the other hand, potentially contain valuable stylistic information. Hirst and Feiguina (2007) is an example of such a study that is based on bigrams of syntactic labels.

Among the linguistically motivated features used in authorship attribution, syntactic n-grams

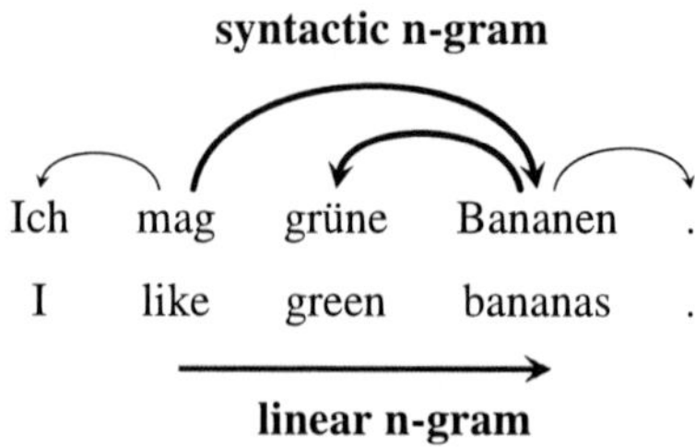

Figure 1: Example of linear and syntactic n-grams: This sentence includes the linear trigram *mag grüne Bananen* and the syntactic trigram *mag>Bananen>grüne*.

are the most promising for our research. Sidorov et al. (2012) suggest a simple concept of syntactic n-grams: Instead of linearly following the text surface as regular n-grams do, syntactic n-grams follow the dependency path in the sentence from head to dependent. Figure 1 shows an example of a linear vs. a syntactic n-gram, spanning the same set of tokens. In contrast to linear n-grams, syntactic n-grams encode syntactically meaningful relations in the sentence. Sidorov et al. (2012) achieve good results in a (non-competitive) authorship attribution task with a model based on syntactic n-grams. Goldberg and Orwant (2013) and Sidorov (2013) augment the concept to n-ary branching subtrees.

The hermeneutic approach is much less prominent than the classification approach and it is dominated by the stylistic investigation of literary works and academic language.

The features used here are primarily token-derived and lexical in nature. A widespread use of this type of analysis working with sequences of words followed upon Biber et al. (1999)'s definition of 'lexical bundles'[2]. This was mainly (but not only) applied to the study of academic language (e. g. Biber et al. (2004); Hyland (2008); Chen and Baker (2010)). Durrant (2015) analyses academic writing by students. By looking at token 4-grams he creates a disciplinary cluster of student writers. Additionally, Durrant interprets the instances found by grouping them into functional categories based on Hyland (2008).

The second field where this type of analysis has proved productive is literary stylistics. Ramsay (2007) bases his analysis of Virginia Woolf on the character-specific frequency of single words.

---

[1] This approach relates to hermeneutics, the distinctive methodology of interpretation in the humanities, cf. Mantzavinos (2016).

[2] We will not adopt this terminology as we see in section 5 that not all phenomena discovered by this method are lexical in nature.

Mahlberg (2007) looks at frequent token n-grams (using the term 'clusters') that function as a type of signature of characters in Charles Dickens' *Bleak House*. Mahlberg (2013) discusses this in more detail and gives a more comprehensive account of Dickens' fiction. She also gives an overview of the varying terminology (e. g. n-grams, clusters, lexical bundles) and different attempts of using these features for stylistics (Mahlberg, 2013, 48-51).

Far fewer studies use more linguistically enriched features and annotations. Boukhaled et al. (2015) include pos annotations in their investigation of classic French novels. Their features are sequences of pos tags that allow for gaps (so-called skipgrams, Guthrie et al. (2006)). Scharloth et al. (2012) use a similar approach that additionally includes combinations of token, lemma and part of speech to compare the style of two social environments in the late sixties in Germany and successfully relate the resulting linguistic features to social features of these two groups.

We consider our study as following the hermeneutic approach. In contrast to most studies, we include the token and pos level as well as syntactic annotation following Sidorov et al. (2012)'s concept of syntactic n-grams. Additionally, we systematically assess the interpretability of n-gram-based features. For measuring the reliability of the interpretations (Krippendorff, 2013, 267-270), we base this judgment on more than one person and give the task to three annotators, as described in section 4.3.

3 Linguistics and literary studies: Linguistic and non-linguistic differences

In this section, we will briefly describe established linguistic and non-linguistic differences between the two disciplines under investigation. We will refer back to these in the interpretation of our own results in section 5.

Academic disciplines are commonly subdivided into hard and soft sciences, which is regarded as a continuum (Biglan, 1973; Hyland, 2004). While linguistics as well as literary studies can clearly be considered disciplines of the soft sciences, most subdisciplines of linguistics tend more to the hard sciences than literary studies does.

Many differences between linguistics and literary studies therefore correspond to the differences between soft and hard sciences, just on a smaller scale. The soft sciences are characterized as being more interpretative, work hermeneutically, show several subjective perspectives and feature plurality of possible objects of study and methods. The hard sciences on the other hand are more analytical, work empirically, have a high agreement on object of study and methods and rely on quantification (e. g. Biglan (1973); Durrant (2015)).

More specifically referring to the two disciplines under examination, Gardt (2007) describes literary studies as focusing on the exemplary analysis of individual objects of study (typically texts) and linguistics as focusing rather on patterns and generalizations. We will come back to these features in the interpretation of linguistic features in section 5.

These non-linguistic features naturally lead to stylistic differences between disciplines, which have been extensively researched so that our overview has to remain illustrative. For instance, Hyland (2004) looks at disciplinary differences along the hard sciences vs. soft sciences continuum. He describes, among other results, that the disciplines vary in their citation practices: The soft fields use more citations than the hard fields and use different types of reporting verbs (Hyland, 2004, 24-29). An analysis of evaluation practices in reviews shows that while the hard fields use more praise, the soft fields use more criticism (Hyland, 2004, 49).

Biber and Gray (2016) investigate academic English in contrast to other registers and with regard to disciplinary differences. They make a distinction between phrasal (e. g. complex noun phrases) and clausal (e. g. subordination) complexity and find that the natural sciences rely more heavily on the former while the soft sciences prefer the latter.

Afros and Schryer (2009) investigate promotional metadiscourse in linguistics and literary studies and find that the style of literary studies sometimes resembles literary texts and addresses aesthetic values of the research community.

When referring to these previously found differences, we have to bear in mind that almost all studies are based on the English language. While many aspects can be expected to be cross-linguistically valid, we know that different (academic) languages have different properties. For instance, Siepmann (2006) gives a summarizing account of differences between the academic writing of English, French and German.

4   Study

We proceed by presenting our data and the way we generated n-grams in section 4.1, our ranking procedure in section 4.2 and the annotation scheme and setup in section 4.3.

4.1   Data and n-gram generation

The present study is based on a corpus of 60 PhD theses. The choice of this text type was motivated by the fact that it serves as a 'gateway genre' (Demarest and Sugimoto, 2014, 3), granting access to the academic world, and is therefore expected to highly conform to the disciplinary norms. Additionally, it is a text type that has about the same status in all disciplines. However, we have to be careful about generalizing the results to academic language in general. We created two subcorpora:

- **subcorpus of linguistics**: 30 PhD theses comprising 1,427,758 tokens,

- **subcorpus of literary studies**: 30 PhD theses comprising 2,151,679 tokens.

Sections that do not belong to the register under investigation or that interrupt the text were extracted semi-automatically: footnotes, citations, examples, tables, figures, title page, table of contents, reference section etc. This preprocessing followed rather simple heuristics and while the results are not perfect, they are sufficient for a quantitative analysis based on this amount of data.

We processed the data using the following tools: the system *Punkt* (Kiss and Strunk, 2006)[3] for tokenization and an off-the-shelf version of MATE dependency parser (Bohnet, 2010) trained on the TIGER Corpus (Seeker and Kuhn, 2012) for lemma, pos and dependency annotation. We evaluated the parser's annotations against a gold standard consensually created by two annotators for a sample of 22 sentences (600 tokens). Given that it is applied to out-of-domain data, the parser performance is good (UAS: 0.95, LAS: 0.93).

We extracted the following data sets from the resulting corpus:

- **linear n-grams** of sizes 2-5 using tokens and pos tags, respectively,

- **syntactic n-grams** of sizes 2-5 using tokens and pos tags, respectively, generated by taking every word of the sentence as a starting point and following the dependency path

backwards by *n-1* steps (following the concept of Sidorov et al. (2012)).

4.2   Distinctiveness and collocational strength: n-gram ranking

For further analysis, only n-grams with a total frequency of more than 10 are included. For these n-grams we calculate their relative frequencies in all 60 texts.

In order to rank the n-grams in a way that is meaningful for later interpretation, two measures are of interest: distinctiveness and collocational strength.

First, we want to identify n-grams with a high difference in frequency between the two subcorpora and thus corresponding to major differences between the disciplines. To achieve this, we use the t-test as suggested by Paquot and Bestgen (2009) and Lijffijt et al. (2014). One of the benefits of the t-test is that it takes variation within the corpora into account. Consequently, a single text cannot dominate the overall result.

Second, we include a measure for collocational strength between the elements of the n-gram. This is necessary because the t-test results disregard the influence of significant substructures of an n-gram. Consider, for instance, that the pos tag CARD[4] is much more frequent in linguistics. Also, the bigram CARD ADJA[5] is much more frequent in linguistics. The latter observation does not necessarily mean that this combination is characteristic of linguistics but can be caused by the high difference in frequency of CARD alone.

A measure for collocational strength tells us whether the bigram is more frequent than we would expect given the corresponding unigram frequencies. Evert (2008) gives a comprehensive overview of different measures and their properties. We use the log-likelihood measure described by Dunning (1993).

While this computation is very straightforward for bigrams, the situation becomes more complicated with higher *n*. We follow the approach of Zinsmeister and Heid (2003), who break down triples of verb, adjective and noun into nested binary tuples ((adjective, noun), verb) to maintain a binary structure.

Our approach comprises the following steps:

---

[3]http://www.nltk.org/api/nltk.tokenize.html, 19.05.2017

[4]Cardinal number. The tagset used here is Schiller et al. (1999).

[5]Adjective in attributive position

1. For each n-gram that is found to be distinctive by the t-test, we generate all possible sub-n-grams contained in the n-gram. For instance, for a distinctive 4-gram, all trigrams, bigrams and unigrams contained are generated.

2. Each list of sub-n-grams is reduced to those sub-n-grams which show a significant difference between the subcorpora themselves and thus are possible candidates for causing the significance of the original n-gram alone.

3. For each of these distinctive sub-n-grams, we calculate the collocational strength between this sub-n-gram and the rest of the original n-gram.

A low log-likelihood ratio indicates that the combination of the two elements does not occur more often than expected. Consequently, it is just one of the elements that causes the distinctive effect. We exclude n-grams from the ranking that contain a combination of elements with a log-likelihood ratio below a threshold of 50.

4.3 Annotating n-grams

The n-gram generation and ranking can be automated to a high extent and is consequently highly replicable. For the following step of interpretation this is much less the case.

Our annotation process aims at objectifying the interpretation of n-grams as far as possible. To this end, the resulting n-grams are annotated by three annotators according to an annotation scheme that was developed in the process of annotating the data (Pustejovsky and Stubbs, 2012, 109).

The n-grams we include in the annotation tasks vary in three dimensions: They are either linear or syntactic n-grams, they are of a size between 2 and 5 and they are either based on tokens or on pos labels.

The sample of token n-grams was taken as Table 1 summarizes: For the n-gram sizes 2-5, we chose at least the 20 highest-scoring linear and syntactic n-grams. If more than 20 instances crossed the significance threshold of p=0.01 in the t-test, the sample size for that group was raised to 40 instances, giving a total sample size of 260 items.

The sample for pos n-grams comprises again the 20 highest-scoring items in our ranking of linear and syntactic n-grams for n=2-5, resulting in 160 items in total. One difference to token n-grams

| | | n-gram type | |
		linear	syntactic
n-gram size	2	40	40
	3	40	40
	4	40	20
	5	20	20

Table 1: Number of instances per category in the sample of token n-grams

is the fact that pos n-grams are more abstract and consequently more difficult to interpret for human annotators. The annotators are therefore provided with five token realizations of the pos n-gram at hand for illustration. These are randomly chosen from the subcorpus of the discipline in which the n-gram is more frequent. In all annotation tasks, the annotators are not provided with any contexts the n-grams appear in as these can be quite divers and our objective was to judge the interpretability of n-grams as such.

We present two annotation tasks: One classifying the structures in the n-gram as nominal, verbal or clausal and a second classifying them as carrying lexical or grammatical information (for token n-grams only).

First, we want to know whether the n-grams capture linguistically interpretable structures and if yes, what kind of structures we find for the two disciplines. Our first annotation scheme is roughly based on Biber et al. (2004, 381)'s 'structural types of lexical bundles' and comprises the following categories:

1. This n-gram contains a verbal structure (V).

2. This n-gram contains a nominal structure (N).

3. This n-gram contains a clausal structure (subordination) (C).

4. This n-gram contains a verbal structure that also indicates a clausal structure (subordination) (V_C).

5. This n-gram does not contain any of the above-mentioned structures (other).

By this annotation scheme we hope to achieve a high degree of abstraction that leads us to a very general characterization of the disciplinary writing styles.

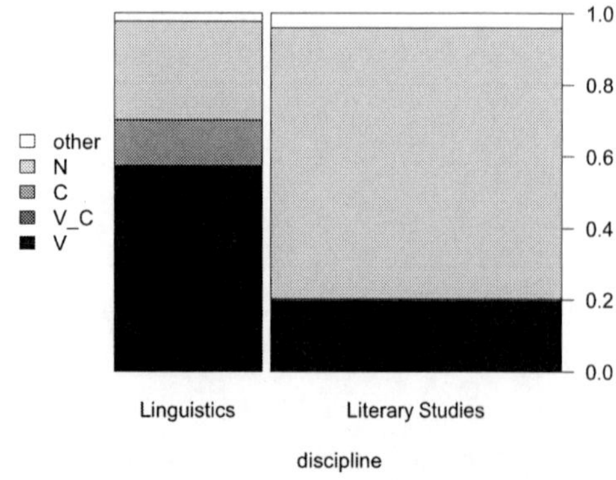

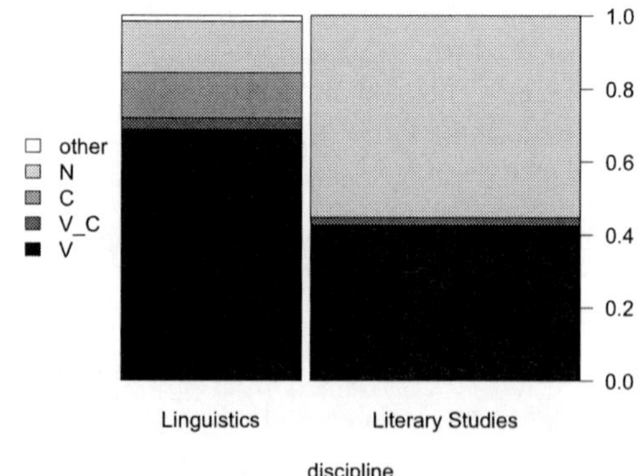

Figure 2: Annotation of structural types of token n-grams dependent on discipline, n=260 (note that the category V_C did not occur here)

Figure 3: Annotation of structural types of pos n-grams dependent on discipline, n=160

For the sample of token n-grams, we made an additional distinction between lexical and grammatical information. This distinction allows for a general assessment of the nature of the differences between the disciplines. These two types of information contribute to style in different ways. For lexical items, it remains to be seen whether they sometimes reflect topic rather than style. The annotation follows these categories:

1. This n-gram contains a (complex) lexical unit (LEX) or overlaps with one (LEX-P).

2. This n-gram contains a grammatical structure (GRAM) or overlaps with one (GRAM-P).

3. This n-gram contains a structure that is ambiguous between lexical unit and grammatical structure (LEX-P_GRAM-P).

4. This n-gram does not contain a (complex) lexical unit or grammatical structure (NONE).

For categories 1 to 3, the annotators were asked to additionally provide the lexical unit or grammatical structure they were thinking of (e. g. relative clause). This results in very concrete phenomena and can be considered the most fine-grained annotation category. At the same time, a generalizing, quantified evaluation of the results is more difficult due to the diversity of phenomena. For the annotation of pos n-grams the differentiation between lexical units and grammatical structures does not apply, as pos tags do not directly refer to the lexical level. Therefore, the annotators are only asked for a label for the grammatical structure represented in the n-gram.

5 Results and Discussion

We will first present the results of the first annotation task about nominal and verbal structures (section 5.1). This is followed by the results related to lexical and grammatical phenomena in token n-grams (section 5.2), and finally by the analysis of these phenomena based on pos tags (section 5.3).

5.1 Nominal vs. verbal style

For the first annotation scheme differentiating nominal, verbal and clausal structures, the three annotators reached an inter-annotator agreement of 0.83 for the annotation of 260 token n-grams, measured by Fleiss' Kappa (Fleiss, 1971). Figure 2 displays the results. In the horizontal dimension we can see the two disciplines. The bars' widths show how many of the distinctive n-grams are more frequent in linguistics and literary studies, respectively. We can see that about two thirds of the n-grams in the sample are more frequent in literary studies than in linguistics. In the vertical dimension, the proportion of the annotation categories is displayed. The distinctive n-grams for the style of literary studies are dominated by nominal structures (in light gray) while verbal structures (in black) are more characteristic of linguistics. The data reveal a significant difference between the disciplines (Fisher's test, p<0.001).

For the annotation of pos n-grams, the annotators reached a slightly lower inter-annotator agreement of 0.69. This could be expected as pos n-grams require more interpretation. When comparing the disciplines, we get a result similar to the token level: In Figure 3 we can see the distribution of nominal, verbal and clausal structures in pos n-grams across the disciplines. Even though the difference is less pronounced than in Figure 2, the difference between the disciplines is also highly significant (Fisher's test, p<0.001).

In the pos n-grams of both disciplines, verbal structures account for a higher proportion than on the token level. This shift emerges as many token instances belong to the same pos pattern, and are mapped to only one pos instance when abstracting from token to part of speech.

To summarize, we found that verbal structures are more characteristic of linguistics and nominal structures of literary studies. Assuming that our nominal structures correspond to Biber and Gray (2016)'s phrasal complexity, this result is in opposition to their observation that the hard sciences rely more on phrasal complexity than the soft sciences. We surmise that this might be due to the fact that the latter study is based on English data only. German literary studies is firmly rooted in the German academic tradition, which might result in this deviation from the English-based expectations.

Furthermore, we can see that among the sample of most distinctive structures in both figures, about two thirds are more frequent in literary studies than in linguistics. The interpretation of this fact is not straightforward and requires a careful review of the underlying patterns (e. g. their absolute frequencies and textual functions) that is beyond the scope of the current paper.

When interpreting these frequencies, we have to keep in mind that (slightly less than) half of the structures under investigation are syntactic n-grams. The dependency path through a sentence always starts with a finite verb and is relatively short in total. Consequently, most of the larger syntactic n-grams include the finite verb at the root, leading to the classification of the structure as verbal. Consequently, verbal structures are much more frequent among syntactic than linear n-grams (Fisher's test, p<0.001). However, this applies to both disciplines and token as well as pos n-grams in the same way. For a more comprehensive comparison of linear and syntactic n-grams, see Andresen and Zinsmeister (2017).

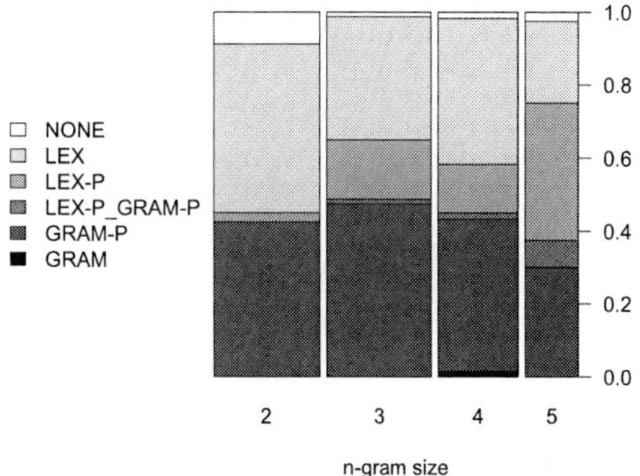

Figure 4: Annotation of information in token n-grams dependent on n-gram size, n=260

5.2 Lexical and grammatical structures in token features

The application of the second annotation scheme, labeling structures as being mainly characterized by grammatical or lexical properties, was more controversial. The inter-annotator agreement is 0.48 and shows that the data is rather ambiguous in terms of the annotated categories. At the same time it indicates the limits of n-gram interpretability: n-grams can invite multiple interpretations that have to be verified carefully. In these annotations, there initially were 20 instances where all three annotators chose different categories. These instances were discussed by two annotators who then agreed on one category. The results presented in the following are based on a majority vote.

In Figure 4, we present the results grouped by n-gram size. The bars' widths reflect the subsample sizes presented in Table 1. For the lexical categories, we can see that with increasing n-gram size the label LEX (in the lightest gray) tends to decrease while LEX-P (directly below) is increasing. This is understandable as LEX-P also covers structures that comprise more than the lexical item itself. With an increase in size, we are more likely to include more than the lexical unit in the n-gram. Also, the proportion of grammatical structures (darkest gray and black) drops slightly for larger n-grams. Ususally grammatical structures are signaled by only few items on the language surface, such as a comma and a subordinating conjunction for an embedded clause, whereas lexical units tend to extend over many words. The category NONE (in white) is most frequent among n-grams of size 2, indicating that this size is too

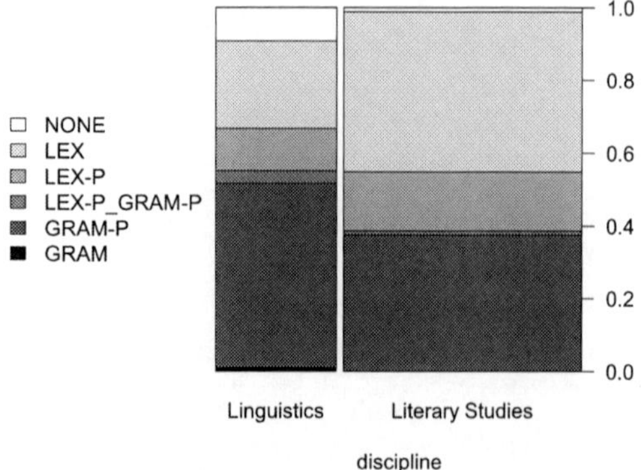

Figure 5: Annotation of information in token n-grams dependent on discipline, n=260

small to fully capture many phenomena.

Figure 5 shows the distribution across the two disciplines. We can see that, even when only taking the rather coarse-grained annotation labels (LEX, GRAM etc.) into account, we find significant differences between the disciplines (Fisher's test, $p < 0.001$). Generally speaking, there are more grammatical patterns distinctive for linguistics and more lexical patterns distinctive for literary studies. When assessing this difference, we have to keep in mind that many of the linguistic phenomena are binary in nature, with one of the variants being more easily detectable by an n-gram analysis. For instance, the grammatical phenomenon 'passive voice' is more frequent in linguistics. The logical consequence is that active voice is more frequent in literary studies. However, only the high frequency of passive voice is visible in the data, as it is realized by a rather stable pattern of auxiliary verbs. This problem of detectability is especially pervasive for grammatical phenomena as they often require the realization of one of a set of options.

In addition to assigning these categories, the annotators provided the lexical or grammatical structure they derived from the n-gram. Here, the annotation is increasingly interpretative. At the same time, clearer differences between the disciplines emerge.

Among the lexical patterns we found to be more frequent in linguistics "in der Regel" ('as a rule, usually') is very prominent. This corresponds to the initial assumption that in linguistics, generalization plays a bigger role than in literary studies. Patterns like "können zurückgeführt werden

auf" ('can be traced back to') show an attempt to give causal explanations. Other words like "Analyse" ('analysis') and "Auswahl" ('selection') mirror the empirical methodology of the discipline. For literary studies, on the other hand, we find many items referring to the temporal dimension: "in dem Moment" ('at that moment'), "in einer Zeit" ('at a time'), "das Ende" ('the end'), "in der ersten Hälfte des" ('in the first half of the'). This characterizes the discipline as being more narrative when referring to the (e. g. temporal) dimensions of the literary object.

Among the grammatical structures literary studies shows a higher frequency of personal pronouns, which is also related to narrative structures and individual objects of study. However, grammatical structures are by far dominated by several patterns introducing relative clauses. This indicates a rather nominal style already found in section 5.1. Interestingly, the relatively few relative clauses more frequent in linguistics all use the relative pronoun "die", which can be feminine but is more likely to be plural. This corresponds to the idea that literary studies rather deals with individuals (mostly male individuals, as the frequencies show) while linguistics deals with groups of phenomena. Other grammatical structures characteristic for linguistics are passive constructions and modal verbs as well as generally more indications of sub- and coordination (structures with "dass", 'that' and "und", 'and').

5.3 Lexical and grammatical structures in pos features

For the pos n-grams, the annotation of lexical vs. grammatical phenomena is less meaningful. But again, the annotators were asked to name or describe the linguistic phenomenon they see represented in the n-gram. This proved to be more difficult than for the token annotation. Often the n-grams were annotated with phenomena that could be derived from a single pos tag in the sequence, e. g. all n-grams including the pos tag PRELS[6] were annotated as relative clause, independent of the other tags in the sequence.

However, the following results can be found: Generally speaking, the phenomena mirror the differences between verbal and nominal structures found in section 5.1. More specifically, passives as well as modals and predicatives are more fre-

---

[6]Relative pronoun

quent in linguistics. For literary studies, complex noun (and prepositional) phrases are more common. In contrast to the results based on the token level, patterns with relative clauses occur in literary studies only. Here, the token level offers an informative differentiation. Many of these noun phrases include possessive pronouns, which are hardly found in linguistics, cf. personal pronouns discussed in the previous section.

6 Conclusion and future work

Our study had the aim of determining the potential of n-grams for linguistically describing style. We illustrated this by a study comparing the German academic languages of linguistics and literary studies. By means of an annotation experiment, we could show that most n-grams are interpretable in the sense that they could be related to some linguistic category. However, interpretations become more challenging with increasing n-gram length and abstractness, e. g. when interpreting parts of speech instead of tokens. Additionally, the results we found can clearly be related to non-linguistic properties of the disciplines: e. g. references to empirical methodology in linguistics, narrative structures in literary studies. Overall, the distinctive structures more frequent in literary studies are for the most part nominal. Linguistics, on the other hand, exhibits more verbal and clausal patterns.

These specific results might help scholars and especially students of the disciplines to reflect on and adapt to disciplinary writing conventions. More generally, we hope to have contributed to a better understanding of how n-gram analysis can add to the linguistic description of style. Last but not least, n-grams can serve as a starting point for subsequent in-depth analyses of language and style.

In the future, we intend to refine our method of dealing with the influence of significant substructures. Between some parts of speech there is a general collocation tendency in languages, e. g., in German a determiner and an adjective generally cooccur more often than expected by their unigram frequencies. Our current approach of using a measure of collocational strength, the log-likelihood measure, does not include this information. It requires a more detailed compositional analysis of n-grams to determine to what extend substructures can serve as a proxy of larger n-grams. In addition, it is necessary to decide whether some of the n-grams are related to topic rather than style. This depends on the specific definition of style and the analysis' objective.

In our opinion, the mathematical decisions behind the ranking of n-grams are especially important when an interpretation by humans is intended. When given an n-gram with the information that it is more frequent in one language variety than in another, humans will usually come up with some kind of interpretation of this fact. If the n-gram's rank is more of a mathematical artifact, this can lead to a highly skewed interpretation of the data.

Acknowledgments

We would like to thank Sarah Jablotschkin for contributing to the manual n-gram annotation, Piklu Gupta for improving our English and the anonymous reviewers for their extensive and detailed comments on our submission. All remaining errors are our own.

References

Elena Afros and Catherine F. Schryer. 2009. Promotional (meta)discourse in research articles in language and literary studies. *English for Specific Purposes* 28(1):58–68. https://doi.org/10.1016/j.esp.2008.09.001.

Melanie Andresen and Heike Zinsmeister. 2017. The Benefit of Syntactic vs. Linear N-grams for Linguistic Description. In *Proceedings of the 4th International Conference on Dependency Linguistics (Depling 2017)*. Pisa, Italy.

Douglas Biber, Susan Conrad, and Viviana Cortes. 2004. If you look at...: Lexical bundles in university teaching and textbooks. *Applied linguistics* 25(3):371–405.

Douglas Biber and Bethany Gray. 2016. *Grammatical Complexity in Academic English: Linguistic Change in Writing*. Studies in English language. Cambridge University Press, Cambridge.

Douglas Biber, Stig Johansson, Geoffrey Leech, Susan Conrad, and Edward Finegan. 1999. *Longman Grammar of Spoken and Written English*. Longman, Harlow.

Anthony Biglan. 1973. The characteristics of subject matter in different academic areas. *Journal of Applied Psychology* 57(3):195–203. https://doi.org/10.1037/h0034701.

Bernd Bohnet. 2010. Very High Accuracy and Fast Dependency Parsing is not a Contradiction. In *Proceedings of the 23rd International Conference* on *Computational Linguistics (COLING 2010)*. Beijing, China.

Mohamed-Amine Boukhaled, Francesca Frontini, Gauvain Bourgne, and Jean-Gabriel Ganascia. 2015. Computational study of stylistics: A clustering-based interestingness measure for extracting relevant syntactic patterns. *International Journal of Computational Linguistics and Applications* 6(1):45–62.

Yu-Hua Chen and Paul Baker. 2010. Lexical bundles in L1 and L2 academic writing. *Language Learning & Technology* 14(2):30–49.

Bradford Demarest and Cassidy R. Sugimoto. 2014. Argue, observe, assess: Measuring disciplinary identities and differences through socio-epistemic discourse. *Journal of the Association for Information Science and Technology* pages 1–14. https://doi.org/10.1002/asi.23271.

Ted Dunning. 1993. Accurate Methods for the Statistics of Surprise and Coincidence. *Computational Linguistics* 19(1):61–74.

Philip Durrant. 2015. Lexical Bundles and Disciplinary Variation in University Students' Writing: Mapping the Territories. *Applied Linguistics* pages 1–30. https://doi.org/10.1093/applin/amv011.

Stefan Evert. 2008. Corpora and collocations. In Anke Lüdeling and Merja Kytö, editors, *Corpus Linguistics: An International Handbook*, De Gruyter, Berlin, Boston, volume 2 of *Handbooks of Linguistics and Communication Science*, pages 1212–1248.

Joseph L. Fleiss. 1971. Measuring nominal scale agreement among many raters. *Psychological Bulletin* 76(5):378–382. https://doi.org/10.1037/h0031619.

Andreas Gardt. 2007. Linguistisches Interpretieren. Konstruktivistische Theorie und realistische Praxis. In Fritz Hermanns and Werner Holly, editors, *Linguistische Hermeneutik: Theorie und Praxis des Verstehens und Interpretierens*, Niemeyer, Tübingen, number 272 in Reihe Germanistische Linguistik, pages 241–261.

Yoav Goldberg and Jon Orwant. 2013. A Dataset of Syntactic-Ngrams over Time from a Very Large Corpus of English Books. In *Second Joint Conference on Lexical and Computational Semantics (*SEM), Volume 1: Proceedings of the Main Conference and the Shared Task: Semantic Textual Similarity*. Association for Computational Linguistics, Atlanta, Georgia, USA, pages 241–247.

David Guthrie, Ben Allison, Wei Liu, Louise Guthrie, and Yorick Wilks. 2006. A closer look at skip-gram modelling. In *Proceedings of the 5th International Conference on Language Resources and Evaluation (LREC-2006)*. pages 1–4.

Berenike Herrmann, Karina van Dalen-Oskam, and Christof Schöch. 2015. Revisiting Style, a Key Concept in Literary Studies. *Journal of Literary Theory* 9(1):25–52. https://doi.org/10.1515/jlt-2015-0003.

Graeme Hirst and Ol'ga Feiguina. 2007. Bigrams of Syntactic Labels for Authorship Discrimination of Short Texts. *Literary and Linguistic Computing* 22(4):405–417. https://doi.org/10.1093/llc/fqm023.

Ken Hyland. 2004. *Disciplinary Discourses: Social Interactions in Academic Writing*. The University of Michigan Press, Michigan.

Ken Hyland. 2008. As can be seen: Lexical bundles and disciplinary variation. *English for Specific Purposes* 27(1):4–21. https://doi.org/10.1016/j.esp.2007.06.001.

Tibor Kiss and Jan Strunk. 2006. Unsupervised Multilingual Sentence Boundary Detection. *Computational Linguistics* 32(4):485–525. https://doi.org/10.1162/coli.2006.32.4.485.

Klaus Krippendorff. 2013. *Content Analysis: An Introduction to Its Methodology*. Sage, Thousand Oaks, CA, third edition.

Jefrey Lijffijt, Terttu Nevalainen, Tanja Säily, Panagiotis Papapetrou, Kai Puolamäki, and Heikki Mannila. 2014. Significance testing of word frequencies in corpora. *Digital Scholarship in the Humanities* pages 1–24. https://doi.org/10.1093/llc/fqu064.

Michaela Mahlberg. 2007. Corpus stylistics: Bridging the gap between linguistic and literary studies. In Michael Hoey, Michaela Mahlberg, Michael Stubbs, and Wolfgang Teubert, editors, *Text, Discourse and Corpora. Theory and Analysis*, Continuum, London, Studies in corpus and discourse, pages 217–246.

Michaela Mahlberg. 2013. *Corpus Stylistics and Dickens's Fiction*. Number 14 in Routledge advances in corpus linguistics. Routledge, New York.

Chrysostomos Mantzavinos. 2016. Hermeneutics. In Edward N. Zalta, editor, *The Stanford Encyclopedia of Philosophy*, Metaphysics Research Lab, Stanford University. Winter 2016 edition.

Magali Paquot and Yves Bestgen. 2009. Distinctive words in academic writing: A comparison of three statistical tests for keyword extraction. In Andreas H. Jucker, Daniel Schreier, and Marianne Hundt, editors, *Corpora: Pragmatics and Discourse*, Brill, pages 247–269. https://doi.org/10.1163/9789042029101_014.

James Pustejovsky and Amber Stubbs. 2012. *Natural Language Annotation for Machine Learning*. O'Reilly Media, Inc., Sebastopol, CA.

Stephen Ramsay. 2007. Algorithmic Criticism. In *A Companion to Digital Literary Studies*, Blackwell Publishing, Malden, MA, number 50 in Blackwell companions to literature and culture, pages 477–491.

Joachim Scharloth, Noah Bubenhofer, and Klaus Rothenhäusler. 2012. Andersschreiben aus korpuslinguistischer Perspektive: Datengeleitete Zugänge zum Stil. In Britt-Marie Schuster and Doris Tophinke, editors, *Andersschreiben. Formen, Funktionen, Traditionen*, Erich Schmidt Verlag, Berlin, number 236 in Philologische Studien und Quellen, pages 157–178.

Anne Schiller, Simone Teufel, Christine Thielen, and Christine Stöckert. 1999. *Guidelines für das Tagging deutscher Textcorpora mit STTS (kleines und großes Tagset)*. Stuttgart, Tübingen.

Wolfgang Seeker and Jonas Kuhn. 2012. Making Ellipses Explicit in Dependency Conversion for a German Treebank. In *Proceedings of the 8th International Conference on Language Resources and Evaluation*. Istanbul, Turkey, pages 3132–3139.

Grigori Sidorov. 2013. Syntactic Dependency Based N-grams in Rule Based Automatic English as Second Language Grammar Correction. *International Journal of Computational Linguistics and Applications* 4(2):169–188.

Grigori Sidorov, Francisco Velasquez, Efstathios Stamatatos, Alexander Gelbukh, and Liliana Chanona-Hernández. 2012. Syntactic Dependency-Based N-grams as Classification Features. In Ildar Batyrshin and Miguel González Mendoza, editors, *Advances in Computational Intelligence*, Springer, number 7630 in Lecture Notes in Computer Science, pages 1–11. https://doi.org/10.1007/978-3-642-37798-3_1.

Dirk Siepmann. 2006. Academic Writing and Culture: An Overview of Differences between English, French and German. *Meta: Journal des traducteurs/Meta: Translators' Journal* 51(1):131–150.

Efstathios Stamatatos. 2009. A survey of modern authorship attribution methods. *Journal of the American Society for Information Science and Technology* 60(3):538–556. https://doi.org/10.1002/asi.21001.

Heike Zinsmeister and Ulrich Heid. 2003. Significant triples: Adjective+ noun+ verb combinations. In *Proceedings of the 7th Conference on Computational Lexicography and Text Research (Complex 2003), Budapest*.

Assessing the Stylistic Properties of Neurally Generated Text in Authorship Attribution

Enrique Manjavacas[1], **Jeroen De Gussem**[2], **Walter Daelemans**[1], and **Mike Kestemont**[1]

[1]University of Antwerp, CLiPS, `{firstname,lastname}@uantwerpen.be`
[2]Ghent University, Department of History, `jedgusse.degussem@ugent.be`

Abstract

Recent applications of neural language models have led to an increased interest in the automatic generation of natural language. However impressive, the evaluation of neurally generated text has so far remained rather informal and anecdotal. Here, we present an attempt at the systematic assessment of one aspect of the quality of neurally generated text. We focus on a specific aspect of neural language generation: its ability to reproduce authorial writing styles. Using established models for authorship attribution, we empirically assess the stylistic qualities of neurally generated text. In comparison to conventional language models, neural models generate fuzzier text that is relatively harder to attribute correctly. Nevertheless, our results also suggest that neurally generated text offers more valuable perspectives for the augmentation of training data.

1 Introduction

In his landmark paper 'Computing Machinery and Intelligence', Turing (1950) quoted Jefferson's 'The Mind of Mechanical Man' (1949): 'Not until a machine can write a sonnet or compose a concerto because of thoughts and emotions felt, and not by the chance fall of symbols, could we agree that machine equals brain'. Strikingly, these early pioneers of modern AI considered the conscious creation of literature as a significant milestone on the long road towards general AI. In recent years, the automated generation of text, such as literature, has received a significant impetus from research in the field of neural language modeling. A variety of recent studies have demonstrated that neural language models can be used to synthesize new (literary) text, even at the character-level.

To a surprising extent, neurally generated text seems to make an authentic impression on readers, due to its ability to mimic certain properties of the text on which it was trained, without it degrading into in a mere reproduction or patchwork of verbatim passages in it. In one particularly visible blog post, Karpathy (2015) demonstrated how a relatively simple character-level recurrent neural network, when trained on Shakespeare's oeuvre, was able to generate new, artificial text which, certainly in the eyes of non-experts, undeniably displayed some Shakespearean qualities. This blog has inspired a wide array of other applications – ranging from cooking recipes (Brewe, 2015) to Bach's sonatas (Feynman et al., 2016).

Much of this work has so far been published in the online blogosphere and the assessment of the quality of neurally generated text has often remained fairly informal and anecdotal, apart from a number of more empirically oriented studies, for instance in the field of hiphop lyric generation (Potash et al., 2015; Malmi et al., 2015). In this paper, we report an attempt at a systematic assessment of the properties of neurally generated text in the context of style-based authorship attribution in stylometry (Stamatatos, 2009). We address the following research questions: (1) *To which extent is the text, neurally generated on the basis of a single author's oeuvre, still attributable to the original input author?* and (2) *To which extent is the neural generation of text useful for training data augmentation in stylometry, e.g. for authors for whom little reference data is available?*

Below, we first present the model architectures underlying our text generation, comparing a modern neural architecture to a more conventional ngram-based language model. Next, we describe the Latin data set which we will use (*Patrologia Latina*) and discuss our experimental set-up (authorship attribution). We go on to present our attribution results; in the discussion section, we in-

Proceedings of the Workshop on Stylistic Variation, pages 116–125
Copenhagen, Denmark, September 7–11, 2017. ©2017 Association for Computational Linguistics

terpret and visualize these results. We conclude by
pointing out viable future improvements.

2   Character-Level Text Generation

We approach the task of text generation with
character-level Language Models (LM). In short,
a LM is a probabilistic model of linguistic sequences that, at each step in a sequence, assigns
a probability distribution over the vocabulary conditioned on the prefix sequence. More formally, a
LM is defined by Equation 1,

$$LM(w_t) = P(w_t|w_{t-n}, w_{t-(n-1)}, ..., w_{t-1}) \quad (1)$$

where n refers to the scope of the model —i.e. the
length of the prefix sequence taken into account to
condition the output distribution at step t. By extension, a LM defines a generative model of sentences where the probability of a sentence is defined by the following equation:

$$P(w_1, w_2, ..., w_n) = \prod_i^n P(w_t|w_1, ..., w_{t-1}) \quad (2)$$

Given its generative nature, a LM can easily be
used for text generation. We start by sampling
from the output distribution at step t and, then,
we recursively feed back the sampled symbol, together with any other previous output, to condition
the generative distribution at step $t + 1$. Equation
3 shows formally the text generation process for a
symbol at step t where w'_{t-1} is the generated symbol at step $t - 1$ and S refers to any given sampling
method.

$$w'_t = S[P(w_t|w'_{t-n}, w'_{t-(n-1)}, ..., w'_{t-1})] \quad (3)$$

An obvious approach towards sampling is to select the symbol that maximizes the probability
of the entire generated sequence (*argmax* decoding). For a large vocabulary (e.g. in the case of a
word-level LM), the search quickly becomes impractical and is usually approximated by means of
beam search (including the extreme case of using
a beamsize equal to 1, which corresponds to picking the most probable symbol at each step). However, when used for generation, the *argmax* decoding approach tends to yield repetitive and dull sentences, and eventually runs into dead-end loops.
Therefore, we instead sample from the LM's output distribution at each step.

The sampling approaches discussed so far attempt to strike a trade-off between variability and

correctness – in the sense of departure from regularities observed in the training data. Beam-search
decoding will tend to generate sentences that are
more formally correct (e.g. more similar to the
sentences observed in the training corpus), while
generating very similar and monotonous output
in the presence of similar histories. Conversely,
multinomial sampling will make the output di-
verge more from the original training data, and
therefore produce a more varied output, but with
a tendency towards more grammatically incorrect
sentences. Focusing on multinomial sampling, the
described trade-off can be operationalized in form
of a parameter τ, mostly referred to as "temperature", that is in charge of modifying the skewness
of the parameters of the multinomial distribution
to encourage more or less variability in exchange
for potentially less or more formally correct output.[1]

A further aspect of our LM approach to text
generation is topical variation. In order to ensure
that during generation the LM explores the topical distribution present in the training data, we
implement the following procedure. After having
generated a fixed number of sentences s, a sentence from the LM's training data is sampled uni-
formly and used to seed the generation of the next
s sentences. Finally, we force the LM to generate fully terminated sentences by including end-
of-sentence symbols (EOS) during training time
and discarding any output sentence that reaches a
maximum number of characters m without having
generated the EOS symbol – thus, we consider the
generation of a single sentence finished whenever
the EOS symbol is produced and we only generate sentences with a maximum number of characters m. This is motivated by the fact that very long
sentences tend to degenerate into poor-quality text.
Our generative system displays a total of 3 generation hyper-parameters: τ (sampling temperature),
s (reset seed every s sentences) and m (maximum
m characters per sentence).

---

[1]Given the multinomial parameters $p = \{p_1, p_2, ..., p_k\}$
for a vocabulary size of V, the "freezing" transformation
$p_i^\tau = p_i^{\frac{1}{\tau}} / \sum_j^V p_j^{\frac{1}{\tau}}$ will flatten the original distribution for
higher values of τ, thereby ensuring more variability in the
output. Conversely, lower values of τ will skew it, thereby
facilitating the outcome of the originally more probable symbol. For τ values approaching 0, we recover the simple
argmax decoding procedure of picking the highest probability
symbol at each step.

2.1 Ngram-based Language Model

So far, we have kept the definition of the LM agnostic with respect to its concrete implementation. In the current study we compare two widely-used LM architectures – an ngram-based LM (NGLM) and a Recurrent Neural Network-based LM (RNNLM). An NGLM is basically a conditional probability table for Equation 1 that is estimated on the basis of the count data for ngrams of a given length n. Typically, NGLMs suffer from a data sparsity problem since for a large enough value of n many possible conditioning prefixes will not be observed in the training data and the corresponding probability distribution will be missing. To alleviate the sparsity problem, two techniques—smoothing and back-off models—can be used that either reserve some probability mass and evenly redistribute it across unobserved ngrams (smoothing) or resort back to a lower-order model to provide an approximation to the conditional distribution of an unobserved ngram (backoff models). Here, however, we implement an unsmoothed LM since we only use the LM for generation, where it is not necessary to compute probabilities for unseen ngrams. An unsmoothed NGLM only has one model hyper-parameter—the ngram order.

2.2 RNN-based Language Model

A RNNLM implements a language model using a Recurrent Neural Network (RNN) to allow left-to-right information flow during sequence processing (Mikolov et al., 2010). As shown in (Bengio et al., 2003), at a given step t, a RNNLM (Elman, 1990) (i) first computes a distributed representation w_t with dimensionality M of the input x_t, (ii) it then feeds the resulting vector into an RNN layer that computes a hidden activation h_t combining it with the hidden activation at the previous step h_{t-1}, and (iii) it projects the hidden activation onto a space of dimensionality equal to the vocabulary size V, followed by a *softmax* function that turns the output vector into a valid probability distribution. More formally, given a binary column vector x_t representing the input symbol at step t, we retrieve its corresponding embedding w_t through $w_t = W_m x_t$, where W_m is the embedding matrix with dimensionality $\mathbb{R}^{MxV}$. The hidden state in the standard RNN is given by

$$h_t = \sigma(W_{ih}w_i + W_{hh}h_{t-1} + b_h) \quad (4)$$

where W_{ih} and W_{hh} are respectively the input-to-hidden and hidden-to-hidden projection matrices with dimensionality $\mathbb{R}^{MxH}$ and $\mathbb{R}^{HxH}$, b_h is a bias vector and σ is the sigmoid non-linear function. Finally, the probability assigned to each entry in the vocabulary at step t is defined by the *softmax*

$$P_{t,j} = \frac{e^{o_{t,j}}}{\sum_k^V e^{o_{t,k}}} \quad (5)$$

where $o_{t,j}$ is the jth entry in the output vector $o_t = W_{ho}h_t$ and W_{ho} is the hidden-to-output projection with dimensionality $\mathbb{R}^{HxV}$.

In practice, training an RNN is difficult due to the *vanishing gradient problem* (Hochreiter, 1998) that makes it hard to apply the back-propagation algorithm for parameter tuning over long sequences. Therefore, it is common to implement the recurrent layer using an enhanced RNN like, e.g. Long Short-term Memory (LSTM) (Hochreiter and Schmidhuber, 1997). An LSTM-based RNNLM only differs from the previous RNNLM in the way the hidden activation h_t is computed. An LSTM cell incorporates three learnable gates—an input, forget and output gate—of shape:

$$i_t = \sigma(W_{ih}^i w_t + W_{hh}^i + b_h^i) \quad (6)$$

$$f_t = \sigma(W_{ih}^f w_t + W_{hh}^f + b_h^f) \quad (7)$$

$$o_t = \sigma(W_{ih}^o w_t + W_{hh}^o + b_h^o) \quad (8)$$

where W^i, W^f and W^o are, respectively, the gates parameters, and a writable memory cell c_t that is updated following

$$c_t = f_t \odot c_{t-1} + i_t \odot \tanh(W_{ih}^c w_t + W_{hh}^c h_{t-1} + b_h^c) \quad (9)$$

(where $\odot$ is element-wise product and $\tanh$ is the hyperbolic tangent non-linear function). Finally, the memory cell is combined with the output gate to yield the hidden activation h_t: $h_t = o_t \odot \sigma(c_t)$. As can be seen from the equations, the role of the gates is to learn to write to and delete from the memory cell based on the input (Equations 7, 6 and 9), as well as to use the memory cell to compute the hidden activation (Equation 2.2).

A RNNLM has as parameter the embedding matrix W^m, the hidden-to-output projection W_{ho}, as well as the input-to-hidden and hidden-to-hidden projections of the RNN/LSTM networks. Theoretically, what sets a RNNLM apart is that it consistently displays a much larger context awareness—because of its ability to carry over information in the hidden state across very large spans—and that it is therefore able to learn syntactic dependencies and structures from the training material. This is in stark contrast with a NGLM, which only reasons on the basis of a very local history and have little abstractive power.

Importantly, however, it should be emphasized that most approaches to AA operate on very *local features*, such as lower-order character ngrams (Stamatatos, 2013; Sapkota et al., 2015; Kestemont, 2014). Most state-of-the-art models for AA indeed depend on document vectors containing normalized character ngram frequencies (typically in the range of 2-4), which are fed to a standard classifier, such as a support-vector machine with a linear kernel. The fact that the RNNLM might generate more realistic sentences than the NGLM does not necessarily entail that it would have an advantage in AA with respect to a conventional NGLM, which will stay closer to the original source documents. An important, if only secondary, question is therefore whether the use of an RNNLM in the context of AA would outperform a conventional NGLM, even if only very local features, such as character ngrams, are included in the model.

3 Experimental setup

3.1 Design

The *Patrologia Latina* (PL) is a corpus containing texts of Latin ecclesiastical writers in 221 volumes ranging a time span of 10 centuries, from Late Antiquity to the High Middle Ages (3rd-13th century). It was first published in two series halfway the 19th century by Jacques-Paul Migne, who mainly based the texts off of 17th and 18th-century prints. Its digitized version is available since 1993, and it has remained one of the most sizable Latin corpora online ($\pm$113M words).

Performing this experiment on the PL, and not on an English corpus, for instance, has been a conscious decision to raise the bar. It has been observed that state-of-the-art AA on an inflected language such as Latin yields poorer results when it is reliant on most frequent words (Eder and Rybicki, 2011). Moreover, the Latin that has come down to us from the 1st century AD onwards is an institutionalized literary language, hardly a natural language, showing only far resemblance, or occasionally no resemblance at all, to the writer's mother tongue (Maes, 2009). Tracing stylistic properties within a heavily formalized language,

and attempting to resuscitate these through generation, is therefore challenging. An additional obstacle for both language generation as AA is that many of the PL's authors cite from similar, authoritative sources such as the Bible or the church fathers' precursory texts, thereby having in common an ecclesiastical vocabulary that could complicate the detection of stable writing style patterns.

Not all authors in the PL have been equally prolific. These circumstances considerably limit the set of authors for whom our task is suited (Eder, 2015). We set the condition that our text data include only texts by authors who dispose of at least 20 authentic, individual documents each. As such we favored document counts over token counts, and lexical variety over mere word quantity. A list of the 18 most prolific authors, their number of documents and the respective average length of these documents is given in Fig. 1.

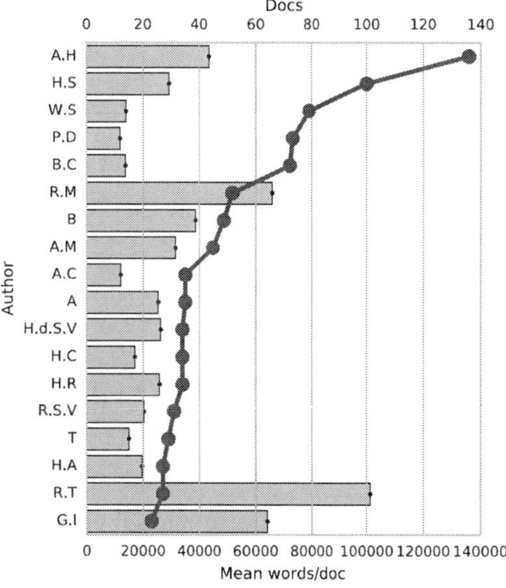

Figure 1: 18 most prolific *Patrologia Latina* authors ranked by document count. The bars yield an average of the document length.

It is not trivial to design an experiment that allows us to study the behavior of generated text in the context of AA. Fig. 2 shows the experimental setup which we propose, and in which we attempt to maximize the comparability of both generated and authentic data. We start by splitting the full corpus into two equal-size document collections (stratified at the author level), α and ω. Only α will be used to train a LM, which then generates a third collection of synthetic documents. For each author in α and ω, we aggregate all documents into a list of sentences per sub-corpus. From these collections, we create 20 documents containing at least 5,000 words to create α and ω, through randomly sampling sentences (without replacement) from the author's sentence collection. For the creation of $\bar{\alpha}$, we would also create 20 artificial 5,000-word documents, but this time through sampling new sentences from the LM. This approach has its limitations, because we limit and balance the available data to a considerable extent. Furthermore, the sampling procedure implies an underestimation in attribution performance, since it strips away all supra-sentential information. Nevertheless, this setup guarantees that the authentic and generated corpora are maximally comparable in terms of number of documents, document length, topical diversity and style mixture—which is our focus in the present study.

Subsequently, 5 classification experiments are defined, where we train and and test on different 2-way combinations of the 3 datasets. In a first pair of experiments, $< \alpha, \omega >$ and $< \omega, \alpha >$, we train and test a classifier on the authentic datasets to assess the classifier's performance under natural conditions. (Note that we apply the classifier in both directions to account for any directionality artifacts.) In a third experiment, we train and test a classifier on the generated data only ($< \bar{\alpha}, \bar{\alpha} >$) to establish to which extent the generated data preserves the data's stylistic structure at the author level (i.e. auto-classification). Fourthly, we conduct an experiment where we train on the generated data in $\bar{\alpha}$ and test on the authentic data in ω ($< \bar{\alpha}, \omega >$). This allows us to verify whether the generated documents retain enough stylistic information to correctly attribute authentic documents. Finally, we train a classifier on the authentic data in ω and test it on $\bar{\alpha}$: this setup ($< \omega, \bar{\alpha} >$) allows to assess whether a classifier, trained on authentic data is still able to correctly attribute the generated materials.

In addition, we conduct a final experiment which can be characterized from the point of view of self-learning or co-learning (Mihalcea, 2004)—a semi-supervised learning technique where a core of training data is expanded with examples from a related but unlabeled dataset that can be classified with high confidence by a classifier trained in the original labeled dataset. In this experiment we compare the NGLM and RNNLM models with respect to their capacity to boost attribution performance by adding synthetic examples to the original training set—which might be a valuable strategy for real-life experiments. Specifically, we perform attribution on ω using a combination of α and $\bar{\alpha}$ as training data ($< \alpha + \bar{\alpha}, \omega >$).

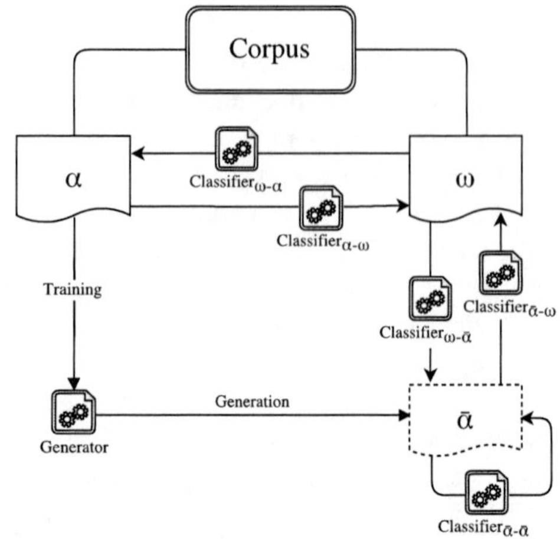

Figure 2: Experimental setup. α and ω refer to 50% splits of the full corpus. $\bar{\alpha}$ refers to the generated dataset (cf. dashed line). Each classifier symbol refers to a classification experiment using the data at the arrow's source (first subscript) for training and the data at the arrow's target (second subscript) for testing (note that training only has to be performed 3 times, one per dataset).

3.2 Language Model Architectures for Text Generation

In Section 2, the text-generation and model parameters were defined. For the present experiments we generate 20 documents of 5000 words each using a τ value of 1 and a m value estimated on each author's dataset. For the RNNLM we reset the seed (parameter s) every 10 successfully generated sentences, whereas for the NGLM we do it after every sentence. This asymmetry is motivated by the fact that NGLM the output distribution of an NGLM at each step is much more skewed and therefore sentences generated from the same seed tend to be be much less varied. For model fitting we set the NGLM order at 6, which, on a subjective evaluation, seemed a sufficiently large value for the comparatively small size of the datasets.

For the RNNLM models the following parameter settings were selected. Embedding dimensionality M was set to 24, the hidden layer dimension was 200 and we stacked up 2 LSTM layers to encourage the model to learn more abstract representations. Parameters were chosen based on common practice and reasonable defaults without further hyperparameter search. Each model was trained during 50 epochs using the adaptive variant of Stochastic Gradient Descent Adam (Kingma and Ba, 2015) with an initial learning rate of 0.001. We set a small batch size of 50, preferring stability over speed during training. Moreover, we clip the gradients before each batch update to a maximum norm value of 5 to avoid the exploding gradients following (Pascanu et al., 2013) and truncate the gradient back-propagation after 50 recurrent steps. We also applied 30% dropout after each recurrent layer following (Zaremba et al., 2015) to avoid overfitting. For each RNNLM we held out a validation set using 10% of the data to monitor and evaluate training. We ensured that validation perplexity was always lower than train perplexity. Average validation perplexity was 4.015 with a standard deviation of 0.183.[2]

3.3 Attribution as Classification

For the AA classification as described in the experimental setup of section 3, we use a linear SVM classifier (Diederich, 2003). We extract shallow linguistic features in the form of Tfidf-weighted character ngrams (from bigrams to four-grams) as style markers by which to determine authorship. Note that the feature extraction of ngrams in the order of 2 to 4 might have important repercussions, since NGLM training fully focuses on capturing that particular distribution, whereas the more expressive RNNLM models full sequences. Furthermore, we refrain from using word-level features such as word ngrams or POS tags, since this would introduce a further asymmetry in the comparison given that the RNNLM can generate unseen words whereas the NGLM can not. The model accuracy of the SVM is fine-tuned by searching over different value ranges for the SVM's parameters. The number of features is set to range from 1,000 to 30,000 max features for each fit, more specifically in the following order: 5,000, 10,000, 15,000 and 30,000 features. For the C-parameter of the SVM we search over values of respectively 1, 10, 100 and 1,000.

---

[2]All software associated with this paper is available from `https://www.github.com/jedgusse/project_lorenzo`.

Source	Experiment	F1	P	R
Real	$< \alpha, \omega >$	0.833	0.818	0.869
	$< \omega, \alpha >$	0.811	0.795	0.853
NGLM	$< \alpha + \bar{\alpha}, \omega >$	0.814	0.809	0.850
	$< \bar{\alpha}, \omega >$	0.706	0.744	0.750
	$< \omega, \bar{\alpha} >$	0.837	0.811	0.881
RNNLM	$< \alpha + \bar{\alpha}, \omega >$	0.872	0.878	0.892
	$< \bar{\alpha}, \omega >$	0.635	0.701	0.658
	$< \omega, \bar{\alpha} >$	0.724	0.778	0.775

Table 1: Mean F1, Precision (P) and Recall (R) scores for all classification experiments.

4 Results

4.1 Examples of Generated Language

What follows are two short extracts from the respective outputs of an NGLM and RNNLM trained on Augustine (A.H.) (most prolific author of the dataset, see Table 1), which gives an anecdotal intuition of how the output of these language models differs.

Ngram-based LM ($\bar{\alpha}$)

(1) * Sed uis   uenire: **quod** postridie,
Yet you wish to come since tomorrow
ascensiones honora   pastorem,
ascensions honoured the shepherd,
nec   sane   reipublicos idem
and not completely republican the same
testis   et   implebitur   tamen
witness also will be fulfilled nevertheless
mentiendum   sit
to be deceived it may be
propitiaberis.
you will be enriched.

RNN-based LM ($\bar{\alpha}$)

(2) * Et idam   precepti,   siue
And that same (?) commandment, be it
ad   sensum   noui:
towards the feeling I know:
nonuulde   sunt enim   Filius
not enough (?) are after all the Son
Domini   substantia,   sed non
of our Lord our substance, but none
sunt   **qui** secururum
are there who amongst the untroubled
superbia   et **perrectus** est, mortalis
through pride also righteous are, mortal
includendi   estus que fiumus
by including fire   and we were (?)
propter   illam uideantur.
because of this   may they be beheld.

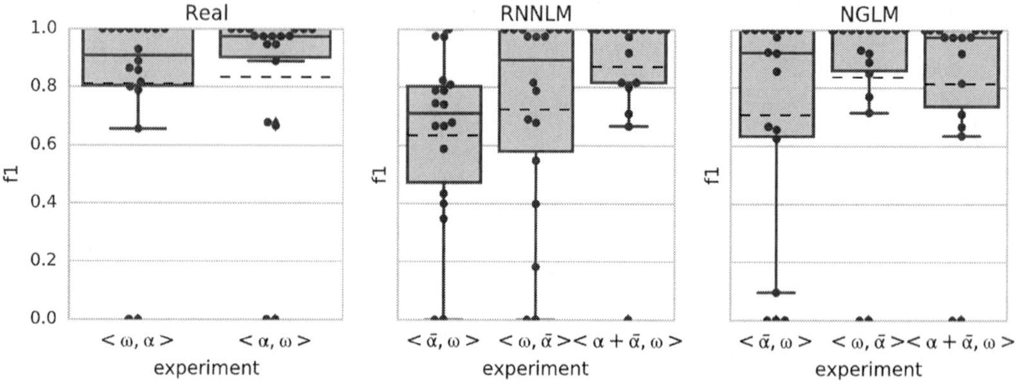

Figure 3: F1 scores for the different combinations of α, $\bar{\alpha}$, and ω.

The extract of RNNLM-generated text as compared to the NGLM demonstrates how the RNNLM is better at reproducing a syntactic logic (which moreover makes translation easier). Note, for instance, how the nominative of the relative pronoun *qui* is maintained towards the end of the subordinate clause in the participle perfect *perrectus*, and even seems to be carried on in the next clause as opposed to the awkwardly placed *quod* in the ngram-based extract. The RNNLM is also arguably better at positioning the verbs in the clauses. Compare, for instance, the NGLM's dense verbal sequence *implebitur tamen mentiendum sit propitiaberis*. Finally, the RNNLM is more apt at generating plausible neologisms. Examples include *idam* (cfr. *idem* and *quidam*), *fiumus* (cfr. *fiemus*), secururum (cfr. *securus* and the genitive ending *-orum* and *-arum*). To a human reader, the RNNLM produces superficially more convincing text.

4.2 Attribution results

The results of the attribution experiments are presented in Table 1 in terms of recall, precision and F1-scores and the distributions are visualized in Fig. 3. We focus on the macro-averaged F1-scores in our discussion, although one should not forget that the scores vary considerably over individual authors (cf. Fig. 3). With respect to the authentic data, classifying α on the basis of ω is slightly more difficult than the reverse direction, which seems a negligible directionality artifact. When we use the generated data as training material to classify authentic material $< \bar{\alpha}, \omega >$, we see that the F1-scores drop significantly for both LMs, although the NGLM seems more robust in this re-

spect. Interestingly, the drop is much less significant for the opposite situation, where we train on authentic material and classify generated material $< \omega, \bar{\alpha} >$. This suggests that enough stylistic information is preserved in the generated text to attribute it to the original author, but that this information in isolation does not suffice to train a convincing attribution system on. When used in isolation, the NGLM outperforms the RNNLM in both setups. However, the situation is clearly different for the augmentation or self-learning setup ($< \alpha + \bar{\alpha}, \omega >$)—c.f. Section 3—, where we train an attributor on the combination of α and $\bar{\alpha}$, and test it on the authentic ω set. Here, we see that the RNNLM performs better than the NGLM in the corresponding experiment – the NGLM in fact even performs worse in this case than in the normal $< \alpha, \omega >$ setup.

4.3 Discussion

To understand the difference in behavior between both LMs, it is useful to inspect Fig. 4. Here, we use a Principal Components Analysis (Binongo and Smith, 1999) to visualize 2500-word samples for 3 three most prolific authors (Augustine of Hippo, Honorius of Autun, and Gregory the Great) using the 150 most common ngrams. We include a mixture of authentic ω data and generated $\bar{\alpha}$ data for each author, comparing the NGLM and the RNNLM. The plots shows that NGLM produces text samples which lie very close in ngram frequencies to the authentic data, whereas the texts produced by the RNNLM follow a markedly different distribution than ω – this difference is very outspoken for Augustine, for instance. As might be expected on the basis of the observation in section 3.3, the NGLM thus produces data that stays very close to the original input, whereas RNNLM yields fuzzier texts, that follow a slightly different distribution. This explains why it is, for example, easier to train an attributor on the data generated by an NGLM than an RNNLM.

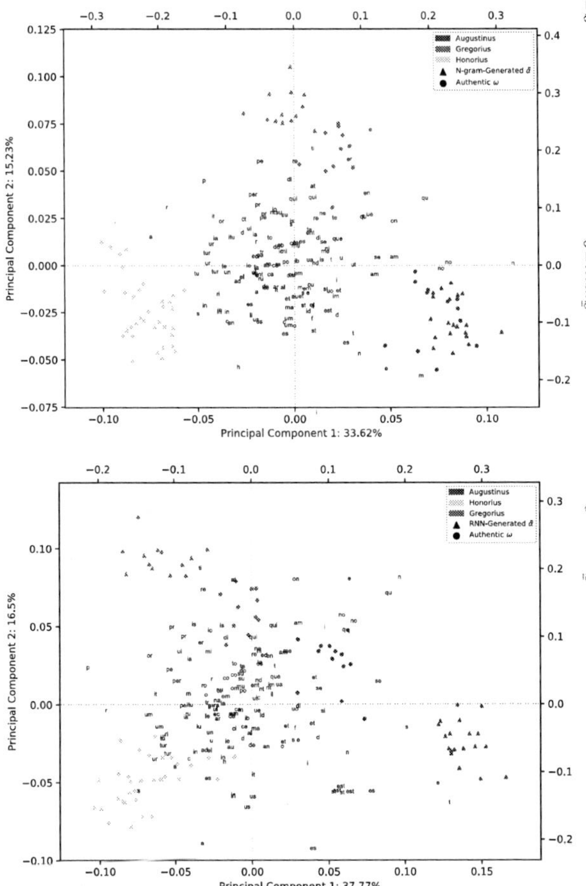

Figure 4: PCA plots (1st 2 PCs) for 3 authors using document vectors representing the normalized frequencies of the 150 most frequent ngrams (order 2-4) in 2500-word sample. We include a mixture of authentic ω data and generated $\bar{\alpha}$ data (*top: NGLM; bottom: RNNLM*).

Conversely, our results show that the situation is different in the data augmentation setup, where we train an attributor on the combination of α and $\bar{\alpha}$ and test it on the authentic ω set. In this case, the NGLM performs worse than in the corresponding the non-augmented setup, whereas the performance of the RNNLM sensitively increases. Arguably, the fuzziness of the RNNLM-generated data adds an interesting complexity to the original core of authentic data, which can be exploited by the classifier.

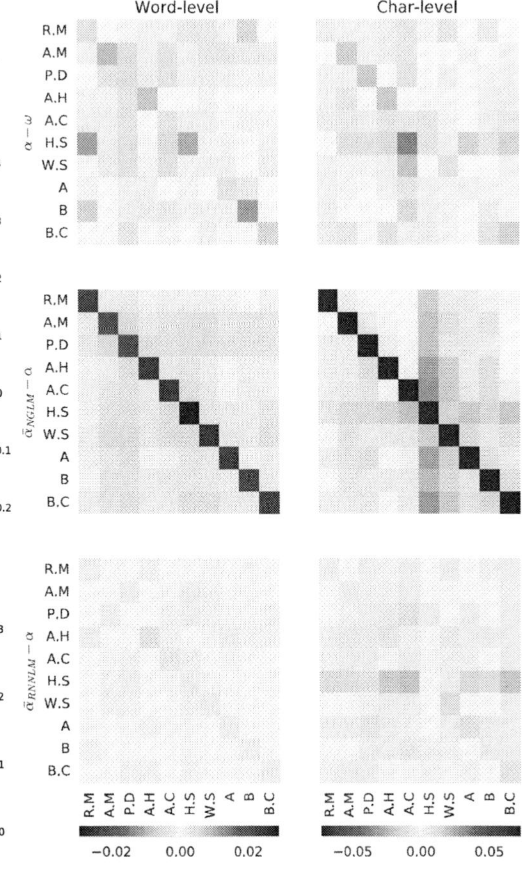

Figure 5: Mean-normalized Jaccard similarity scores between 10 most prolific authors using word (left column) and character (right column) bigrams to fourgrams, comparing real data (first row), RNNLM-synthetic data with real data (second row) and NGLM-synthetic data with real data (third row).

While these results indirectly show that the RNNLM did not simply overfit on α, it is an interesting question to which extent α and $\bar{\alpha}$ display (lexical) overlap in the case of both LMs. If the overlap would indeed be larger for the NGLM than the RNNLM, this would support our interpretation. In Fig. 5, we show mean-normalized, pairwise Jaccard similarities for the 10 most prolific authors in both α and $\bar{\alpha}$ for each LM. The dark diagonals in the second row of the heatmaps visually support the observation that the NGLM displays a much more outspoken overlap between α and $\bar{\alpha}$. Such an effect is much more faint in the case of the RNNLM and in this respect it remains more faithful to the real data (first row for α and ω).

5   Conclusion

Our preliminary results confirm that the texts generated by a traditional NGLM are relatively 'dull' and 'conservative' in the sense that they stay relatively close to the local distribution of the source data on which they were trained. Conceptually, the RNNLM has a clear advantage in terms of expressiveness and capacity with respect to the NGLM. In practice, given the small size of AA datasets, an underfitted RNNLM yield fuzzier examples, which explains why the NGLM outperforms the RNNLM when the classifier is *restricted* to the generated data ($< \bar{\alpha}, \omega >$ and $< \omega, \bar{\alpha} >$). At the same time, the training data augmentation setup ($< \alpha + \bar{\alpha}, \omega >$) shows that whereas NGLM-generated data adds comparatively little to the authentic data—reproducing a subset of the original feature distribution, as shown in Fig. 5—, the RNNLM-generated data presents a valuable data contribution which does result in an absolute increase in attribution performance with respect to the real classification setup $< \alpha, \omega >$. Although further research into the matter is needed, this clearly suggests that the complexity of the RNNLM data is useful for training data augmentation, arguably capturing stylistic nuances which a simpler LM cannot.

In the future, we will explore the flexibility of the general RNNLM framework to develop generative architectures that better capture the style of the training data. In particular, following (Linzen et al., 2016) we hypothesize that forcing the RNN to model more linguistic structure—e.g. jointly modeling words and POS-tags—, should result in better language generation and better style preservation. Furthermore, we plan on exhaustively testing the capabilities of author-specific generative models for self-learning in AA, investigating the effect of adding different amounts of synthetic data and selectively adding synthetic data based on the confidence with which it can be correctly classified by a classifier trained on real data.

Additionally, we would like to investigate pre-training in out-of-domain data as well as more compact ways of modelling author-specific language—such as conditional language models (Tang et al., 2016)—as means to alleviate underfitting of the RNN models on small datasets.

References

Yoshua Bengio, Réjean Ducharme, Pascal Vincent, and Christian Janvin. 2003. A Neural Probabilistic Language Model. *The Journal of Machine Learning Research*, 3:1137–1155.

José Nilo G. Binongo and M. Wilfrid A. Smith. 1999. The application of principal component analysis to stylometry. *Literary and Linguistic Computing*, 14(4):445–466.

Tom Brewe. 2015. Do androids dream of cooking? https://gist.github.com/nylki/1efbaa36635956d35bcc.

Joachim Diederich. 2003. Authorship attribution with support vector machines. *Applied Intelligence*, 19.1(4616):109—123.

Maciej Eder and Jan Rybicki. 2011. Deeper delta across genres and languages: Do we really need the most frequent words? *Literary and Linguistic Computing*, 26(3):315–321.

Maciej Eder. 2015. Taking stylometry to the limits: Benchmark study on 5,281 texts from "patrologia latina". In *Digital Humanities 2015: Conference Abstracts*, pages 1919–1924.

Jeffrey L. Elman. 1990. Finding structure in time. *Cognitive Science*, 14(2):179–211.

Liang Feynman, Mark Gotham, Marcin Tomczak, Mathew Johnson, and Jaimie Shotton. 2016. The bachbot challenge. http://bachbot.com/.

Sepp Hochreiter and Jürgen Schmidhuber. 1997. Long Short-Term Memory. *Neural Computation*, 9(8):1735–1780.

Sepp Hochreiter. 1998. The Vanishing Gradient Problem During Learning Recurrent Neural Nets and Problem Solutions. *International Journal of Uncertainty, Fuzziness and Knowledge-Based Systems*, 06(02):107–116.

Geoffrey Jefferson. 1949. The mind of mechanical man. *British Medical Journal*, 1(4616):1105–1110.

Andrej Karpathy. 2015. The unreasonable effectiveness of recurrent neural networks. http://karpathy.github.io/2015/05/21/rnn-effectiveness/.

Mike Kestemont. 2014. Function words in authorship attribution. from black magic to theory? In *Proceedings of the 3rd Workshop on Computational Linguistics for Literature*, pages 59–66. Association for Computational Linguistics.

Diederik P. Kingma and Jimmy Lei Ba. 2015. Adam: a Method for Stochastic Optimization. *International Conference on Learning Representations 2015*, pages 1–15.

Tal Linzen, Emmanuel Dupoux, and Yoav Goldberg. 2016. Assessing the Ability of LSTMs to Learn Syntax-Sensitive Dependencies. nov.

Yanick Maes. 2009. Continuity through appropriation? In Jan Papy, Wim Verbaal, and Yanick Maes, editors, *Latinitas Perennis. Volume II: Appropriation and Latin Literature*, chapter 1, pages 1—10. Brill, Leiden.

Eric Malmi, Pyry Takala, Hannu Toivonen, Tapani Raiko, and Aristides Gionis. 2015. Dopelearning: A computational approach to rap lyrics generation. *CoRR*, abs/1505.04771.

Rada Mihalcea. 2004. Co-training and self-training for word sense disambiguation. In *CoNLL*, pages 33–40.

Tomas Mikolov, Martin Karafiát, Lukas Burget, Jan Cernocký, and Sanjeev Khudanpur. 2010. Recurrent neural network based language model. In *Interspeech*, number September, pages 1045–1048.

Razvan Pascanu, Tomas Mikolov, and Yoshua Bengio. 2013. On the Difficulties of Training Recurrent Neural Networks. *Icml*, (2):1–9.

Peter Potash, Alexey Romanov, and Anna Rumshisky. 2015. GhostWriter: Using an LSTM for Automatic Rap Lyric Generation. *Proceedings of the 2015 Conference on Empirical Methods in Natural Language Processing*, (September):1919–1924.

Upendra Sapkota, Steven Bethard, Manuel Montes, and Thamar Solorio. 2015. Not all character n-grams are created equal: A study in authorship attribution. In *Proceedings of the 2015 Conference of the North American Chapter of the Association for Computational Linguistics: Human Language Technologies*, pages 93–102, Denver, Colorado, May–June. Association for Computational Linguistics.

Efstathios Stamatatos. 2009. A survey of modern authorship attribution methods. *Journal of the American Society For Information Science and Technology*, (60):538–556.

Efstathios Stamatatos. 2013. On the robustness of authorship attribution based on character n-gram features. *Journal of Law and Policy*, 21(2):421–439.

Jian Tang, Yifan Yang, Sam Carton, Ming Zhang, and Qiaozhu Mei. 2016. Context-aware Natural Language Generation with Recurrent Neural Networks. *arXiv preprint arXiv:1611.09900*.

Alan Turing. 1950. Computing machinery and intelligence. *Mind*, 49(4616):433–460.

Wojciech Zaremba, Ilya Sutskever, and Oriol Vinyals. 2015. Recurrent Neural Network Regularization. *ICLR*, pages 1–8.

A   Author names with abbreviations

Abbrv	Author
H.S	Hieronymus Stridonensis
G.I	Gregorius I
A.H	Augustinus Hipponensis
A.M	Ambrosius Mediolanensis
B	Beda
H.C	Hildebertus Cenomanensis
H.d.S.V	Hugo de S- Victore
R.T	Rupertus Tuitiensis
W.S	Walafridus Strabo
T	Tertullianus
P.D	Petrus Damianus
H.A	Honorius Augustodunensis
H.R	Hincmarus Rhemensis
B.C	Bernardus Claraevallensis
A	Alcuinus
R.M	Rabanus Maurus
A.C	Anselmus Cantuariensis
R.S.V	Richardus S- Victoris

Author Index

Association for Computational Linguistics
209 N. Eighth Street
Stroudsburg, Pennsylvania 18360

ISBN 978-1-5108-4763-7